FADE OUT

Also by the Author:

Destinies

Thy Kingdom Come

FADE OUT

The Calamitous Final Days of MGM

PETER BART

WILLIAM MORROW AND COMPANY, INC.
New York

Recognizing the importance of preserving what has been written, it is the policy
of William Morrow and Company, Inc., and its imprints and affiliates to have the
books it publishes printed on acid-free paper, and we exert our best efforts to that
end.

Library of Congress Cataloging-in-Publication Data

Bart, Peter.
Fade out : the calamitous final days of MGM / Peter Bart.
p. cm.
ISBN 0-688-08460-5
1. Metro-Goldwyn-Mayer.   I. Title.
PN1999.M4B37   1990
384'.8'0979494—dc20   89-77812
                                                                                            CIP

Printed in the United States of America

    2   3   4   5   6   7   8   9   10

BOOK DESIGN BY PAUL CHEVANNES

This book is for Blackie.

■
ACKNOWLEDGMENTS

Many colleagues and onetime employees of MGM and United Artists were very helpful to me in preparing this book. I thank them all for their generous assistance and guidance while honoring their requests to remain anonymous. You know who you are!

■
CONTENTS

■
INTRODUCTION

My odyssey with Metro-Goldwyn-Mayer began, like many Hollywood stories, at the Polo Lounge of the Beverly Hills Hotel.

Seated across the table from me was an intense little bulldog of a man named Frank Yablans, whose darting black eyes continued to roam the room even as we talked. Though it was still a few minutes before eight on that March morning in 1983, the room already resonated with the fervid buzz of power breakfasts.

From the table on my left: "...Either he does the two weeks of reshoots, or he never works in this town again."

From the table on my right: "...If he's so unhappy with his deal, tell him to find another sucker willing to pay him a million bucks for four weeks' work, plus gross at cash break." The dialogue of intimidation was getting off to an early start this morning.

But while egos were being eviscerated all around me, my colloquy with Frank Yablans was taking a far different course. As the newly appointed chief of MGM, Yablans was offering me a job, but it sounded as though he was also recruiting me for a mission.

"What we face here is a once-in-a-lifetime opportunity—the chance to save a great studio," Yablans intoned gravely. "Kirk has

11

given me an open checkbook. I can make any deal, go after any project!"

The "Kirk" in question was Kirk Kerkorian, the ever-mysterious and reclusive financier who owned not only MGM, but also its sister company, United Artists, which he had merged to become MGM/UA. At their zenith, both companies had occupied an almost mythic stature in the film industry, but both had now fallen on lean times.

"This is his last shot," Yablans explained. "If we succeed, it's back to the halcyon days."

"And if not? . . ."

"Kirk locks up the studio and throws away the key."

Having laid out this dark scenario, Yablans went on to explain the role he intended me to play. "You'll be senior vice president for production, reporting directly to me. You'll have a two-year deal, half a million guaranteed, and bonuses. Plus the usual perks— new car, all that stuff. I'll back you all the way."

Yablans continued to marshal his arguments as to why this was an irresistible opportunity, but I found myself listening instead to a small, cautionary voice within me warning, "Watch yourself; this isn't what it seems to be." MGM/UA was a deeply troubled company—that much I knew. And while Frank Yablans was a volatile and unpredictable figure, Kirk Kerkorian was an even greater enigma. Besides, why is it that "once-in-a-lifetime" opportunities usually turn out to be more like death sentences?

I accepted the job, of course. It seemed preordained that I would do so.

But even the cautionary voice did not prepare me for what lay ahead. In signing my contract, I signed on to a hallucinogenic roller-coaster ride during which I would witness not the long-awaited renaissance of MGM, but rather its utter and complete devastation. Within five years of my arrival, the studio would be totally dismantled, its executives dismissed, its back lot sold, its valuable library of films stripped away. Not only would Frank Yablans fall victim to the onslaught, but so would his high-profile successors such as Alan Ladd, Jr., Lee Rich, and Jerry Weintraub.

All these men, like Yablans, had developed their blueprints for "saving" MGM/UA. What they hadn't realized, however, was that Kerkorian, ever the savvy Las Vegas game-player, had evolved a scheme of his own to harness Hollywood's myth-making machinery to serve his personal objectives. The end result: Kerkorian emerged a billionaire. His companies emerged a shambles.

In witnessing the debacle, I felt much like a befuddled archae-ologist who got lost on an important dig. There I was, scratching around for relics of past greatness, and all I found was Kirk Kerkorian, playing poker in the ruins.

This, then, is an account of the decline and fall of two great movie companies. It is a story with a colorful cast of characters, all of whom found themselves propelled across an Alice-in-Wonderland landscape, littered with dashed hopes and bitter betrayals.

On one level, the events that overtook MGM/UA pose a vivid illustration of the scenario that gripped much of American business in the 1980's. Companies created by innovators fell captive to corporate pirates—the ubiquitous "leveraged buyout" specialists, among whom Kerkorian was one of the pioneers. The inevitable casualties have been the hapless workers (in this case, the filmmakers) and the customers (in this case, the moviegoers).

There will always be movies to see, of course, but they will not be true MGM movies. They will not emanate from the time-hallowed stages where Garland once sang and Astaire once danced and where Andy Hardy came of age. That legacy is no more.

CHAPTER ONE

■

THE SUMMONS

1983

THE installation of a new regime at a movie studio is reminiscent, in nuance and ritual, of the transfer of power within a powerful Mafia clan. The atmosphere crackles with high expectations, mixed with an undercurrent of fear. The wizened *consigliere* hovers close by as the new "capo" receives a succession of ceremonial visitors. Would-be friends and allies position themselves in the corridors, awaiting some impromptu dispensation. Courtiers and courtesans gossip about the new pyramid of authority, even as those pushed from power grimly await their exile. And all the while, the flowers and champagne keep arriving at the gates, and the phone lines clog with incoming calls.

Some years ago, as a young studio executive supervising the production of *The Godfather*, I spent many hours in the company of "the family," schooling myself in the rituals of Mafia power. And now, moving through the corridors of MGM at the side of Frank Yablans, I was overtaken with a curious feeling of *déjà vu*.

This was just a movie studio, to be sure, whose fortunes were built on illusion, not crime. Nonetheless, there was no mistaking the portents in Yablans's jaunty stride and steely stare as he assumed his duties as chief operating officer at MGM in early 1983. Heads were about to roll, careers would rise and fall, and hundreds of millions of dollars would be dispensed on a handshake or a nod of the head. It was all about power, and Frank Yablans wore the mantle.

Other executives had come and gone in the fourteen years since Kirk Kerkorian first acquired control of the proud old Culver City studio, but this transfer of power carried special meaning. The new regime, Kerkorian let it be known, would be supported by an infusion of new capital that would be directed not only to motion pictures, but also to television, video, and other realms of the fast-expanding, global entertainment industry. The time had come to restore tattered old Leo the Lion to his former glory.

All this represented an abrupt turnaround for the unpredictable financier who for fourteen years had pursued a program of benign neglect at MGM, sharply curtailing film production and selling off valuable studio assets. Hollywood had long dismissed Kerkorian as someone who had exploited the studio to build his gambling empire in Las Vegas and Reno.

Then, in 1981, Kerkorian startled the filmmaking community by laying out $380 million to acquire United Artists, the great company founded by Mary Pickford, Charlie Chaplin, and their friends. In another surprise move, Kerkorian then turned to the newly recruited David Begelman, who had recently been fired by Columbia Pictures in a celebrated check-forging scandal, to spearhead an ambitious program of films.

The Begelman experiment self-destructed, however. Kerkorian and his advisers liked Begelman's flamboyance, but disdained his style—the lavish budgets, the slapdash administration, the fat deals for talent. The studio needed product, to be sure, but it also needed fiscal restraint. When Begelman's first few movies bombed, Kerkorian pulled the plug.

The power vacuum brought the studio to a grinding halt once again. Management was a shambles. The United Artists acquisition had never been fully digested to begin with. Elaborate plans had been initiated to spin off the casinos and the video company into separate, publicly owned entities to generate new capital, but the most urgent problem was that of creating a sense of order.

Enter Frank Yablans. He and Kerkorian had met several times during Yablans's tenure as president of Paramount Pictures. Kerkorian had been impressed by his street-corner brashness.

Yablans was the son of an immigrant Brooklyn cabdriver, Kerkorian the son of an immigrant Armenian farmer. There was a bond there, too.

But could Yablans do the job? At least he'd had ample experience in corporate management. The trouble with David Begelman, Kerkorian felt, was that he was basically an agent, a hand-holder, a man who knew how to service clients, not how to run a company. But Yablans had departed Paramount under curious circumstances—that would have to be looked into.

Unlike the owners of other entertainment companies, Kerkorian, a private, almost reclusive man, had never constructed a network of industry sources to call upon at moments like this. His friends were, by and large, Las Vegas types—men who, like Kerkorian, wore leisure suits and ate in rib joints. A handsome and roisterous playboy-attorney named Gregson Bautzer, Jr., functioned as Kerkorian's eyes and ears in the filmmaking community.

And Bautzer was getting good reports on Yablans.

In part, Yablans was orchestrating these reports. He wanted the MGM job—wanted it badly. It had been eight years since he'd been eased out of Paramount. He'd put himself up as a candidate for other positions in the industry, but the high-profile investment bankers and corporate attorneys who influenced decisions of this sort had not been in his corner. Yablans was a diamond in the rough.

That's why the MGM situation posed a unique opportunity. There were no Ivy League types to take note of his lack of a college education or to scrutinize his family tree. Kerkorian and Bautzer were street-fighters like him. If only he could get that message across.

The calls went out, to agents, actors, exhibitors—even a few Vegas friends. And finally the summons came: Greg Bautzer would like to see him. There was an opportunity at MGM. . . .

The deal was straightforward: two years at $600,000 a year, plus performance incentives that would bring total compensation to the $1 million level if things went well.

Frank Yablans did not waste time negotiating. This was more than a job—it was like a new lease on life. It was the second chance he'd been yearning for.

Even after eight years, he still bore the scars of the Paramount debacle. He still felt he'd been the victim of corporate politics, forced out of a company that he himself had helped to build.

Frank Yablans had been a lowly assistant sales manager when he first caught the eye of Charles Bluhdorn, the bombastic,

Austrian-born chairman of Gulf + Western Industries, which had bought Paramount in 1967. Bluhdorn was a brilliant, if erratic, corporate carnivore, who would randomly consume companies irrespective of what field they might be in.

Having already acquired a mixed bag of companies that did everything from mine zinc to manufacture automobile bumpers, Bluhdorn coveted his glamorous new film studio, while at the same time realizing it was in deep trouble. Another corporate raider, Kirk Kerkorian, had just acquired MGM, but while Kerkorian had embarked on his austerity program, the impulsive Bluhdorn pumped millions into Paramount, financing a series of expensive, ill-conceived movies. There was *Paint Your Wagon*, a bumbling musical that began and ended the singing careers of both Lee Marvin and Clint Eastwood; and there was *Darling Lili*, in which Julie Andrews and Rock Hudson awkwardly posed as passionate lovers and spies.

Having turned out these turkeys, Bluhdorn became intrigued by a ferocious young salesman who, far from moaning about the dismal product, as did his colleagues, went out into the field and came up with sizable advances for the films. In Bluhdorn's failures, Yablans saw his own opportunity for success, and it paid off. Suddenly, Bluhdorn's luck started to turn. Along came *Love Story*, and instead of derisive laughter, there were suddenly lines around the block. Though it danced gingerly around the edges of mawkish melodrama, *Love Story* became one of the first genuine "blockbusters" of the postwar years. Filmgoers lined up to see it not once, but over and over again.

Frank Yablans, who by now was head of distribution, was credited with propelling what might have been a modest success into a runaway hit. A generous and instinctual man, Charles Bluhdorn was duly impressed; in his euphoria, he rewarded Yablans with the presidency of Paramount.

Love Story brought immediate rewards to others, as well. For Robert Evans and myself, *Love Story* meant a mandate to make whatever films we wanted. Evans was the executive vice president and I, having joined Paramount two years earlier, was vice president of production. Together, we constituted essentially the studio's entire West Coast creative staff. Frank Yablans, as the new president stationed in New York, pledged his support for our endeavors. Out of that collaboration over the next four years came a stream of successful films such as *The Godfather, True Grit, Chinatown, Goodbye Columbus, Harold and Maude, Rosemary's Baby, Paper Moon, The Conversation*, and *The Longest Yard*, among others.

With the studio on a winning streak, Yablans worked diligently to improve his presidential style. He sought out appropriate mentors to upgrade his attire, hone his manners, and advise him on the arts. He moved his wife and three children into a rambling home in an upscale section of suburban Scarsdale. Even as he functioned as a hard-hitting executive, Frank Yablans was diligently reinventing himself.

The task of reinventing Charles Bluhdorn proved more demanding, however. In accepting the presidency, Yablans had asked Bluhdorn for the same measure of autonomy that Yablans had granted his creative team. In the past, Bluhdorn's involvement in the studio had been so intense that he'd functioned effectively as president of Paramount, as well as chairman of Gulf + Western. Though Bluhdorn had promised to change his ways, it soon became clear that this was impossible. Without realizing it, he'd become a movie "junkie," habitually second-guessing Yablans's strategies and negotiating impromptu deals without telling anyone. He would fly off, ostensibly to buy a zinc mine, and end up concocting a $20 million Italo-Russian co-production to be directed by some obscure Eastern European "auteur."

Yablans was continually humiliated by these intrusions. At the same time, he discovered that his job offered many "perks" that more than compensated for them. There were private jets at his disposal, suites in the finest hotels, the best tables at restaurants, the company of celebrities. And with the studio churning out success after success, culminating in *The Godfather*, Yablans's name began to acquire a certain "buzz" in the industry. Here was a "comer," it was said. Here was an executive who understood how to maximize the talents of those around him, how to turn an ordinary movie opening into "an event."

Charles Bluhdorn was noticing all this, too, but he was also noticing how assiduously Yablans was working to enhance his own image. There were constant interviews in the press, for example, including a piece in *New York* magazine in which Yablans boasted of the total autonomy with which he operated at Paramount—a boast that Bluhdorn did not exactly appreciate. Yablans was even telling reporters that his Paramount job was just a warm-up for him, that he planned before long to run for the presidency of the United States!

Then there were the awards; barely a month went by without Frank Yablans being annointed "humanitarian of the year" or "man of the hour" by one group or another, and Paramount could always be counted on to make a hefty contribution to the charity in question. It became an industry joke that Paramount executives always kept their tuxedos hanging in their offices lest they be summoned unexpectedly to a new Frank Yablans award banquet.

Even more irritating to Bluhdorn, however, were Yablans's unexpected acting ambitions. The Gulf + Western founder was under intense pressure from the Securities and Exchange Commission concerning several major stock transactions; Bluhdorn, in response, was eager to depict his company as a wholesome, clean-cut example of American free enterprise. He was, therefore, apoplectic to learn one morning that one of his top executives, Frank Yablans, had accepted a role playing a Mafia hood in a forthcoming Elaine May movie. Indeed, Yablans was already in rehearsal for the film, entitled *Mikey and Nicky*, without having notified his boss.

Charles Bluhdorn decided it was time to clamp down on his unpredictable young corporate climber. Yablans arrived at work one morning to find a team of auditors from the parent company digging through ledgers and deal memos. Other Bluhdorn aides, meanwhile, were probing a report that Yablans had placed his mother on the company payroll, and that he had appropriated two valuable paintings belonging to Gulf + Western for his personal collection.

Under siege from all directions now, Yablans was hit with even more alarming news. Bluhdorn had decided to recruit a new member to Paramount's management team—a fast-rising young TV executive named Barry Diller. As the new chairman of Paramount, Diller would occupy a position parallel to that of Yablans, who would remain president. The resulting competition between the two, Bluhdorn told colleagues, would serve to hold Yablans's rampant ego in check, and would elicit the best work from both young executives.

Yablans was stung. He could not believe that Bluhdorn could turn on him so fiercely after all he had contributed to the company.

Yablans struggled to bury his pride as he watched Bluhdorn lavish attention on his new protégé. To the European-born Bluhdorn, who still spoke with an Austrian accent, working with the witty, sophisticated Diller was a pleasant relief after years of Yablans's blunt, confrontational style. Bluhdorn admired the deftness with which Diller negotiated deals and handled subordinates.

Diller became a frequent guest at Bluhdorn's sumptuous hacienda in the Dominican Republic, to which he invited not only friends, but also influential leaders such as Henry Kissinger and "Punch" Sulzberger of *The New York Times*.

Indeed, as the personal bond between the two men continued

to grow, Bluhdorn confided to his French-born wife, Yvette, that he was determined to find a suitable wife for his new corporate protégé. Under his tutelage, Bluhdorn declared, Barry Diller would become not only a corporate statesman, but also a father (a goal that was never realized).

To Bob Evans and myself on the West Coast, it was clear that new winds were blowing. Having worked at Paramount for over seven years, I had begun to feel the need for a change of scene. Early in 1974, I resigned to head an independent production company, financed by private investors. By the end of the year, Yablans, too, had left to begin his new career as an independent producer.

The transition for Yablans was not an easy one. He had never developed a script or produced a film. As a studio president, he could issue edicts and write the checks to back them up. As a producer, he now had to cajole, persuade, negotiate. Agents who formerly would interrupt their own phone calls to receive his would now get back to him a day or two later, or not at all.

To ease the transition, Yablans decided to take in a partner. The combination of Yablans and Martin Ransohoff struck many as a natural. Both were short, gruff, and trigger-tempered. As a producer, Ransohoff had been responsible for a string of hit TV shows (*The Beverly Hillbillies, Petticoat Junction*) and movies (*The Cincinnati Kid, The Sandpiper*). The first joint Ransohoff-Yablans production, *Silver Streak*, starring Richard Pryor and Gene Wilder, was a hit, but the two producer partners immediately terminated their partnership amid angry recriminations. On his own, Yablans went on to produce a vividly realistic movie about pro football, *North Dallas Forty*, but that did not satisfy him. He desperately wanted the cachet of having produced a superhit. He yearned to be a George Lucas or a Ray Stark.

The burden of these expectations, however, made the process even harder. *Monsignor*, a lame thriller about the Vatican, proved an embarrassment, as did a melodrama entitled *The Other Side of Midnight*. *Mommie Dearest*, a gauche soap opera about Joan Crawford and her daughter, caused audiences to laugh when they were supposed to cry. And even as Frank Yablans was negotiating for his MGM job, he knew he was leaving behind at Twentieth Century-Fox two films that were destined to be flops, *Star Chamber* and *Kidco*.

Those final efforts had underscored the fact that Frank Yablans was not cut out for a producer's life. He desperately missed the lordly accoutrements that a studio chief commanded. He missed the limos and the lackeys, the authority to bark orders and close deals and change the course of someone's career on a whim. He missed the action.

Now, thanks to Kirk Kerkorian, all those indignities would be forgotten. He would have a second chance to prove his managerial skills. He was older and more mature now. And there was no Charles Bluhdorn to contend with at MGM/UA. Kerkorian, Yablans knew, had no taste for the nitty-gritty of the movie business. He never second-guessed deals, and rarely even attended meetings of the executive committee. Kerkorian was interested only in the bottom line.

There was another key "player" at MGM whose role had to be taken into consideration, however—a more ambiguous figure. This was Frank Rothman, whom Kerkorian had appointed chief executive officer. A litigator by training, with no background either in management or in the film industry, Rothman's appointment two years earlier had caused considerable surprise in the industry. A tall, gawky man, Rothman looked like an academic who had wandered by mistake into Hollywood's executive corridors. No academic, however, received the sort of money Rothman did—a basic salary of $609,865, plus incentive awards totaling $425,000. And it was Rothman, not Yablans, who occupied the vast, baronial office that had once belonged to Louis B. Mayer.

Moreover, despite his calm, pedantic demeanor, there was no doubt that Rothman could be a ruthless corporate manipulator. He had shown this months earlier when the order came down to dump Begelman. Frank Rothman had been Begelman's friend and attorney five years earlier during the long and painful legal proceedings stemming from the Columbia forgeries. Indeed, Begelman had publicly thanked Rothman as the man whose loyalty and legal brilliance had kept him out of jail. Yet it was Frank Rothman who now, on January 7, 1982, marched into Begelman's office and told him he was through at MGM/UA. Further, there would be no settlement of his contract—not a penny. Begelman could take it or leave it. And given his reputation in the community, Rothman told his former client, his recommendation was that Begelman go quietly.

This was the man Yablans would now work with on a day-to-day basis—a man who could be smooth and amicable on the outside, but who clearly had no qualms about whatever deeds his "client," Kirk Kerkorian, wanted done.

Yablans understood all that, and he felt he could deal with it. The important consideration was that Rothman, like Kerkorian, wanted nothing to do with operations. It was up to Yablans to decide which motion pictures would go before the cameras, which TV shows would be developed, which filmmakers would be signed to long-term deals. Managing the company was Yablans's responsibility. He would leave it to Rothman to "manage" Kirk Kerkorian.

Yes, Yablans thought, it had been a long wait, but once again, his time had come.

Yablans could not sleep the night before he was to start the new job. He yearned to get to the studio, sit behind the desk in his new office, and let the reality of it all seep in.

Finally, an hour before dawn, he could hold back no longer. He eased behind the wheel of his silver Rolls—his special gift to himself for landing the job—and started for the studio.

The guard at the gate studied him blearily—a small man in a very large car, materializing out of the predawn mist. Then it clicked: He recognized the face from the photo in *Variety*. Quickly, deferentially, he led the newly appointed studio chief to the parking place that had been allotted him. It was the spot closest to the Thalberg Building, a vast white presence that seemed to hover above him in the early gloom.

Once inside, Yablans paced the long executive corridor, peeking into offices. His office was adjacent to Rothman's and smaller, but it nonetheless occupied that vaunted space that had once been the lair of the Mayers, the Thalbergs, and the other fabled personages of MGM history, whose portraits stared down from the walls. It was here that Gable and Garbo and Garland had been summoned to receive their assignments—or suspensions. The paneled conference room, the creaky corridors, the now-boarded-up secret elevators and passages—all of it represented history, tradition. Yablans had been schooled on the legendary clashes that took place within these walls: Irving Thalberg informing the imperious William Randolph Hearst that *his* protégée, Norma Shearer, not Hearst's, Marion Davies, would star in *The Barretts of Wimpole Street*, even though, as Hearst threatened, Miss Shearer's name would never again appear in the Hearst papers. Or Louis B. Mayer's rage when he learned of a new project to combine two of his favorite "series." Andy Hardy would contract a venereal infection in a forthcoming film, then go to Dr. Kildare for a cure. The proposed film was an elaborate practical joke, but the humorless Mayer had raged for days about this sordid notion.

Yes, the place had seen its share of history, but now the rooms smelled musty and abandoned. It was as though the clock had stopped twenty years ago. People had continued to occupy these spaces, yet their presence had left no impact either on the studio or the craft.

If ever there was an institution that cried out for energy and innovation, this was it, Yablans thought. This was, after all, Hollywood! All that was needed to turn things around was one picture that would grab everyone's attention. One blockbuster. MGM needed a *Godfather*!

Frank Yablans sat slumped in a chair in the darkened studio theater, watching the images that flickered before him on the screen. He had been seated there, alone, for several hours, but to him it seemed like several days. He had been asked by Frank Rothman to screen some films that had been produced under the auspices of the previous regime—"troubled product," Rothman had called it, with his usual bent for euphemism. To call these movies "troubled" was like calling the sinking of the *Titanic* a yachting accident.

At first, Yablans had been determined to see each film from beginning to end, but soon his resolve had begun to crack. He had watched an incoherent comedy called *Nothing Lasts Forever*, which featured what had been described as "brilliant cameos" by the stars of *Saturday Night Live*. Yablans blinked, and hence missed Bill Murray's star turn. Then came an alleged medical black comedy called *The House of God*—not even the most drastic surgery could save it, Yablans had concluded. *Eureka* was a Caribbean thriller without thrills. *Exposed*, directed by James Toback, had left him numb. *Jinxed*, a Bette Midler film, defied rational explanation.

On and on they went. Yablans felt as though he'd been appointed to judge a film festival produced in a lunatic asylum. He could not imagine how any of these films had gotten made, or what could have gone wrong in their making.

Now and then, Yablans caught glimpses of studio aides peeking at him from the dark recesses of the theater. It was as though these old-timers, who had served their years in the MGM lab or editing rooms or wherever, were curious to see whether he'd stick it out, or whether he'd just bolt from the room in total discouragement. Frank Yablans was now sharing their secrets, as though some distinguished old family were parading out its illegitimate children.

He'd realized that a number of "clinkers" had been stashed away, of course. Having studied the numbers, Yablans knew that even those MGM films that had been released had generally turned in a dismal performance at the box office over the past three years'. And the record at UA hadn't been much better. Some $200 million had been spent on production at UA since 1980, but the only winners had been the two sequels, *Rocky III* and *For Your Eyes Only*, the latest James Bond epic. Together, they had accounted for nearly $100 million in U.S. film rentals—the money paid back to the distributor by movie theaters. Nothing else had clicked commercially.

The meaning was vividly clear: Except for these two "franchises," both MGM and UA were essentially out of the movie business. Only two years before, UA had managed to drop a staggering $35 million on *Heaven's Gate*—one of the film industry's most celebrated debacles. But at least *Heaven's Gate* had been formally written off; MGM had not written off the clinkers he was seeing now—they sat there in limbo. It was one thing to survey the numbers, but another to sit in a theater and stare numbly at the product itself.

The projectionist had now shifted into higher-profile films inherited from previous regimes. There was *Brainstorm*, a clunky melodrama that starred Natalie Wood, who had recently drowned in a boating accident off Catalina Island before the film had finished shooting. A decision now had to be made whether to complete the film, using stand-ins, or to abandon it and let the insurance company pay the freight. What complicated the decision, Yablans now saw, was that one of the key scenes in the movie showed Natalie Wood sitting in a small boat, sipping wine, and then falling overboard—an eerie foreshadowing of her real-life death scene. Obviously, the scene would have to be eliminated were the film to be released.

Then, finally, came the *pièce de résistance*—Barbra Streisand's *Yentl*. By including it in this oddball film festival, no one at the studio was suggesting that *Yentl*, too, was unreleasable. Quite the contrary. Even the hard-nosed marketing executives at the studio greatly admired the dedication and craftsmanship displayed in Streisand's maiden directing effort. Her stubborn campaign to get her film made had become legendary in the community. At one point, in an effort to elicit the support of Norbert Auerbach, then president of United Artists, Streisand had even sung him the entire score of the movie. Then, peering into the elderly Auerbach's face, she exclaimed that he would be perfect to play the part of her father in the film.

Streisand later claimed this had been a facetious suggestion, but the literal-minded Auerbach had taken her at her word.

The problem posed by *Yentl* was one of marketing strategy: How does a studio interest a mainstream American audience in a period love story set in a small Jewish shtetl in Eastern Europe? Even the title *"Yentl"* did not summon up the same universal response as, say, *The Sound of Music.*

Now, driving home in his Rolls, an exhausted Yablans struggled to rekindle his salesman's bravado. The soaring optimism that had overtaken him earlier had been severely deflated. His job was more complex than he'd thought. Not only must he build a future for this company, he must also overcome its recent past.

In one area, he would be resolute. If Kirk Kerkorian had allowed previous production chiefs to finance unreleasable movies, then the company would now have to eat its mistakes. At Paramount, Yablans had learned the futility of trying to "chase grosses" with lavish advertising campaigns. He could see his energies consumed in trying to market films that, in reality, had no market.

This, after all, was the start of the Yablans era at MGM, he told himself. The sleeping giant would shake off its cobwebs and be gripped by a new exhilaration—the excitement of deals being made, of important filmmakers returning to Culver City. The Lion would roar anew.

By the time I arrived on the lot to assume my new duties, Yablans had been on the job for two months, and the initial traumas of adjustment had been smoothed over. Rothman and Yablans had begun to evolve a *modus operandi*; the atmosphere was one of optimism.

Yablans himself exuded confidence. My first day at MGM was immortalized by a ceremonial dinner at Morton's, a restaurant that functions as Hollywood's executive commissary. Yablans was accompanied by Tracy Hotchner, his live-in girlfriend. My wife, Leslie, accompanied me. The maître d', who keeps abreast of hirings and firings on a minute-by-minute basis, immediately ushered us to a prize table in recognition of Yablans's exalted status. And within moments, the procession of visitors started—agents, producers, and assorted hangers-on, all filing to the table to greet Yablans and pay their respects. At Morton's, visitations between tables have long been ritualized in accordance with rank and seniority. The "vendors," whether producers or agents, are expected to pay their respects to the "buyers," i.e., those who run the studios. And the "buyers," in turn, are expected to pay theirs to the stars, who array themselves in yet another, even more favored section of the room.

As we received our visitors, I could see that Yablans was relishing his role. It was as though eight years had been instantly erased, and we were back in the Paramount times once again. Yablans himself sensed it. As one prominent agent departed, he leaned over the table and confided, "That son of a bitch wouldn't return my phone calls for eight years, and look at him now. He's like a shark who's gripped by a feeding frenzy."

Apart from enjoying the occasion, Yablans was also using it to spread his message. Over and over, he repeated his litany: "MGM is about to become a major buyer once again," he declared. "The studio is debt-free. We've got the big bucks to spend, and we'll give you the fastest answers in town."

The message was not falling on deaf ears. One could hear the wheels turning as Yablans spread the word. Two or three producers even promised to drop off their scripts the next morning—major "elements" were involved, they promised.

"We've got to get the excitement going," Yablans reiterated, peering across the table at me. "This has got to be your job as well as mine. Spread the word—we want to see everything first. Everyone gets a 'yes' or a 'no' within a week."

"You'll have a thousand screenplays on your desk by the end of the week!" Tracy exclaimed.

"That's great," Yablans enthused.

"Except we have no staff to help review them," I pointed out.

"Then we hire the staff."

I glanced over at him. "Frank, this line about MGM having no debt..."

"That's been one of my major projects. When Kirk bought UA, he amassed a gigantic bank debt. That debt has now been retired."

"You just don't make debt disappear, Frank...."

He looked at me and smiled. "I forgot who I was talking to— Mr. Hot Shit London School of Economics."

In the Paramount years, Yablans would needle me often about my London School of Economics training, insisting that it had been greatly inferior to his "Brooklyn Street-Corner School of Economics."

"Look," he explained. "Rothman and I have been doing this dog-and-pony show for investment analysts. We've sold four hundred million dollars' worth of bonds. It's been fucking amazing."

What Yablans was referring to was an effort orchestrated by a young financier named Michael Milken of Drexel Burnham Lambert to sell MGM bonds—later to be called "junk bonds." It was one of Milken's first coups, which succeeded in easing the pressure of the crushing short-term debt that Kerkorian had accumulated. Milken had accomplished this by putting Yablans and Rothman and other MGM executives on the road, stressing the value of the MGM library, projections of future earnings, the growth prospects of the entertainment industry, etc. It had been quite a show that Milken had staged—one that he would replicate time and again for other companies.

Of course, junk bonds carried high interest rates. MGM was far from "debt-free," as Yablans was telling his fans at Morton's. It was just a different form of debt.

"You have to tell people what they want to hear," Yablans observed with a twinkle. "They want to see the color of our money."

He polished off his drink with a contented smile.

"This is gonna be a lot of fun," he said, grinning. "A lot of fucking fun."

CHAPTER TWO

■

THE GAMBLE
1969

BY any rational yardstick, it seemed like an inept move. Inept and self-destructive. Friends had tried to warn him off. So had his bankers.

Metro-Goldwyn-Mayer had been a magic name in its time. "There were giants in those days...." said Spencer Tracy, invoking the Book of Genesis at the funeral of Louis B. Mayer, MGM's founder. But by 1969, the giants were long gone, and the magic had worn thin. Debts had spiraled to $85 million, and the studio was about to default on its bank loans. Studio management was so panicked by its new slate of pictures that it was pondering an immediate $45 million write-off.

Nor was MGM alone in its woes. Television was king in 1969, and five of the seven major motion-picture companies were in the red. Movie theaters had lost well over half of their customers in the generation since World War II.

Kirk Kerkorian was not intimidated by these numbers. He was a gambler, a man ruled by gut instinct. An Armenian farm boy with an eighth-grade education, he did not have hit squads of Harvard MBAs at his beck and call, eager to crunch numbers and

29

chart industry trends. Kerkorian had made his fortune buying and selling old airplanes, then using them to fly gamblers to Las Vegas.

He knew Wall Street had soured on MGM, and that didn't bother him, either. Time Inc. owned a big stake in the studio, but now it was trying to get out. Xerox and Metromedia had taken a hard look, then backed away.

A year earlier, Edgar Bronfman, the forty-year-old scion of the powerful Seagram dynasty, had bought control of MGM, but his regime was now hemorrhaging, and Sam, the fierce patriarch of the clan, was urging that his son unload his holdings.

It would require a major infusion of capital to turn MGM around, and Kerkorian was already stretched thin, but that, too, was all right. He was, after all, a creature of Las Vegas: In Vegas, when you're on a roll, you keep plunging. And over the last twenty months, Kerkorian had been on a remarkable roll.

Taking advantage of the sudden vogue of so-called supplemental airlines (i.e., charter services), Kerkorian had sold his jerry-built charter to the fast-expanding Transamerica Corporation. He then quickly unloaded his Transamerica stock to make a surprise tender for a "real" airline—a $73 million transaction that gave him a 30 percent stake in Western Airlines.

Its suspicions aroused by the lightning speed of these transactions, the Civil Aeronautics Board immediately subpoenaed the financial analyses and other studies prepared by Kerkorian before mounting his Western takeover bid. The regulators were chagrined to find that Kerkorian had nothing to give them—just numbers scrawled on the back of a napkin.

Fueled by additional bank loans, Kerkorian next scooped up the old scandal-torn Flamingo Hotel and Casino in Las Vegas. And he started construction of yet another casino, the International, placing the two under the umbrella of a trendy-sounding, publicly held company called International Leisure Corporation.

Aides were urging Kerkorian to take time to digest these moves, but the rough-hewn onetime boxer from the San Joaquin Valley was hungry for bigger prey. His good friend and attorney Gregson Bautzer had already set off abject panic among MGM's board of directors by clumsily dropping hints about takeover possibilities. The board had assumed Bautzer was acting on behalf of his *other* Las Vegas client, the dreaded Howard Hughes. Kerkorian figured they'd be relieved when the "raider" turned out to be a more benign presence.

He was mistaken. Despite the precarious condition of the company, the MGM board was united in its determination to resist the takeover until a suitable "white knight" could be found—a buyer who understood the entertainment industry and who had the capital to reshape the old studio. Kerkorian was clearly not that individual.

Undeterred, Kerkorian started buying MGM stock at its depressed price of twenty-five dollars a share. The "breakup" value, he figured, was somewhere around seventy dollars a share. Now that the takeover was public knowledge, the price of MGM shares was rising sharply, but Kerkorian kept buying. Within a month, the shares were heading toward forty dollars, and Kerkorian still had not secured control. The deal was going to cost him more than he had calculated—indeed, more than he could afford, in the opinion of the MGM board. Kerkorian, they noted, had already borrowed up to his limit from U.S. banks against his stock in Western Airlines and International Leisure. In the opinion of Wall Street, Kerkorian had no choice but to pack up and go away.

They were right—for two weeks. Then, suddenly, he was back again, claiming now to have accumulated a war chest from foreign investors that he said was in excess of $70 million. The source of the money, he declared, was a consortium of banks in England and West Germany, but "the Street" had its own unsubstantiated rumors. It was Onassis money, it was Arab money, it was laundered money from the syndicate. MGM lawyers marched on federal court, seeking an injunction against further stock purchases on the grounds that Kerkorian lacked legitimate collateral. The court responded that it had no grounds on which to issue such an injunction.

By mid-September, two months after starting his raid, Kerkorian acquired a final 620,000 shares at $42, giving him 40 percent control. His opposition, unable to raise new capital to continue the fight, surrendered. The deal, analysts estimated, had cost Kerkorian over $100 million—an extraordinary expenditure for a studio that was struggling to keep its head above water.

Yet Kerkorian was ecstatic. The man who had never expected to own anything more glamorous than a battered secondhand jet now controlled the mythic kingdom of Mayer and Thalberg—the studio where he'd once worked as a day laborer. "Kirk felt he'd bought himself a little immortality," observed his friend Bautzer.

As he would soon learn, Kerkorian had also bought himself a nightmarish web of problems that would soon threaten his reputation, as well as his fortune.

* * *

Seizing control of his new toy, Kirk Kerkorian was keenly aware of his most pressing need—management. Kerkorian himself knew nothing of the intricacies of the entertainment business. His advisers were men who understood casinos, not movies. The man needed to run MGM, he concluded, must not only understand filmmaking, but also must inspire the confidence of the bankers and stockholders.

A meeting had been arranged between Kerkorian and the onetime cereal executive Louis F. "Bo" Polk, who now headed MGM, but the session had been a disaster. Kerkorian did not like squeaky-clean business-school types who spouted statistics; he also didn't like men who nicknamed themselves "Bo." Send Polk back to his cornflakes company, Kerkorian ordered. Someone more formidable was needed for MGM.

And he thought he had the man for the job. One of his favorite tennis-playing friends in Beverly Hills was Herb Jaffe, a solid, respected onetime literary agent who was now in charge of West Coast production for United Artists. Kerkorian had flown him to Las Vegas to confide his takeover plans for MGM, and Jaffe had seemed keenly interested. Having now offered Jaffe the job, however, Kerkorian was running into static. Jaffe said he would need time to think it over. His family was frightened about Kerkorian's supposed "connections." His colleagues at United Artists were warning of Kerkorian's uncertain finances. Why would he want to quit the secure respectability of United Artists for this character from Las Vegas?

Reluctantly, Herb Jaffe phoned his regrets. He still wanted the job, he confessed, but he'd been browbeaten to the point where he would have to turn it down.

Kerkorian was stung by his friend's rejection, but Greg Bautzer moved quickly to fill the vacuum. With Jaffe out, the only other man to run MGM, he asserted, was none other than Jim Aubrey, the "Smiling Cobra" who four years earlier had been dismissed as president of CBS. Aubrey was tough, said Bautzer. He was a sound businessman who had proved he could keep the creative types under control.

On the surface, Kerkorian and Aubrey seemed an unlikely match. Aubrey was the rich man's son who'd gone to Princeton. Kerkorian's father could neither read nor write, and Kerkorian's grammar could best be described as "basic Vegas." The tall, lean Aubrey looked as though he'd fallen out of a Brooks Brothers ad. Kerkorian showed up for meetings unshaven and wearing a battered windbreaker. Aubrey was schooled in the sophisticated power plays of

Madison Avenue. Kerkorian knew what it was like to take off from an unlighted runway with marshals racing after him, waving repossession notices.

Yet there were subtle areas of similarity. Both affected soft-spoken, almost diffident styles, as though to conceal their lethal natures. Kerkorian sensed the predator in Aubrey. Here was a man who could take the heat for the massive cutbacks that lay ahead if MGM were to survive.

To be sure, Aubrey was purely a creature of TV. He had never made a movie; indeed, rarely saw one. But, as Bautzer kept insisting, maybe this was an advantage. He would not be beholden to Hollywood's power elite.

And no one could quarrel with Aubrey's achievements at CBS. During his regime, *The Beverly Hillbillies, The Dick Van Dyke Show, Green Acres, Petticoat Junction*, and *Gilligan's Island* were all brought to the air. These shows hadn't exactly been cultural landmarks, but they'd made CBS number one, which was what William Paley, its founder, had always wanted.

Himself a "bottom line" sort of fellow, Aubrey understood that while Paley enjoyed reminiscing about the great days of Edward R. Murrow and CBS News, what really mattered to him could be reduced to one word: ratings. And Aubrey had delivered.

The Smiling Cobra's abrupt dismissal by Paley in 1965 was the subject of more scrutiny and speculation than a Kremlin coup. One school held it was strictly a business decision. Three of his new shows had gone over budget and flopped—and all had been produced by a partying friend named Keefe Brasselle, an ex-actor with a dark reputation. And that, in turn, led to juicier theories that the whole affair had been triggered by Aubrey's exotic personal habits. Gossip about wild parties and ribaldry had caused disquiet among key sponsors, it was said.

The mythology that Aubrey had created about himself had come back to haunt him. Robin Stone, the womanizing hero of Jacqueline Susann's *The Love Machine*, was blatantly Aubreyesque. An Aubrey-like character was prominent in Harold Robbins's *The Inheritors*, and, of course, there was the nonfiction best-seller *Only You, Dick Daring!* Most blatant was the turgid novel written by Brasselle himself, *The Cannibals*, in which Aubrey turns up as the ruthless Jonathan J. Bingham, a network president who exploits an actor-turned-producer reminiscent of Brasselle. The Bingham character, among other things, likes his bed partners in sextuplet. "He's a real bad scene," confides one fictional hooker.

The face Aubrey presented to the world was that of the controlled tactician, the master of cool. The after-hours Aubrey was a whole different animal—hard-drinking and feral. Jack Gould, the eminent television critic of *The New York Times*, had written of "the jungle that prevails at the executive level of TV programming." And Aubrey had become its ultimate product; he had become the fabled "Jungle Jim."

During his four years in exile, since his CBS dismissal, Aubrey had traveled and relaxed in an effort to get his turbulent personal life under control. He had left CBS with some 18,642 shares worth $55 each, and had made some prudent investments. His friend Greg Bautzer had occasionally come to him with business offers. He'd even introduced Aubrey to Howard Hughes, who had decided to buy the ABC television network and install Aubrey as its chief. Hughes abruptly canceled the deal, however, when informed he'd be required to make an appearance before the Federal Communications Commission. Since Hughes had locked himself away in a Las Vegas hotel suite, such an appearance would have been inconceivable.

The disappointment over the Hughes deal was one reason why Aubrey reacted eagerly to Kerkorian's invitation. Here was this Hughes-like figure, younger and less crazed than Hughes, offering him a chance to rebuild MGM. He felt he understood Kerkorian's hard-edged approach to business.

Under the deal they negotiated in 1969, Aubrey's salary would total $208,000, compared with the $224,000 he'd earned at CBS, and he would also have options to purchase 17,500 shares of MGM stock. But there would be no contract. "Kirk lives by his handshake," Bautzer told him.

Aubrey's introduction into MGM's affairs was accomplished with his customary aura of mystery. Several key executives from the studio had been summoned to New York to discuss a plan involving the sale of the Culver City studios to real estate developers and the construction of a new studio in the Conejo Valley, a two-hour drive away. Career MGM officials knew the plan made no sense whatsoever, but Bo Polk's holdover MBAs dragged on hour after hour with their charts and statistics.

Four hours into the meeting, the door to the conference room opened, and a tall man entered and moved to the table. "Sorry for interrupting," the stranger announced, "but I'm Jim Aubrey, your new president." Then, turning to the MBAs, he added, "Now, if we can move on to my agenda..."

Aubrey's personal agenda, to be sure, did not include most of the people around the table. Within a week, Polk's MBAs were history. Aubrey and Kerkorian had both moved into new offices at the studio. Typically, while Aubrey's parking space had his name painted on it, Kerkorian's had no name—just the "lucky" number 21.

Upon assuming his new duties, Aubrey quickly armed himself with epithets about trimming costs and modernizing what he termed "the studio's archaic methods of doing business." He said he intended to trim bureaucracy, appoint a solid management team, and shape a new program of modestly budgeted films to take the studio through its hard times. It would all be accomplished in an orderly, cool-headed way, the way things had been done at CBS.

Within a week, however, Aubrey realized that he'd walked into a whipsaw. There was no time for orderly, cool-headed planning; the studio was in a state of abject chaos. Creditors were hammering at the doors. Huge commitments had been made for new films that the studio could not even begin to afford. These weren't cautious "step deals" for low-budget projects; these were firm "pay-or-play" commitments (everyone would get paid even if the films were canceled) involving some of the world's most important, and expensive, filmmakers. Three of the projects alone, *Man's Fate, Ryan's Daughter*, and *Taipan*, would cost the studio some $60 million if they went forward as planned.

Jim Aubrey now knew how the members of the Civil Aeronautics Board had felt when they demanded to see Kerkorian's "due diligence" reports on Western Airlines. The acquisition of MGM had been marked by a complete absence of research and preparation. Kerkorian had told his new president that the studio was financially strapped. He hadn't told him that the studio was in a state of siege, with bankruptcy looming.

The first priority, clearly, was to deal with the staggering picture commitments, and that meant a quick trip to the European battlefront. It would turn out to be a legendary tour—one that would set the tone for the Aubrey regime at MGM.

Rome was the first stop. Michelangelo Antonioni, the distinguished Italian director who'd scored a hit with *Blow Up* two years earlier, wanted to show Aubrey a cut of his first American film, *Zabriskie Point*, which MGM was going to release. Aubrey arrived on a Friday afternoon, and that night screened the film with Antonioni and his producer, Carlo Ponti. Ponti was the man responsible for *Doctor Zhivago*, the film that had kept MGM afloat through the mid-sixties.

Zabriskie Point, however, was another story—a disconnected and profoundly boring canvas of couples coupling and triples tripling against the surreal backdrop of the Mojave Desert. Though it incorporated the obligatory youth-versus-establishment theme, it somehow got it all wrong. And, to complicate matters, it would certainly get an "X" rating, which would sharply inhibit the scope of its release.

Jim Aubrey rubbed his weary eyes and mumbled a few polite words to the filmmakers, adding that he would offer some specific suggestions at their meeting the following morning. Ponti and Antonioni, eager to retire to their country homes for the weekend, politely urged that they have the conversation now. Ponti not only wanted to talk about *Zabriskie Point*, he also wanted to question the new MGM president about plans for his other MGM film, *Man's Fate*, which was in preproduction in London under the direction of Fred Zinnemann. But Aubrey would have none of it. "Talk to you tomorrow," he said, striding from the room, leaving Ponti and Antonioni standing there.

When the two Italians turned up for the meeting the next day, Aubrey was not there. A hotel clerk informed them the MGM president had checked out in the middle of the night and had left no message.

Aubrey had, in fact, flown to London, where the *Man's Fate* kettle was already boiling. Lee Steiner, Ponti's American attorney, had arrived in London at the same time as Aubrey. Indeed, they'd passed one another at Heathrow—Aubrey had nodded but dodged off. No sooner had Steiner checked into his hotel than he received a phone call from the company's general counsel in New York. "The picture's off," snapped Ben Melniker, the MGM executive. "Tell Ponti."

"My God, has anyone informed Fred Zinnemann?" Steiner asked.

"That's your job," Melniker shot back.

"He's not even my client!" Steiner replied, but Melniker was already off the line.

Steiner immediately tried to track down Aubrey, but as he attempted to do so, even more bad news was emanating from the studio. MGM, it seemed, was taking the position that Zinnemann was personally responsible for the $3.5 million spent on the film to date. Preproduction expenditures had been channeled through Zinnemann's English-based company for technical reasons, relating to co-financing treaties, with the specific understanding that MGM would reimburse all expenses. Now, the $3.5 million suddenly had become Zinnemann's sole responsibility. When Zinnemann's attorneys protested, an MGM official replied, "What's the hassle? Tell him to file for bankruptcy."

The Viennese-born Zinnemann, who had reached preeminence with such films as *High Noon* and *A Man for All Seasons*, was enraged. He demanded an audience with Jim Aubrey, but no one could find him. Aubrey, it seemed, had already accomplished his purpose in London, and was off to his next battlefront, Dublin, where David Lean was preparing to shoot yet another MGM epic, *Ryan's Daughter*.

Though Aubrey had been determined to cancel *Man's Fate*, an expensive film based on André Malraux's classic novel set in the Orient, his mission to Dublin was less apocalyptic. He hoped that by citing the studio's financial difficulties, he could persuade the crusty, sixty-year-old filmmaker to sharply reduce his budget. Studio aides had warned him that trying to cut a David Lean budget was like negotiating with the Pentagon: You get him to drop a sailboat, but you end up with an aircraft carrier. Nevertheless, Aubrey was confident of his powers of persuasion.

The summit meeting, however, got off to a rocky start. Philip Kellogg, Lean's agent from the William Morris Agency, happened to be in Dublin at the time, and Lean decided to invite the gentlemanly Kellogg to the meeting. Learning of this, Aubrey sent forth the dictum No agents. And Lean replied, No meeting.

Now, it was Aubrey who backed off. The meeting was held, with Kellogg in attendance, and Aubrey pleaded his case. Lean listened respectfully and said little. Even as Aubrey shook hands to leave, he sensed his mission had failed.

The bloodbath was not yet over. Aubrey flew back to Culver City to cancel some fifteen other projects that were either in preproduction or advanced preparation. Among them was *Taipan*, yet another expensive production set in the Orient, based on the James Clavell best-seller. The producers of *Taipan*, the ubiquitous Carlo Ponti and Martin Ransohoff, were informed by studio lawyers that they, too, would be held responsible for preproduction costs, in this case some $2.5 million.

The cocky, combative Ransohoff wasted no time in marching on Aubrey's office. In his career as a TV producer, it was Ransohoff who'd delivered *The Beverly Hillbillies*, *Mr. Ed*, and *Petticoat Junction*, which had made Aubrey a hero at CBS. And now his old colleague was going to stiff him!

Ransohoff launched into his tirade as Aubrey sat with the usual impassive look on his face. Lawyers flanked him. Finally, the Smiling Cobra broke in.

"Marty, you're missing the point."

"What's the goddam point?"

"The goddam point is that we have no goddam money," Aubrey said.

"You have a firm pay-or-play deal...."

"No money, Marty," Aubrey repeated. "No fucking money. Get the message?"

The meeting ended.

In canceling these commitments, Aubrey had saved the studio tens of millions of dollars—an accomplishment that greatly pleased Kirk Kerkorian. At the same time, Aubrey had effected these savings in a manner that seemed designed to maximize indignation in the filmmaking community. Lawsuits already had been filed by Zinnemann and Ransohoff. In addition, the widely venerated Zinnemann had fired off an irate public statement condemning Aubrey and the studio for its immoral business practices. His position was supported by other filmmakers in a trade ad. If MGM did not change its ways, it was warned, the Dark Ages would soon close in on Culver City.

If the lawsuits and trade ads were designed to intimidate Aubrey, they would prove a ringing failure, for he was just warming to his task. At the January 15, 1970, annual stockholders' meeting, Aubrey announced that the company had lost $35 million during the past year and, as a result, planned a new round of stringent measures. The studio work force, he said, would be cut by a staggering 50 percent. Over a third of MGM's acreage in Culver City would be put up for sale, and so would the two thousand acres the company had purchased in the Conejo Valley.

Moreover, a twenty-five-year-old whiz kid named Mike Curb had been hired to take over the music division, which, Aubrey said, "had nearly disintegrated."

As Aubrey introduced the baby-faced Curb, a stockholder asked from the floor: "Who is this kid—Kerkorian's son-in-law?"

Studio morale was decimated by the cutbacks. Veterans of the back lot, it seemed, were being fired at random. Studio assets were being sold off with almost giddy abandon. Huge chunks of the studio's 187-acre lot were sold at far lower prices than could have been obtained in a more orderly process, senior executives charged. MGM SWAPS ASSETS FOR PROFITS screamed a *Variety* headline.

One studio officer, desperate to stop the selling frenzy, insisted on walking Aubrey and several top Kerkorian aides around the lot to point out the wealth of tradition that was being squandered. Patiently, deliberately, he showed his odd little tour group the tank and jungles for the Tarzan films, the railway from *The Harvey Girls*, Andy Hardy's small town square, Chinese streets from *The Good Earth*, the Dickensian buildings from *David Copperfield*, the sprawling lake that still harbored the tug from *Tugboat Annie*, the lavish Fifth Avenue set from *Easter Parade*, the rolling lawns from Garbo's *Camille*, the handsome mansion from *The Philadelphia Story*, the huge tank that doubled as Esther Williams's swimming pool, the army camp built for the *Private Hargrove* pictures, the eight Victorian mansions from *Meet Me in St. Louis*.

The tour was not a success. Fred Benninger, a big, burly man whom Kerkorian befriended when they were both pilots, stared blankly at the historic sets and props and said, "How often is this stuff used? It's just lying around all over the place."

Aubrey, too, was irascible. "I don't want to hear any more bullshit about the old MGM," he snapped. "The old MGM is gone."

As if to prove his point, he ordered that the Thalberg Building be renamed the Administration Building. A bust of Thalberg was removed, along with a commemorative plaque. Both were surreptitiously preserved by a studio veteran and restored to their places of honor four years later, after Aubrey himself had been fired.

Meanwhile, the fire sales continued. The studio's movie theaters overseas were sold for $6.4 million. Boreham Wood, MGM's handsomely appointed London studio, was sold for $4.3 million. The studio's camera department was peddled to Panavision.

Even as all this was happening, the public-relations men were struggling to put a positive face on the transactions. *The Wall Street Journal* dutifully carried a story headlined HOW AUBREY IS REVIVING MGM BY CUTTING OUT THE FAT AND NOSTALGIA. Other business publications, too, explained how "modern business practices were bringing new life to the studio."

In reality, of course, they were draining the life from the studio— indeed, stripping it clean. The ultimate metaphor for the process was the eighteen-day-long series of auctions that were held in May 1970, during which the studio's treasure trove of wardrobe, props, vintage cars, etc., were sold to the highest bidders. The pathetic occasion was akin to a once-proud dowager selling off her furnishings to pay the rent.

The event had been set up by David Weisz, a professional auctioneer, who'd advanced $1.5 million for the props, wardrobe, etc.—enough to fill several soundstages. Kerkorian aides who'd made the deal had vastly underestimated the value of the goods, not realizing that much of the furniture, chandeliers, and other props, dating back to the studio's "golden era," were not reproductions or fakes, but valuable antiques. Apart from the nostalgia value, there was true commercial value in these goods.

The auctions received remarkably little attention in the press, almost as if the community wanted to ignore the embarrassment. Those industry people who attended felt uncomfortable at being there. "If you saw somebody you knew, you pretended not to recognize them," said actor Roddy McDowall, who'd grown up among the props being sold.

The array of paraphernalia was staggering. There were ancient swords and armor, branding irons, spears, and ceremonial axes, and great quantities of model planes and ships. There were ancient radiators, sitting baths, brass hair-curlers, incense burners, ramrods, Egyptian plaques. A vast display of peace pipes sat next to another of powder horns. There were all manner of contraptions and vehicles, ranging from sod cutters to rickshas, canoes to antique railway cars. One could bid on an entire ship's lavatory or a wide array of antique organs and other musical instruments.

The wardrobe itself represented an exercise in wish-fulfillment. Women could buy Judy Garland's white cotton dress from *Meet Me in St. Louis.* Or Elizabeth Taylor's powder-blue gown from *Raintree County.* Or a two-piece dark gray velvet suit worn by Greta Garbo in *Queen Christina.* Or Debbie Reynolds's turquoise velvet outfit from *The Unsinkable Molly Brown.* Or a feather-trim lavender chiffon dress worn by Susan Hayward in *I'll Cry Tomorrow.*

For the men who wanted to acquire a different look, there was the Oriental brocade outfit Paul Muni wore in *The Good Earth.* Or Stewart Granger's purple cape from *Young Bess.* Or Tarzan codpieces for the warmer weather.

The auctions were a great success, at least for the auctioneer. Those still charged with the responsibility of making films wondered how they were supposed to mount their productions if the cupboards were bare.

That is, if MGM was still in the business of making pictures. According to the rumor mill, an announcement was imminent that MGM would officially withdraw from filmmaking. Finally, with the auctions over, Aubrey decided to put that report to rest. The studio, he declared, would definitely keep making films, but with a lid of $2 million for each project. "At that kind of figure," he explained, "we know we can't lose much money." Clearly, at those numbers, the days of the *Doctor Zhivago*s were over.

The task of making and marketing these $2 million movies, Aubrey said, would be assigned to Douglas Netter and Herbert Solow. Netter, a brash, tough-talking distribution man, was already in the process of shutting down MGM's East Coast offices so that all marketing functions could be consolidated at Culver City. As a crony of Aubrey and a man who loved exploitation pictures, Netter seemed a natural "fit" into the new MGM setup.

Solow, on the other hand, did not. The lone holdover from the Bo Polk era, Solow had known Aubrey when both worked in TV, but they had never been close. While Aubrey was the tight-lipped corporatist, Solow was an informal man, totally devoid of managerial affectation. Aubrey and Netter, prowling the lot in suits and ties, would see Solow, clad in tan slacks and workshirt, sipping coffee with a film crew.

In sensibility, Solow was a "sixties person." As head of production, he had made such whimsical exercises as Robert Altman's *Brewster McCloud*, which dealt with a crazed youth (Bud Cort) who was intent on building mechanical wings to help him fly.

Solow also had given the green light to the darkly satiric Paul Mazursky film *Alex in Wonderland*, whose central character was a deranged director (Mazursky himself did a comedy turn as a paranoid producer).

Under the previous regime, all proposed film projects had been scrutinized by Bo Polk's whiz kids, who, armed with their computer readouts, claimed an ability to predict the precise demographic results of each film. Having discovered the burgeoning "youth market," the whiz kids instructed Solow to make such films as *The Magic Garden of Stanley Sweetheart* and *The Strawberry Statement*, two "youth comedies" about sex and social protest. Both bombed.

Now, Solow found himself freed from the tyranny of the computer readout, but confronting instead the hard-nosed assessments of Aubrey and Netter. As a TV executive, Aubrey had been renowned for his cynical assessment of public tastes. Aubrey believed, as George Bernard Shaw had put it, that "the audience receives the art it deserves," and, to Aubrey, it deserved *Mister Ed*.

If Solow wondered how this cynicism would transfer itself to films, he did not have to wait long to find out. To Aubrey, the kind of movie that made sense was *Shaft*, a gory exploitation picture about a black private eye. (Aubrey went on to make two sequels.)

He exhibited similar enthusiasm for *Kansas City Bomber*, in which Raquel Welch (a frequent Aubrey date) played a roller-derby queen.

To elicit Aubrey's approval, Solow concluded, a project had to meet two criteria. It had to be cheap. And it had to appeal to a clearly defined segment of the audience.

Movies with sex and violence stood the best shot at meeting

these criteria. Solow had shot down a project called *Angel Loves Nobody*, in which a high school student systematically hacked his teachers to death. Aubrey and Netter resurrected it.

Similarly, sex films such as *Private Parts* and *Percy* popped up with regularity on MGM's slim production schedule ("Percy" was the name of a penis). Aubrey even invited Gerald Domiano, the "auteur" of *Deep Throat*, to meet with studio executives, but they couldn't agree on a project, to Herb Solow's considerable relief. Paradoxically, when Robert Littman, MGM's production chief in London, proposed a deal for *Last Tango in Paris*, the project was rejected by the studio.

Given the paucity of low-cost product, MGM's release schedule was padded with curious pickups and co-financed projects from around the world—projects bearing such eccentric titles as *Every Little Crook and Nanny; The Lolly Madonna War; My Lover, My Son;* and *In the Black Belly of the Tarantula*. It was not a distinguished program of pictures, and it did not produce distinguished box-office results. Indeed, other than *Shaft*, the "new MGM" of Kirk Kerkorian was bombing with alarming consistency.

It wasn't taste alone that was working against the success of MGM's films. Talented filmmakers were steadfastly avoiding the studio, with few exceptions. In part, this stemmed from the Zinnemann controversy over *Man's Fate*. MGM, to many directors, was now hostile territory.

And the feeling was mutual. Jim Aubrey distrusted Hollywood's top directors and producers. He often alluded darkly to "the club"—movie people who "took care of" their friends and allies at the expense of the studios. As president of MGM, he was determined to prove that he didn't need the support of "the club" in order to succeed.

On those rare occasions where a prominent filmmaker found his way into MGM's ranks, the result was usually war.

Blake Edwards was a case in point. Acknowledging that the studio needed at least an occasional movie with recognizable stars, Aubrey agreed to make a film called *Wild Rovers* starring William Holden and Ryan O'Neal, with Blake Edwards directing. It was a good-spirited, picaresque western about two cowboys with a penchant for getting into trouble. To Aubrey, the picture was nothing but trouble. The imperious, often petulant Edwards found himself challenged repeatedly by an equally contentious Aubrey. No detail seemed too small to battle over.

A prime example was a derby worn by O'Neal in the film. To Edwards, the derby represented realism. Not everyone in the West wore conventional cowboy hats, he pointed out. Perhaps not, Aubrey countered, but cowboys in MGM movies always wore cowboy hats. By the time Aubrey first seized on the issue, the film had already been shooting for two weeks. Ordered to switch hats, Edwards was adamant. It was too late to switch, he argued. The derby had already been established as part of O'Neal's character.

"Change hats or shut down," was Aubrey's edict—an extraordinary threat in view of the fact that *Wild Rovers* was the only "high profile" picture in production at the studio.

The battle of the derby escalated. Edwards remarked in an interview that "Jim Aubrey doesn't know as much about film as a first-year cinema student." Aubrey, meanwhile, let it be known that he didn't think too much of Edwards's work, and that he might have to hire his own editor and cut the film himself.

In the end, Edwards buckled. Grimly, he wrote an expository scene in which the Ryan O'Neal character explained his change in haberdashery. Thereafter, he wore a cowboy hat in the film.

Nevertheless, Edwards fared better than Sam Peckinpah, the volatile director of *Pat Garrett and Billy the Kid*. A hard-drinking man with a formidable persecution complex, Peckinpah seemed ideally suited for his role as an Aubrey adversary.

Even under the best of circumstances, *Pat Garrett* seemed destined to be a troubled project. Its script was extremely violent and oddly fragmented, and its cast, at best, inexperienced. Kris Kristofferson had had little acting experience at the time; his co-star, cult hero Bob Dylan, had absolutely none. Peckinpah wanted lots of rehearsal time and a leisurely shooting schedule to ensure time to work with his actors. The studio, just prior to production, chopped the fifty-eight-day schedule to thirty-six days. Peckinpah wanted to shoot in New Mexico. MGM decided Mexico would be cheaper.

The studio was determined that the film be brought in for $3 million. Peckinpah thought that figure was absurd.

By the time the film finally started shooting, both Aubrey and Peckinpah were primed for a fight. An innocuous scene about river-rafting provided the unlikely flash point.

The scene depicted Pat Garrett and Billy floating blissfully down a river. The peaceful bucolic setting is violently interrupted when a man who has been sunning himself at river's edge suddenly picks up his rifle and starts shooting at the raft. Billy and Pat frantically paddle away.

As he saw dailies that night, Aubrey demanded, "What the hell is that all about?"

There was silence in the room. Aubrey turned to an aide who was charged with responsibility for the film and repeated the question. "Don't you understand your own movie?" he asked.

The aide blanched. "I spoke with the producer about it," he replied. "In Sam Peckinpah's movies there are always scenes like this. They're metaphors, really—metaphors for the existential violence that existed in that period."

Aubrey fixed a lethal stare on the aide. "The scene comes out of the movie," he directed. "I don't want any of this existential horseshit in my movies, is that clear?"

The battle of wills continued throughout the shoot, with angry phone calls and telegrams bouncing back and forth between the studio and the location. But open hostilities did not resume again until Peckinpah turned in his first cut. It was two hours and forty minutes long.

Aubrey was in a state of shock. He decreed that a full hour be taken out of the movie. Moreover, he informed his director that the film's release date had been moved up two months. This would leave Peckinpah only three weeks to make the drastic changes.

Working night and day, Peckinpah had his cut ready for the designated preview date, only to discover that Aubrey had secretly made a copy of the print and had put his own editors to work preparing a "studio version." Peckinpah's cut was two hours long, Aubrey's ninety-six minutes.

Instead of attending the preview, Peckinpah filed a lawsuit charging not only breach of contract, but also, imaginatively, invasion of privacy. MGM proceeded to release its own version to unfavorable critical response and dim business.

By the time Peckinpah filed suit, Aubrey was already doing battle with other filmmakers at the studio.

Michael Laughlin, the producer of *Chandler*, took a full page ad in the *Hollywood Reporter*, signed by himself and his director, Paul Magwood, which stated, "To those who may be interested: Regarding what was our film, CHANDLER, let's give credit where credit is due. We sadly acknowledge that all editing, postproduction, as well as additional scenes, were executed by James T. Aubrey, Jr. We are sorry."

Two days later, Laughlin received a telegram from Robert Altman, stating, "I understand you're having your problems with the cowardly lion, MGM. . . . I am pleased that you are attempting to bring public and judicial attention to their used car lot type of dealing, but I am afraid it will fall on deaf ears. The law is too complicated, slow and expensive to reach them before they die of a natural corporate death."

Meanwhile, Bruce Geller, a top TV producer, demanded his name be removed from *Corky*, which he'd directed. And Herbert Leonard, who produced and directed a Robert Mitchum film, *Going Home*, charged his film, too, had been disastrously reedited.

Even in cases where their films weren't altered, directors were startled to find tunes stuck on the beginning or end. The man responsible was Mike Curb, Aubrey's twenty-five-year-old music protégé, who had made a minor splash in the pop-music field with the Mike Curb Congregation. As the new head of MGM Music, Curb had quickly earned a reputation as a minor-league Aubrey by firing 239 of this division's 240 employees. (A press agent was the sole survivor.) It was Curb's notion that by sticking a pop song at the end of such films as *Zabriskie Point* or *Kelly's Heroes*, he could generate a surprise hit single. It did not occur to him to notify filmmakers, who usually did not learn about the added songs until they saw their films in the theater.

The net result of all this was that MGM was becoming the favorite whipping boy for the industry, and the press was gleefully joining in. Reviews would not only knock the studio's films, but also attack MGM as a company. Even the studio's advertising campaigns came in for derision.

When ads for *Wild Rovers* appeared, showing a grinning Ryan O'Neal mounted behind William Holden on a horse, his arms around Holden's waist, *Variety* asked, "Could this perhaps be a story of two homosexuals? Why is O'Neal smiling? Is the horse involved?"

Aubrey's response was to bar *Variety* from the lot and its critics from studio screenings. After a few weeks, the bans were lifted, and the *Wild Rovers* campaign was subjected to radical surgery.

"Morale at the studio has never been higher," Jim Aubrey told an interviewer from the *Los Angeles Times* in 1971. The quote was immediately emblazoned across walls all over the studio. The truth, of course, was that morale was nonexistent. Almost everyone still working at the studio (employment had plummeted from sixty-two hundred to twelve hundred) was circulating résumés all over town. Herb Solow, the production chief, was about to leave, and Roger Mayer, the erudite attorney who had long headed the studio's physical plant, also was job-hunting. The joke among filmmakers was that MGM was the *last* place you went with a project—right after the unemployment office.

At a time when truly innovative films were emerging from rival studios—films like *The Godfather, Clockwork Orange,* and *Deliverance*—MGM's output seemed downright squalid. This fact drew angry complaints at the 1971 stockholders' meeting. The shareholders were rewarded in kind: For the first time, there was no free lunch and no free movie.

Though maintaining his usual cool, Aubrey himself felt trapped and demoralized. Kerkorian, he believed, had either misrepresented or misunderstood the true condition of the company when he'd brought Aubrey aboard. And since that time, Kerkorian seemed to be standing back, watching him twist in the wind. The longer he worked for Kerkorian, the less Aubrey felt he knew him. Just when they seemed to strike a personal connection, Kerkorian would distance himself once again.

Fred Benninger, the man whom Kerkorian had delegated to "keep an eye" on the studio, struck Aubrey as being flagrantly hostile, not only toward him, but toward the studio as well. Aubrey always referred to the burly, tough-talking aide as "the Prussian." He half-jokingly suggested that the wardrobe department suit him up in a Nazi uniform.

In the face of all this, Aubrey grew progressively more irritable with colleagues and employees. He was drinking too much. His personal habits were becoming increasingly self-destructive. Always a creature of the night, Aubrey was hanging out in the wrong places with the wrong people. His most frequent companions were his sales chief, Doug Netter, and a homosexual ex-agent named Billy Belasco, who abrasively demanded special favors at the studio because of his close ties with Aubrey.

Aubrey's behavior now reminded friends of his final days at CBS. It was almost as though he were courting the dark rumors about wild parties, fights, and orgies.

"Some people go on automatic pilot when they're in trouble," said one Aubrey colleague. "Jungle Jim goes on automatic self-destruct."

MGM, which once seemed like a great opportunity for Aubrey, now seemed like a growing embarrassment. And the studio was starting to have the same affect on Kirk Kerkorian. Before the MGM takeover, Kerkorian had relished his anonymity. He operated like a financial phantom who, with lightning speed, could scoop up companies and swing spectacular deals.

Now, despite all efforts, he was the subject of intense public scrutiny. Magazines were poking around in the shadows of his past, analyzing his strategems, assessing his wealth. A piece in *Fortune* estimated his worth at $272 million, but said his MGM holdings within the first year already had lost over 10 percent of their value. *Barron's* ran a similar story, ticking off every Kerkorian asset, including his $4 million DC-9, his $1 million yacht docked in San Diego, his homes in Las Vegas and in the Bel Air section of Los Angeles.

All this made Kerkorian acutely uncomfortable. A scrupulously private man, Kerkorian had an instinctual fear of the spotlight. Further, he knew some heavy bills were coming due, and he needed room to maneuver. He couldn't afford to have the press looking over his shoulder.

The most immediate pressure stemmed from the $72 million in European loans that had enabled him to complete his MGM takeover. The one-year, 13 percent loans were coming due in the summer of 1970, at the very time that the stock market was tumbling.

And MGM was tumbling along with it. Wall Street, it seemed, had concluded that Kerkorian was not serious about rebuilding the studio, but was simply intent on peeling off its assets.

Because of the falling market, Kerkorian found himself pledging more and more of his stock as collateral against his loans. Something would have to be done to ease the pressure.

The answer seemed foolproof: International Leisure would hold a secondary offering. The deal would bring a much needed $28.5 million to Kerkorian, while still enabling him to retain a 72 percent stake in the company.

But a totally unexpected obstacle now loomed. The Securities and Exchange Commission refused to permit the secondary. When he'd acquired the Flamingo Hotel in Las Vegas a year earlier, it seemed Kerkorian had not submitted a financial statement covering its previous three years of operation. The reason he had not done so, Kerkorian explained, was that the sellers had refused to turn the records over to him. It wasn't his fault.

The government, to Kerkorian's astonishment, was adamant. No records, no secondary. It was as simple as that.

Kerkorian smelled a rat. This had nothing to do with financial records, he now understood. Something more important was at stake.

What was at stake, it turned out, was a long-standing government investigation into alleged "skimming" at the casino during the two years prior to Kerkorian's ownership. By holding up the secondary, the government hoped to persuade Kerkorian to co-operate with the investigation. Some $36 million in casino earnings had been concealed by the Flamingo in its skimming operation. And at the center of the scheme was none other than Meyer Lansky, financial kingpin of organized crime, who had fled to Israel.

Kerkorian was beside himself. If there was one thing he did not need in his life, it was to be tied in some way to Meyer Lansky. Kerkorian reiterated his complete ignorance of the Lansky operation. He was just the guy who happened to come along and buy the place.

The government was dubious. Kerkorian, after all, had been a "player" in Las Vegas for a long time. As early as 1950, he'd put down fifty thousand dollars for a small piece of the Dunes—and lost his money.

Furthermore, in buying the Flamingo, Kerkorian knew he wasn't exactly purchasing a monastery. This had been Bugsy Siegel's headquarters. Even its swimming pool had achieved a curious Vegas-style immortality: One day, Bugsy had forced his press agent to splash around the edges of the pool while Bugsy fired his .38 over his head.

No, Kerkorian's self-depiction as the innocent who accidentally stumbled into a nest of thieves did not sit well with the zealous investigators. And the press seemed to be leaping on the bandwagon. The *New York Post* ran a headline declaring MGM HEAD TALKS TO MAFIA, referring to a newly discovered 1961 phone tap in which a mob gambling figure named Charlie "the Blade" Tourine was heard talking to Kerkorian. The conversation had been routinely taped by Manhattan district attorney Frank Hogan, who had been tapping the phones of underworld figures such as Tourine.

Kerkorian's colloquy on the tape was indeed opaque. Kerkorian promised Charlie "the Blade" that he would send him a check for $21,300 made out to George Raft. Raft would cash it and then turn it back to Charlie. Kerkorian warned Tourine not to endorse the check himself "because the heat is on."

Investigators assumed the call related to Kerkorian's gambling losses (he was a high roller in the 1960's). Kerkorian's attorneys, however, would only reply that "Kerkorian has never knowingly associated with any member of a criminal organization."

Even the austere *Wall Street Journal* joined the chorus of press critics now, analyzing Kerkorian's relationship with such a "questionable figure" as George Raft, who had been barred from England in 1967 after fronting for a large London casino.

The *Journal* emphasized it could find no hard evidence of business links between Kerkorian and underworld figures, but it could not resist speculating about the source of Kerkorian's European financing. Did the money really come from Aristotle Onassis? Or even from Howard Hughes?

The SEC's action in blocking the secondary had put Kerkorian in a major crunch. Unless he could raise some major money fast, he would be forced to liquidate assets. *Barron's* magazine, which had published a puff piece only a year earlier, was now stating that all of Kerkorian's assets were tagged for sale, including his airplane, his yacht, and his pride and joy, the International Hotel.

And meanwhile, the market continued to fall like a stone. Kerkorian's stock in Western Airlines had dropped below seven dollars, representing a paper loss of about $10 million. The MGM stock, bought at an average price of thirty-six dollars a share, had fallen to thirteen dollars. Even International Leisure, which had peaked at sixty-six dollars per share, now was hovering at ten dollars.

At a federal hearing, Kerkorian was quizzed relentlessly about his financial problems.

> Q: So the total value of your assets has diminished from about $553 million to about $89.7 million, is that correct?
> KERKORIAN: I wouldn't say my total assets. We have other assets also that I haven't gone into...
> Q: What other assets are those?
> KERKORIAN: Just other assets...

The questioner kept persevering until he was called off by the chairman.

Clearly, a momentous decision was at hand. With the government blocking him at every turn, Kerkorian would have to bail out of at least one of his ventures. Associates like Benninger and Walter Sharp favored dumping MGM. But Kerkorian resisted. Even though the MGM caper had been a desperate disappointment, he still had his own private scenario for the company—plans he was not as yet prepared to reveal.

Instead of dumping the studio, he would instead sell his hotels. His colleagues were crushed, but Kerkorian's mind was made up. In late 1970, Kerkorian disclosed he'd sold half his holdings in International Leisure to Hilton Hotels. The deal, which could have yielded him $90 million six months earlier, now brought him a meager $16.5 million. In subsequent transactions, Hilton increased its holdings to 85 percent.

With the money from the Hilton sale, Kerkorian paid down his European debts. He still owed some $25 million to the Bank of

America—money he had used in part to pay his taxes—but at least he was "whole" again.

By the end of his crisis, analysts estimated his wealth had shrunk to between $50 million and $100 million. He was still an enormously wealthy man, but no longer the "high flyer" the headlines had dubbed him a year before.

Throughout his ordeal, Kerkorian had sustained his stoic exterior. There had been no theatrics, no public tantrums. But friends noticed a seething anger they had not detected before. Everyone—the government, the press—had put the squeeze on him, Kerkorian felt. He had allowed himself to show a brief moment of vulnerability and, as a result, he had been practically skinned alive.

It would not happen again.

On October 14, 1971, the press was surprised to receive an invitation to a rare news conference to be held in the administration building on the MGM lot. Reporters were escorted to the fourth floor of the broad, cathedrallike structure and led into the austere paneled room that had once been Louis B. Mayer's private dining room.

Rumors were flying about the nature of the pending announcement. According to one theory, Aubrey would announce his resignation. Another held that Kerkorian would disclose a sale of the studio.

Both theories were off the mark. Jim Aubrey strode in, accompanied not by Kerkorian, who, as usual, was absent, but by the man he especially disliked, Fred Benninger, Kerkorian's Las Vegas overseer.

After introducing several members of the board of directors, Aubrey read a press release disclosing plans for "a far-reaching diversification program into the leisure field."

The announcement did not even give passing mention to the entertainment business. Rather, it heralded a plan to build three $18 million cruise ships that would offer lavish gambling facilities. It also stated that the company would build a vast new resort hotel in Las Vegas. After an absence of less than a year, Kirk Kerkorian was back in business in Las Vegas.

The company went out of its way to stress Jim Aubrey's important role in all this. The new ships, like the projected hotel, would require the services of top entertainers. "Talent is the name of the game in Las Vegas, and Jim Aubrey knows talent," Kerkorian was quoted as saying in the press release.

There was no masking the press's hostility toward Aubrey, however. The tough questions were directed at him, not at Benninger, who sat at his side. Asked one reporter, "Mr. Aubrey, Las Vegas has fallen on hard times lately, so why does the company believe that an investment there would now be profitable?"

Aubrey paused to glare at the reporter. Then he replied, "On what do you base the assumption that it has fallen on hard times?"

There was muffled laughter. Las Vegas's financial problems had been amply documented in the press of late. The reporter replied, "The economy is in a semirecession. Is this proposed investment based on secret information about a projected recovery?"

Again there was derisive laughter. "We are optimistic," Aubrey retorted, "about the ultimate recovery of the economy, and we believe we can operate profitably under current conditions."

There were more hostile questions. Did this mean, a reporter asked, that MGM would become even less important in Kerkorian's overall plans?

"Not at all," Aubrey said. "We believe in MGM's future as a filmmaker. There is no intention to get out of the film business." Again reporters around the room exchanged skeptical glances.

The hostile response of the press was abundantly evident the following day. The trade press hinted strongly at the imminent demise of MGM. The *Los Angeles Times,* however, instead of trumpeting Kerkorian's return to Las Vegas, focused on another aspect of the story not disclosed at the press conference. MGM, it seems, had paid some $5 million for the site of the projected new hotel, which was adjacent to the old Bonanza Hotel. The person to whom the money had been paid was none other than Kirk Kerkorian, who had bought the property two years earlier, sold it, and subsequently bought it back again prior to MGM taking the parcel off his hands.

Not only had Kerkorian personally profited from the transaction, according to the *Times,* he had made his deal with a group that included Moe Dalitz, a longtime Vegas operator whose name had for quite a while been cropping up in underworld investigations. The press, in citing Dalitz's name, usually described him as "a former Cleveland organized-crime figure."

In fact, Dalitz belonged to what was colorfully known as the Mayfield Road Gang, which dominated the Cleveland territory for some years, and ultimately moved on to Las Vegas where Dalitz's operations connected him with several well-known figures. Dalitz sold the Desert Inn to Howard Hughes in 1967. Additional real estate dealings involved Merv Adelson, a co-founder of Lorimar.

Kerkorian's deal with Dalitz, however, inevitably regurgitated the denials of a year earlier. In an effort at damage control, Kerkorian was persuaded by his press agents to take an unprecedented step—namely, to grant an interview to *Forbes* magazine.

Kerkorian met with the two reporters at his office at the Beverly Hilton Hotel, where he placed himself under life-sized portraits of his two daughters, Tracy and Linda. While Kerkorian had been primed to direct the conversation toward his expansion plans, it became immediately clear that his interviewers had other priorities. All the old names were popping up—Dalitz, Lansky, Tourine, etc. Kerkorian bristled, but managed to keep his customary cool.

After the reporters had left, Kerkorian informed his press advisers that this would be his first and last interview. The "professional talkers" could deal with the press, he said. He was not a "talker."

That was abundantly clear in the resulting interview that appeared in *Forbes* magazine. It stated:

"Kerkorian insists he is 'clean as a whistle.' He told Forbes: 'I have never knowingly dealt with anyone with any criminal activity. I swear on my children that is true.'

"What about testimony given before the New York State Joint Legislative Committee on Crime in September, stating that Mafioso Charlie Tourine tried to arrange a $5 million airplane loan for Kerkorian in 1961 or 1962? 'I talked to people all across the country about that loan. I can't say whether I talked to Tourine or not.'

"And what about Lansky, who apparently owned a piece of the Flamingo when Kerkorian came along to buy it in 1967? 'I don't know the man. When we negotiated the Flamingo deal, we dealt 100 per cent with Morris Lansburgh and Sam Cohen.'"

Turning to the Dalitz deal, *Forbes* quoted Kerkorian thus: "I don't see anything wrong with buying a piece of vacant property from these people. What's wrong with Moe?"

Forbes concluded its story with Kerkorian stating, "I do the right thing. And I trust that everything will be all right. We pay heavy taxes—more than $25 million in the last four years. Would you say that a guy who pays as heavy taxes as I do is a bad guy?"

Forbes added, "The issue isn't whether or not Kirk Kerkorian is a 'bad guy.' The real question is, is Kerkorian's direction good for MGM?"

Skepticism about Kerkorian's private agenda surfaced again at the December stockholders meeting, which was held not at the MGM theater, but in the austere surroundings of the Culver City

Recreation Center. The meeting was attended by a phalanx of stockholder gadflies such as Evelyn Y. Davis and John Gilbert, and they were quick to fixate on Kerkorian's absence. "You should at least give us a picture, so we can see what he looks like," Gilbert suggested sarcastically.

Aubrey tried to cast a positive note on the proceedings by announcing net income from operations of $7.8 million, reflecting the success of *Shaft* and *Ryan's Daughter*. He also disclosed the sale of yet other MGM properties, including a theater chain in Australia.

But the moment he opened the floor to questions, the Kerkorian issue arose again. "I'm Ethel Rudick," said a small woman in a white hat, "and I am a holder of five hundred shares. Mr. Aubrey, during the past year, has Mr. Kerkorian met with you?"

"I see him regularly," said Aubrey. "He attends board meetings. I see him personally at least every two weeks."

"Then doesn't it seem ironic to you that at a shareholders meeting, he chooses not to appear?"

"You'll have to direct that to Mr. Kerkorian."

Several stockholders promptly proposed that Mrs. Rudick run for a position on the board of directors instead of Kerkorian.

Despite his pronouncements, Jim Aubrey was having an increasingly difficult time maintaining the illusion that MGM was still in the movie business. Aubrey himself was spending more and more time working on the Las Vegas operation, traveling often to New York to raise money for construction.

His staff was also being preempted for Las Vegas activities. Studio press agents were grinding out releases portraying the architectural magnificence of the new hotel. The structure, said one release, would be "centered around a 25-floor tower with curtain walls of glass soaring 263 feet into the air." Suites would be named after characters in famous MGM films—a Rhett Butler Suite and even a Lara (from *Doctor Zhivago*) Suite.

Tony Seininger, the top MGM advertising man, who normally would be working on campaigns of new films, presented a design for the public rooms of the new MGM Grand. Each room would be modeled after a famous MGM picture—*Show Boat*, for example. The disco would resemble the set of Kubrick's *2001: A Space Odyssey*.

Fred Benninger, Kerkorian's Vegas functionary, drew the line, however. "People who come to Vegas want gold and burgundy," he admonished. "They want it to look like a whorehouse, not a movie set." Benninger prevailed.

To maintain the illusion of studio activity, Aubrey began shopping around for a successor to Herb Solow, his well-liked production chief, who had departed late in 1971. Not surprisingly, most candidates wondered why Aubrey wanted to fill the job, since there didn't seem much production to supervise.

Finally, Aubrey settled on Jack Haley, Jr., the son of the actor who played the Tin Man in *The Wizard of Oz*. A jovial, high-spirited filmmaker who had worked in features as well as TV, Haley had no interest in such corporate conventions as presiding over production meetings. And he openly disdained Aubrey's continuing civil war with the directing fraternity. Nonetheless, with Aubrey's assurance that he would show greater restraint, Haley signed on as MGM's new production chief.

No sooner was Haley in place than Aubrey got a better idea. A former associate from TV, Daniel Melnick, was in the process of getting a divorce and was looking for a career change. Melnick had been David Susskind's partner in Talent Associates, a prestigious TV production company, and had recently produced a film Aubrey greatly admired. It was *Straw Dogs*, directed, oddly enough, by Aubrey's favorite adversary, Sam Peckinpah.

Melnick refused to accept the job unless he could meet Kerkorian in person to win his assurance that the studio seriously intended to remain in the film business. Aubrey dutifully set up the meeting, but immediately regretted it. Kerkorian was unshaven and distracted; he had just flown in from Europe and was about to fly off again to New York. But he shook Melnick's hand and started reciting, as if by rote, his pledge to keep MGM active in motion pictures. The studio will make twelve films a year, he promised. Aubrey listened skeptically, trying to figure out whether his boss really meant what he said or was simply eager to get the meeting over with as quickly as possible.

Melnick himself didn't believe a word Kerkorian had said, but he decided to take the job anyway. How many chances does one have to climb into the shoes of an Irving Thalberg? he reasoned.

Aubrey, meanwhile, now had to persuade Haley to accept a lesser title, vice president for creative affairs. Haley seemed relieved. He was just as happy to have someone to insulate him from the corporate wars.

Upon assuming his new responsibilities in February 1972, Melnick's suspicion that his taste in films bore no relation whatsoever to Aubrey's was quickly confirmed. The urbane and well-read Melnick favored New York writers like Paddy Chayefsky and filmmakers like Sidney Lumet and Herbert Ross. Aubrey's line of "B" pictures, he was persuaded, had run their course, and so had the strict $2 million lid that had been arbitrarily imposed on budgets.

Taking advantage of Aubrey's focus on Las Vegas, Melnick began to slip through some more promising projects. Michael Crichton, the young doctor-turned-novelist-turned-director, had created a fresh concept for a fantasy western entitled *Westworld*, in which the "heavy," Yul Brynner, turned out to be a robot.

Equally offbeat was a thriller called *Slither*, starring James Caan, Louise Lasser, and Sally Kellerman. Another first-time director, Howard Zieff, who'd made his name in commercials, did an excellent job on a restricted budget.

Was there hope at MGM?

The limits of this new freedom were put to the ultimate test when Melnick and Haley proposed a deal for a nautical thriller that would far exceed their budgetary limits. To enhance their case, sketches of special effects were prepared. Experts in undersea shooting were standing by to offer their comments about efficacy. A meeting was scheduled at which the entire production staff would confront Aubrey with its collective enthusiasm.

Jim Aubrey looked and listened—and shook his head. "I don't like the story," he stated. "Besides, how do you get a shark to do all those tricks?"

Jaws was vetoed. Melnick and his colleagues were despondent. How could Jim Aubrey fail to see the potential of such a remarkable project? Their judgment, of course, was borne out, but another studio, Universal, would be the beneficiary. (The film would become one of the first whose grosses would soar past the hundred-million mark.)

While *Jaws* went down to defeat, another project, *Mister Ricco* received an instantaneous green light. It was an utterly innocuous murder melodrama, but Dean Martin, whose movie career had been fading badly, wanted to star in it—and "Dino," in return, would agree to perform at the opening of the MGM Grand. To everyone in the company, by now, it had become abundantly clear that the hotel opening was all that mattered. Jack Haley, Jr., was under pressure to persuade Jackie Gleason, an old family friend, to perform. The function of the studio was now to serve Las Vegas.

With this in mind, Fred Benninger unleashed a band of foragers to roam the back lot in search of what he called "souvenirs." The purpose, Benninger explained, was to stock up a gift and memento shop to be located in the basement of the new hotel. "Trinkets for the tourists," he put it.

Melnick, Haley, and Roger Mayer, who administered the studio, protested adamantly. The auctions had already stripped the place clean, they pointed out. But it was to no avail. Benninger's marauders fanned out across the lot, filling their bins with cartoon cels from old MGM shorts, sketches for sets and costumes, original copies of screenplays, and other artifacts missed by the auctioneer.

Roger Mayer made a final try: Why not contribute this material to a university archive and take the tax write-off? he suggested. But the Las Vegas executive again overruled him, and the bins were carted off. A year later, Haley was to find William Wyler's personal shooting script of his Oscar-winning *Mrs. Miniver*, replete with notes and stage directions, on sale in Las Vegas for twelve dollars. Haley bought the script.

The continued "looting" of the MGM archives was all the more painful to Haley because of another unsuccessful fight he'd been waging. Haley had noticed that some of the MGM "classics" were suffering from extreme deterioration—the film was literally crumbling as it ran through the projector. To a cinephile like Haley, this was like watching a part of the national heritage turn to powder.

Soliciting Melnick's help, he made an appeal to Aubrey and Netter for an emergency allocation to salvage the old films. They were turned down.

Now, the cause became obsessive. Haley found himself spending his lunch breaks and evenings sorting through old film clips, sensing that he might be the last man ever to see them. He started splicing the clips together, showing them to Melnick. Some of the material was familiar, such as Fred Astaire's walls-and-ceiling dance from *Royal Wedding*. Some of it was arcane, such as Judy Garland's debut in a short entitled *Every Sunday*, or Jean Harlow's oddball performance in the long-forgotten *Reckless*.

Almost without Haley's realizing it, the body of work continued to grow. Sequences featuring Bing Crosby, Frank Sinatra, Gene Kelly, and Mickey Rooney were added. And editorial costs continued to soar, as well. Expenses were initially buried in executive operating budgets and expense accounts, but soon it became apparent that five-thousand-dollar lunch tabs would not be overlooked for long.

Melnick had made a quick, offhand stab at eliciting Aubrey's approval for continuation of the project and had met with a quick, offhand rejection. "You've really gone Hollywood, haven't you, Danny?" Aubrey responded. Melnick's proposal embodied everything Aubrey had opposed since becoming president of MGM—an obsession with "the old MGM." If management support was to be obtained, Jack Haley would have to prepare a full-fledged presentation, which would have to be shown under the most ideal of circumstances.

Haley went to work. His compilation of clips was expanded and enhanced. The MGM studio theater was booked. The seats were filled with the elite corps of "survivors"—those long-term MGM employees who could still remember the "good old days." There were secretaries, film editors, workers from the lab, drivers, guards, commissary waitresses. None had been told what they were about to see. And just before the lights dimmed, Aubrey and Netter strode into the room.

The material they saw, of course, was the nucleus of what would ultimately be known as *That's Entertainment,* which was later augmented by a witty narration by Fred Astaire. But even without the narration, the cumulative impact of the extraordinary material thrilled the captive audience. It was as though the viewers, having numbly endured the studio's recent films, were suddenly reminded once again of what MGM had once stood for—opulence, imagination, vision!

Aubrey stood quietly to one side after the screening as Melnick approached nervously. "What do you think?" he asked.

"You have my okay to move ahead," Aubrey replied. "What the hell—we can always sell it direct to TV."

By the spring of 1972, Jim Aubrey sensed a distinct cooling in his relations with Kerkorian, but he did not understand the cause. Aubrey had tried to faithfully play the "good soldier" in helping engineer Kerkorian's triumphant return to Las Vegas. He'd participated in the dog-and-pony shows for financiers, presided over press conferences, played host at countless receptions. At the groundbreaking of the MGM Grand in April 1972, he'd "delivered" his friend Raquel Welch to stand next to Cary Grant while the ceremonial dynamite charge was set off.

But Kerkorian was still unhappy with him. He'd needled Aubrey over the studio's continued losses—$2.3 million for the third quarter of 1972—forgetting, it seemed to Aubrey, the grave restrictions under which he'd been forced to operate. Kerkorian bristled when Aubrey, in turn, criticized a Kerkorian-engineered sale of MGM's music subsidiaries in the United States and England. Aubrey felt these highly profitable entities had been vastly underpriced.

The reason for the hastily negotiated sales, Aubrey knew, was that Kerkorian was again strapped for money. Kerkorian had figured he would end up with a $90 million windfall in American Airlines stock as a result of the planned merger of American and Western Airlines, the company Kerkorian controlled. But in July 1972, after frantic lobbying, the Civil Aeronautics Board had voted four to one against the merger, and Kerkorian once again was left holding the bag.

Faced with these setbacks, Kerkorian initiated talks with several industry leaders on a plan that would boldly reduce MGM's overhead. Kerkorian's notion was to spin off the studio's marketing and distribution operations. MGM would continue to make an occasional film, but someone else would have to worry about getting it out into the marketplace.

Jim Aubrey, among others, vehemently opposed this plan. Unless MGM controlled the distribution of its product, he argued, it might as well pull out of the movie business.

As usual, however, Kerkorian kept his own counsel. Though he had previously discussed his problems with Lew Wasserman of MCA and Charles Bluhdorn of Paramount, the man he felt most comfortable with was Arthur Krim, who ran United Artists. Indeed, he'd once confided to a startled Krim that he was his role model in the film business—Kerkorian had always hoped to model his operation after UA.

Even as Krim and Kerkorian sat down to serious negotiation early in 1973, Krim was surprised to receive a phone call from Frank Yablans, who was then president of Paramount. Yablans said he'd got wind of Krim's talks with the MGM chief and that he'd advise Krim to "butt out." Kerkorian had already agreed to a deal with Bluhdorn and Wasserman, Yablans declared—the ship had sailed.

Unnerved by this intervention, the methodical, lawyerly Krim decided to set aside his talks with MGM, but Kerkorian had no intention of dropping the issue. Since everyone seemed interested in MGM's future product, he would divide his largess. UA would pay MGM some $15 million for the right to distribute the studio's films in the United States for the next ten years. And Cinema International Corporation, which was jointly owned by MCA and Paramount, would pay $17 million to distribute the projects overseas.

Jim Aubrey tried to put a brave face on all this. The company had been forced to take these actions, he told the press, because "the bottom has fallen out of the market.... Audiences are totally rejecting the average film." This pronouncement was a little bearish in view of the considerable success other studios were having with their films, including *The Poseidon Adventure, Last Tango in Paris, Paper Moon, The Way We Were* and the new James Bond movie, *Live and Let Die.*

Aubrey understood this, of course. He had fought the deal but had lost. Benninger and the other "Vegas boys" had persuaded Kerkorian that he would do better simply selling out to United Artists. Even Aubrey's friend Greg Bautzer, who Aubrey thought would take his side of the argument, folded and threw his support to Benninger.

Aubrey was furious. The UA deal had been so badly negotiated, he told friends, that if he were an ordinary stockholder, he would file a stockholder suit. As it was, Aubrey dispatched a letter to Kerkorian, stating that he wanted to go on the record as opposing the deal.

The letter did not please Kerkorian, who summoned Bautzer to his house. Team players, Kerkorian said, accept management decisions and do not put their arguments "on the record," as Aubrey had done. It wasn't acceptable behavior.

The following day, Bautzer asked Aubrey to drop by for a drink. In his gruff, gravelly voice, Bautzer imparted the message from "the boss." Said Bautzer, "Kirk wants you out. It is over."

Aubrey was stricken but not surprised. Since he had no signed contract, he asked Bautzer what sort of settlement Kerkorian might have in mind.

"Kirk doesn't believe in contracts, and he doesn't believe in settlements, either," Bautzer told him. There would be no money, nothing.

For a few brief moments, Aubrey sat there reviewing in his mind all the money men he had visited, trying to raise funding for Kerkorian, all the people he'd fired, all the ill-conceived deals he'd felt compelled to rush into. And for all that, the settlement was "nothing."

At the age of fifty-four, Jim Aubrey was unemployed. The four years at MGM had been grueling, frustrating, and ultimately defeating.

As it would turn out, Aubrey would never again hold an important executive job.

Life magazine had once said about Aubrey, "No man in history ever had such a lock on such an enormous audience."

The most talked-about and most written-about executive in the entertainment industry had, however, lost touch with his audience; slowly, he receded into the shadows.

Ironically, long after Aubrey's departure, Kirk Kerkorian did a historic flip-flop on United Artists. In 1981, eight years after his clash with Aubrey over the UA distribution deal, Kerkorian announced that he would acquire United Artists in its entirety. As a result, UA would no longer be distributing MGM's films; the MGM organization would effectively be distributing UA's.

Jim Aubrey had won his battle, but lost his war.

CHAPTER THREE

■

EUPHORIA

1983

IN his initial weeks in office in 1983, Frank Yablans decided to try to create an atmosphere of orchestrated euphoria. The studio, he felt, must radiate confidence and excitement. In phone calls to major agents, his message was direct: "We're buying. If you're selling, see us first."

The process of reinventing MGM/UA as the center of the film-making universe was not going to be easy, he well understood. There were no pictures shooting at the studio, and hardly anything was left in the pipeline. The studio's management was still fragmented, its credibility compromised. How, then, was he going to achieve an instant turnaround?

"We do it with mirrors," Yablans asserted cheerfully. "How does anything get done in Hollywood?"

Indeed, the pronouncement that the studio was in a buying mode did unleash a considerable reaction. MGM's aged switchboard suffered a near-meltdown with the volume of incoming calls. Agents and producers lined the corridors, waiting to make their pitches. Even the lowliest story editor found his appointment calendar clogged.

Yablans's strategy provided quick results in volume, but not in quality. With few exceptions, the tidal wave of projects that swept over Culver City represented material that had previously been seen and rejected by every other studio. Tracking the submissions, the story department counted literally hundreds of scripts that had been logged in four or five times before. Many now bore different titles, always fresh new covers, but the projects still had the stamp of familiarity.

Yablans had anticipated this; the gambit of inviting the deluge of submissions was a publicity stunt of sorts. The studio's most urgent need was not the random screenplay or treatment, but that magic "package" that could form the basis for a Christmas or summer release. As a onetime distribution man, Yablans knew that movies, like books, are a seasonal business. And if MGM/UA were to become competitive once again, it would have to find its potential "blockbuster" just in time to entice those big holiday crowds.

To qualify as a "hot package," a project would have to offer the following attributes: There would have to be a star attached, or at least a star director. And there would ideally be some "pre-sold" aspect to the property. Perhaps it was based on a best-selling novel or a hit play, or, even better, was a sequel to a hit film.

Projects like this, to be sure, were hard to come by.

Fortunately, the acquisition of United Artists had already provided the company with two great film "franchises"—the Rocky films and the James Bond series. A new Bond film, bearing the self-consciously licentious title *Octopussy*, was due out that summer. Yablans hadn't seen the film as yet, but that didn't matter. Starting in 1962, there had been twelve Bond pictures released, and each of the last three had approached $200 million in worldwide receipts.

The *Rocky* films were not far behind. Only three had been made, but the last, *Rocky III*, released in 1982, had done $184 million. Unfortunately, given the UA sale and the constant changes of regime, no new *Rocky* film was in preparation or even negotiation.

There was yet another "franchise" rattling around the company, the *Pink Panther* sequels, but these appeared to have run their course. The sixth, *Trail of the Pink Panther*, had been a flop, and the seventh, *Curse of the Pink Panther*, did not hold out better prospects.

"We've got to focus on our 'crown jewels,'" Yablans announced at a production meeting. "Somewhere there's a great sequel or remake that has been overlooked."

By "crown jewels," Yablans was referring to the MGM classics.

And there was one in particular that attracted his attention—Stanley Kubrick's memorable film entitled *2001: A Space Odyssey*. Produced in great secrecy at MGM's English studio in 1967, the film had seemed ahead of its time (several leading Hollywood figures walked out of the first screening), but it finally established itself as the ultimate cult film. Eventually, *2001* did a respectable, but not exalted, $24 million in domestic rentals, only slightly more than the studio's schlocky *Clash of the Titans*.

In Yablans's mind, however, filmgoers were now ready to accept a new *Space Odyssey*—namely *2010*. The sounds and imagery that had seemed hallucinatory fifteen years earlier would now seem completely acceptable. The strains of *The Blue Danube* and *Thus Spake Zarathustra* would be heard in the land once again.

The notion, while intriguing, ignored certain obstacles. For one thing, Stanley Kubrick agreed with Ring Lardner that "a sequel is an admission that you've been reduced to imitating yourself." A stubbornly obsessive man, Kubrick also was angry with the studio because one of its myriad regimes supposedly had cheated him out of some video monies. There was clearly no chance of persuading Kubrick to direct the sequel. And it would ultimately take some $250,000 to convince him to allow a sequel to be made with another director.

Though he had not as yet informed his colleagues, Yablans had already decided on the identity of that director. It would be Peter Hyams, who had just directed Yablans's final producing effort at Twentieth Century-Fox—a film called *Star Chamber*.

Choice of Hyams for this pivotal assignment did not generate excitement at MGM. Advance word on *Star Chamber* was not good. And Hyams's previous films, including *Outland*, *Hanover Street*, *Capricorn One*, and *Busting*, though competent, were oddly unexciting. There was nothing in Hyams's work that suggested Kubrickian genius.

It was Freddie Fields who raised the issue at the next production meeting. A lone holdover from the Begelman years, Fields now held the much-circulated title of president of MGM and was nominally the head of production—at least until Rothman and Yablans could agree on a successor. Always a tactful negotiator, Fields pulled out a list of potential directors for *2010*, which he began to read. Yablans quickly cut him off.

"I've offered the project to Peter Hyams . . ." Yablans interjected.

"I understand that," Fields persisted, "I just thought it would be helpful to examine other possibilities. . . ."

"...And Hyams has accepted it," Yablans said with finality.

"I'm just concerned, Frank, that his work is a little...wooden," Fields offered.

"Okay, maybe if we took six months, we could find someone else to direct it," Yablans retorted. "But Peter Hyams can write it, produce it, direct it, even be his own cameraman—and he can guarantee us a picture for next Christmas. Can anyone else do that?"

There was silence around the room. No one, it was clear, was of a mind to challenge Hyams on the grounds of versatility.

While the *2010* negotiations were moving forward, the studio was also closing on several other projects, thus reinforcing the desired image of "action." And some of the acquisitions carried formidable price tags.

A producer named Aaron Russo had brought in a provocative script called *Teachers*—then announced that he wanted $1 million for the script and his producing services. Russo, a onetime manager of Bette Midler and a co-producer of *Trading Places*, did not have the credentials to justify this kind of fee. But Yablans, over the objections of his business-affairs staff, gave it to him anyway. One reason was that Russo's "package" involved the commitments of Nick Nolte to play the teacher and Arthur Hiller to direct. It was a case of good timing. Hiller had directed Yablans's *Silver Streak*. And Nolte had starred in *North Dallas Forty*, another Yablans production. Hence, Hiller ended up with a $1.2 million directing fee, and Nolte ended up with $2 million for his acting services.

These numbers were deemed profligate by some competitors, especially in view of the film's subject matter. This was not an action picture, not a thriller, not a hot comedy—it was a rather serious-minded $12.5 million film about the problems facing inner-city teachers. Its focus was the controversial decision of a high school to grant a diploma to a youngster who was technically illiterate.

Other deals also began to fall into place. John Milius was signed to direct *Red Dawn*, a thriller dealing with a hypothetical Russian occupation of the United States. Mickey Rourke and Eric Roberts agreed to co-star in *The Pope of Greenwich Village*, an offbeat gangster story set in New York. Christopher Reeve signed on for a period adventure called *The Aviator*, and Mel Gibson was cast opposite Diane Keaton in another period piece—a romantic thriller titled *Mrs. Soffel*.

Negotiations were also concluded for Jack Nicholson and Tim Hutton to co-star in a contemporary western entitled *Road Show*, which was the lone project remaining from the previous regime.

Martin Ritt, whose credits included *Hud* and *Norma Rae,* was set to direct.

As MGM's spending spree continued, even the world-class directors who had been ducking Yablans were suddenly returning his phone calls. Steven Spielberg checked in to say yes, there was a possibility he would be interested in directing a script called *Always,* but not as his next picture. John Boorman wanted to discuss *Emerald Forest,* set in the wilds of the Amazon. The inscrutable David Lean was even on the phone to talk about *A Passage to India,* the film he wanted to base on the famed E. M. Forster novel. And Alan Pakula dropped by with a thriller called *Dream Lover.*

Frank Yablans's spirits were soaring. He had been on the job for only a couple of months, and already some of the world's most celebrated directors and producers were courting him—men who had long avoided the studio or its functionaries. The skeptics had warned it would take years to "respectabilize" MGM/UA again, but he was accomplishing the feat in a matter of weeks.

Each evening after seven, once the phones had ceased their assault, he would hold court in his office, pouring drinks for whichever members of his staff wished to drop by. Freddie Fields would often stop for a visit, and so would I. Also present would be Yablans's former assistant at Twentieth Century-Fox, Ileen Maisel, who had now been made a vice president. Various members of the MGM "Old Guard" would also appear from time to time—Frank Davis, the courtly white-maned head of business affairs, and perhaps even Rothman. Never in attendance was Kirk Kerkorian, who would drive himself to work each day in his BMW, march directly to his office, looking neither left nor right, and remain there until the end of the day. "The gray phantom," the guards called him.

The informal after-hours cocktail parties gave Yablans the opportunity to vent his corrosive wit. A friend once described him as the sort of man who, when he smells flowers, immediately starts looking for a coffin. Yablans did pride himself on being a connoisseur of greed. As such, he would enjoy citing each day's most outlandish demand, whether from a star or a filmmaker. "Contrary to what you may think, I didn't go for that deal, Warner Brothers did," he might add with a sly grin.

Yablans understood full well that his free-spending ways were coming under criticism, but he felt that his critics misunderstood him.

"I don't mind paying the prices for the right director on the right project," Yablans would say. "We just have to be sure they understand one thing: Just 'cause we pay their price, that doesn't mean we're also gonna pay their overages." Budgets would be rigorously enforced, he warned.

In holding forth about the directing community, a frequent target was Robert Altman, who was one of Freddie Fields's favorite filmmakers (and a former client). Indeed, Fields was persistently advocating Altman for different projects, including a property entitled *O.C. & Stiggs*, a dark satire about two teenagers growing up in Arizona. The project had recently fallen out at Paramount, where Mike Nichols had been set to direct. Now, there was a possibility MGM/UA could pick it up, with Altman taking over for Nichols.

While Fields was eagerly supporting the deal, Yablans was skeptical as to whether the burly, iconoclastic Altman could still direct a commercial movie.

"He did *M*A*S*H*," Fields insisted.

"That was fourteen years ago," Yablans replied. "What's he done since? *Health* and *Quintet* and esoteric shit like that."

"It's still the same man," said Fields.

"The trouble with Altman," Yablans countered, "is that he turns everything into the same movie. Same cast, same crew, same everything."

"I know how to handle him," Fields replied.

Yablans was not placated. "I don't want him 'handled,'" he shot back. "I want him challenged. I want him intimidated!"

"Bob can get a little hot. . . ." Fields cautioned, but Yablans was not to be put off. "You're not in the agency business anymore, Freddie, you're in the studio business. Bring Altman in here tomorrow, and I'll show you what I mean."

The next day, a nervous Fields ushered Robert Altman into Frank Yablans's office. Yablans assessed his visitor as they shook hands. A bear of a man, with thinning gray hair, a booming growl of a voice, and angry eyes that seemed set too close together, Altman did not look like the sort of person one could tinker with, but Yablans was determined to tinker nonetheless.

"They tell me you are interested in directing *O.C. & Stiggs*," said Yablans, getting quickly down to business.

"I think it could be a damn good picture," Altman replied, his face frozen.

"Well, I would love to see you direct the film on one condition. I want this to be an MGM film, not a Bob Altman film."

Yablans peered at Altman, awaiting the predicted outburst. Altman just stared back, like a poker player determined not to show his hand.

"I don't think I follow you," Altman replied finally.

"I mean I want a commercial movie."

"So do I."

"This time around you don't get script approval or cast approval. I don't want Altman's road company in this picture. I want fresh faces."

Altman glowered, but kept his cool. "I always use the best actors I can find."

"You'll edit here, not in New York."

"I like New York. If *you* want to edit the goddam picture . . ."

"No, I want *you* to edit the goddam picture, but you edit it here." There was another lull. Then: "What else?"

"We see dailies every day. We talk."

"Look, Mr. Yablans, let me make one thing clear. The idea of making a 'youth comedy' represents a big risk for me. If I try to make a commercial movie and it turns out to be a flop, then I'm royally fucked. Do you follow me?"

Yablans smiled expansively. "I think we understand each other."

"It looks that way."

Altman and Yablans shook hands. Then the director left the room with Fields, who looked as if he'd just been through a root canal.

After the door was closed, Yablans grinned. "A few more meetings like that, and Freddie Fields may understand what it means to run a studio."

Having set an array of projects in motion, Yablans turned his attention back to his "franchises"—*Rocky* and Bond.

Negotiations over a possible *Rocky IV* seemed hopelessly stalled. Sylvester Stallone, mindful that *Rocky III* had been responsible for two thirds of the total film rentals pulled in by MGM/UA during 1982, decided, not surprisingly, that he deserved a hefty boost in pay. And he wanted it up front—Stallone did not want to be at the mercy of some anonymous studio accountant to compute the film's gross and report his cut. "The only way to resolve this is to offer Stallone fifteen million dollars in cash," MGM's negotiator recommended.

Freddie Fields was aghast. "Let's forget the fucking movie," he flared.

Tensions were further heightened when Stallone's office called Yablans to arrange a face-to-face meeting. Yablans's secretary replied that he was leaving town. The response from Stallone: If Yablans can't schedule a meeting, Stallone can't schedule the movie. Yablans delayed his trip, and closed the deal on Stallone's terms.

But now negotiations with the co-producers, Irwin Winkler and Robert Chartoff, had reached a crisis point. Yablans informed the pair, who had guided their "Italian Stallion" through ten years of combat, that he would not need their services. Yablans would personally supervise *Rocky IV* himself. He offered Winkler and Chartoff $2 million to "go away." Winkler and Chartoff fired off a telegram to Kerkorian, promising a lawsuit. Within an hour, Yablans was on the phone, suggesting a meeting. "There's been a little misunderstanding," he said.

Nor were things going smoothly on the Bond front. In studying the returns of the latest Bond pictures, Yablans had noted that while the overseas results had continued to be bountiful, the U.S. audience seemed to be tapering off. The 1981 Bond, for example, entitled *For Your Eyes Only*, had brought in rentals of only $28 million in the United States—the same amount as it had cost to make.

Perhaps Roger Moore was getting too old for the part (Moore himself propounded this theory). But then the same could be said about the producer, Albert "Cubby" Broccoli, the one-time Long Island farmhand who, at the age of seventy-four, still ran his "Bond business" as though it were a family farm (Broccoli's ancestors had been growing broccoli for generations in Calabria, Italy; hence the family name). All three of Broccoli's children worked on his films now. Even Michael G. Wilson, the co-producer and co-writer, was the son of Broccoli's wife, Dana, by a previous marriage.

Broccoli, who had gotten his start in movies escorting Jane Russell around the set of the Howard Hughes film *The Outlaw* (he ultimately was accorded assistant director credit), had pitched the idea for the James Bond films to Arthur Krim a quarter of a century earlier, and he had no intention of changing his *modus operandi* for some newcomer like Frank Yablans. Indeed, when the MGM/UA team blithely suggested its intention of having more input on the next Bond film, the proposal was quickly stonewalled. If MGM/UA wanted another Bond picture, Broccoli declared, the studio would have to play by the customary rules. This meant advancing as much as $6 million before studio executives caught even a glimpse of an outline—forget about seeing a script. That was the way it had been done in the past, and that was the way it would continue.

*   *   *

As the workload of projects continued to rise, along with the
level of submissions, the inevitable fissures began to appear in the
production staff. From the outset, the staff had been an odd patchwork. Arrayed around Fields was a tight-knit little development
group that had worked with him earlier when he'd been an agent
or producer. Madeline Warren, Lynn Arost, Bonni Lee, and the
others all understood Fields's idiosyncratic work habits and taste
in material.

Inevitably, just as Fields looked to his staff for feedback, so
Yablans, in turn, looked to his coterie—namely Ileen Maisel, myself, and, later, David Wardlow, a former ICM agent.

There was nothing intrinsically wrong with this arrangement
except for one fact: It soon became clear that Freddie Fields had
his own agenda of projects, which did not conform with those
favored by Yablans. Indeed, each disdained the other's "picks."

A clear struggle of wills was brewing.

Fields had been carefully nurturing his own "wish list" since
arriving at the studio a year before Yablans. In a few cases, the
projects had been co-owned by himself and David Begelman during
the brief time they'd been partners in a production company.

They were an eclectic array. *Millennium*, which Fields had developed with Richard Rush, who'd directed *The Stunt Man*, was a
high-budget science-fiction film. Its plot concerned a group of ma-
rauding space aliens bent on kidnapping earthlings to repopulate
their dying planet.

A second project, *Turn Left or Die*, was a black comedy about
air controllers, which Bob Clark, the director of *Porky's*, had developed. *Hartman*, a third, was a survival drama set against an
Arctic dog race.

Yablans was excited by none of these. The studio, he felt, could
afford but one expensive sci-fi epic, namely, his sequel to *2001*.
Fields believed *Millennium* was far more accessible than *2010*, and
that Rush was a more inventive director than Peter Hyams.

As for *Turn Left or Die*, Yablans did not admire Bob Clark, whose
most recent MGM film, *A Christmas Story*, struck him as flat and
uninspired. Fields, on the other hand, believed that Yablans's two
favorite screenplays, *The Pope of Greenwich Village* and *Teachers*,
both set in urban slums, were too downbeat.

Their disagreements did not emerge in the form of open debate.
Fields's many years as an agent for such strong-willed personalities
as Steve McQueen and Paul Newman had taught him that low-key
persuasion was more effective than confrontation. Quietly, unobtrusively, Fields kept reiterating his viewpoint. *Turn Left or Die*

kept turning up with new script revisions and new casting suggestions. On *Millennium*, he even staged a reading of the script at his home, replete with professional actors and background music, to which Yablans was invited. But none of it turned Yablans around.

If their assessments of material differed, so did their work habits. Yablans was a voracious reader who would take home stacks of screenplays each weekend and be prepared Monday to argue his fiercely held opinions. Fields disliked reading; he would prefer to sit in his office while an aide analyzed a script for him, or read him the synopsis. His favorite "storyteller" was a young story editor named Chris Bomba, who spoke in an adenoidal monotone that put others to sleep but that Fields found oddly soothing. Producers who had devoted years of their lives and hundreds of thousands of dollars to fine-tune their scripts would gladly have hired professional storytellers to read their synopses, had they known that their fate would rest with Bomba's monotone.

With all their surface differences, there was nonetheless an unspoken bond linking Fields and Yablans. Both had been Brooklyn street kids from poor Jewish homes. Fields's real name had been Fritzie, not Freddie; his brother had been Shep Fields, the bandleader. Both Yablans and Fields, too, grew up on the tough edge of the movie business—Fields hustling talent, Yablans hustling exhibitors. The craft of filmmaking was something neither really identified with. Their craft was negotiation and deal-making, and they were brilliantly inventive at it.

Both men also relished the perquisites of their success. Both drove to the studio in Rolls-Royces. Both wore custom-made suits and spent lavishly on their personal lifestyles.

In their subtle game of one-upmanship, Fields clearly won in the category of homes. Having been separated from his wife, Ruth, for some years, Yablans had surrendered his opulent home in Bel Air for a comfortable but relatively modest condominium apartment in Century City, which he leased from Fields (Yablans later moved to a comfortable home in Coldwater Canyon). Fields, his landlord, on the other hand, lived with his Greek-born wife, Corinne, in a lavish Mediterranean villa, complete with tennis court, screening room (whose construction had been subsidized by the studio), and manicured gardens. It was an exquisite house, a showpiece, Freddie Fields's pride and joy.

Fields, indeed, had proven his mastery at upgrading his lifestyle with the help of company subsidies. He enjoyed relating how his old agency, CMA, had purchased his first home in Beverly Hills for him, which he had successfully traded up into bigger and better homes in Malibu and now Benedict Canyon and other places—indeed, he now bought, sold, and traded elegant homes as a hobby.

When Yablans and his girlfriend, Tracy, the daughter of author A. E. Hotchner, visited Fields, there would occasionally be banter about Fields's baronial lifestyle.

"How come everyone who works for me lives better than I do?" Yablans would demand.

"Because living well *is* the best revenge," Fields would respond, and there would be slightly pained smiles all around.

Whatever tensions existed between Yablans and Fields, both shared the overriding goal of bringing about a "renaissance" in Culver City. If that were to happen, the rewards, both in terms of money and prestige, would suffice for both of them. All it would take was one hit.

And there was one project they agreed could provide the basis for that hit. There were risks inherent in it, to be sure, but the potential was there. It had a unique idea, big stars, a solid script, though each had his own list of revisions. But it was a winner—both of them sensed it.

The project was called *Road Show*.

The morning after I signed my contract with MGM/UA, a studio van pulled up to my house, and the driver handed me a script. I could sense him peering at me as I signed for it.

"You one of the new boys?" he asked.

I nodded. "Is that a capital offense?"

The driver did not smile as he glanced at the script. "Hope this one's better than the crap we been making lately," he said, turning to go.

The delivery may have been unorthodox, but I was relieved that at least he'd brought only one screenplay. I had geared myself for a veritable truckload. Reading through the backlog of work-in-progress was one of the numbing rituals of studio transition. At least, someone had selected this one script as the precursor.

A brief note was attached. "This is *Road Show*," it said. "It starts shooting in July." There was no name or signature.

The anonymity seemed curious, but at least I knew about the project. It had been generating a "buzz" around town. Jack Nicholson and Tim Hutton were committed to play the leads, I knew, and a widely respected director named Martin Ritt was also attached.

If all this were true, then *Road Show* had the makings of what Hollywood likes to call a "slam dunk." It could be the big summer picture every new regime hungers for.

That night, however, after reading the script, I was overcome by a keen sense of disappointment. It wasn't that the script was bad. The writing was, in fact, quite polished and professional. The problem was that *Road Show* was a metaphor in search of a movie. It was one of those stories where you didn't believe for a minute that the characters would really behave as they do, except to fit the arcane requirements of the plot.

Why would Nicholson and Hutton want to play these roles? I wondered. And why would Martin Ritt, the man who gave us *Hud* and *Norma Rae*, want to devote a year of his life to this curious antique?

Two days later, I confessed my reservations to Freddie Fields as we walked down a corridor in the Thalberg Building, past posters of *Singing in the Rain* and *The Philadelphia Story*.

"You read *Road Show*, kiddo?" he asked. Freddie called almost everyone "kiddo."

"Yeah. I don't get it."

"It's a western."

"Exactly. And it reminded me why no one makes them anymore."

"It's *Red River*, kiddo."

"I wish it read that way."

"Frank Yablans thinks it's a classic."

"Then I'm the lone dissenter."

"Trust me, kiddo. This one's a slam dunk."

"A slam dunk," I repeated, trying to persuade myself.

Fields's enthusiasm, I quickly learned, was unanimously shared by his development staff—"D-girls," as they're known in the trade. All expressed confidence that while the script needed sharpening in places, the project had "blockbuster" written all over it. Listening to them, I couldn't help but ask myself, Is this really what they think, or is it what they want to think? This was, after all, the glossiest "holdover" project from the former regime. In a sense, *Road Show* validated their previous year's work.

Driving home that night, I told myself the story of *Road Show* once again. It *sounded* like such a sound story—why didn't it *read* that way?

The central character was a rock-solid American cattle rancher named Spangler (Jack Nicholson) who finds himself besieged by voracious creditors. When thieving truckers try to charge an outrageous price to transport his 250 head of cattle to Kansas City, Spangler opts for the ultimate act of defiance. He will drive his herd to market the old-fashioned way—a classic cattle drive past the turnpikes and the billboards and the Holiday Inns and the Big Macs. Assisting him will be his wife, Opal, and his friend Leo (Tim Hutton), a schoolteacher who is desperate to learn what the "real world" is like. Along the way, there is danger and adversity, but Spangler prevails—he gets his cattle to Kansas City.

The notion of a classic hero embarking on a contemporary cattle drive is a catchy one—the kind of one-liner that is very seductive in a community that thrives on one-liners. Indeed, this one was strong enough to keep the project afloat for six long years, as it drifted from one development deal to the next.

Back in 1977, Donna Dubrow was a young executive at a now-defunct company called Filmways when she persuaded her superiors to option a novel called *The Last Cattle Drive* by Robert Day. A screenwriter named Robert Getchell, who had written such fine pieces as *Bound for Glory* and *Alice Doesn't Live Here Anymore*, was hired to adapt the novel. Ed Feldman, who then was head of production at Filmways, was sufficiently impressed by the piece to renew the option, but not impressed enough to put the film into production.

At Filmways, as at many movie companies, regimes kept changing with the seasons, and Dubrow faithfully kept regrouping and resubmitting. Four production heads all looked at the project; all four liked it—but not quite enough to finance it.

Finally, when Dubrow herself was set adrift by Filmways in 1981, she shelled out her own money to option the property and once again start the excruciatingly slow process of submission. This time, she decided to take aim at prospective stars, rather than battle-weary production executives.

The actors proved more receptive. There were the usual "ifs, ands, and buts"—but the glimmer of hope was there.

Jack Nicholson, for example, liked the idea of playing an imperiled cattle rancher. Not for his next picture, mind you—but maybe after that. To the studios, Jack Nicholson was a hot item.

Trouble was, Nicholson's "next picture" turned out to be a dud entitled *The Border*, and by the time it was released, the studios were less exuberant about Jack Nicholson. Unless, of course, another ingredient could be added to the mix.

The "other ingredient" turned out to be Tim Hutton, who wanted to work with Nicholson and also liked the idea of a contemporary western. Trouble was, Hutton, a notorious procrastinator, was just in the process of switching agents, and the new agent didn't think his part in *Road Show* was important enough for a recent Academy Award winner (he'd won his Oscar for *Ordinary People*). Unless, of course, another ingredient could be added.

Enter Martin Ritt. A rotund, gravel-voiced man who dresses like a longshoreman, Ritt had had success with westerns and liked the cast. Nicholson and Hutton, in turn, liked Ritt. Under his guidance, perhaps the film could become the contemporary *Red River* that everyone kept predicting.

Dubrow took her package to MGM. Freddie Fields was interested. It was just the sort of prestigious package he was looking for.

Hence, six years after beginning her quest, Donna Dubrow had pulled off a hat trick. The neophyte producer had assembled two major stars. She had a suite of offices at proud old MGM, and a producing salary of $175,000 plus $25,000 deferred.

And best of all, everyone, including Dubrow, was pay-or-play. That meant that even if the studio decided to cancel the film, it would still have to fork over the salaries, which aggregated almost $6 million. Surely, no company in its right mind would want to get out of a picture *that* badly.

There was, as usual, one potential glitch. As had happened to her at Filmways, MGM, too, was changing regimes. Frank Yablans and his entourage were coming in. David Begelman's entourage was checking out, except for Freddie Fields, who had been the strongest advocate of *Road Show*, and who promised to champion the project through the transition.

Yes, it was finally going to happen!

Dubrow was all but immobilized by her sudden good fortune. Having survived all the setbacks and rejections, what could she now do to freeze this magic moment?

She decided to take a vacation in Hawaii. It seemed corny, but somehow appropriate.

The vacation was not a success. Even as she was swimming and sunning, Dubrow felt a curious foreboding. It was all so wonderful—yet somehow it would never come to pass.

Her foreboding, as she would learn in the coming weeks, was justified. Those seers who had predicted that *Road Show* someday would become a legend were only partially right. It would be a legend in that dread corner of the movie industry known as Development Hell.

*   *   *

"Green light"—the two most cherished words in the Hollywood lexicon. When a movie earns its green light, that means it is officially approved to go into production, that its key personnel are all firmly in place, and that a start date has been set. In the case of *Road Show*, the magic date was to be July 15, 1983.

When a studio gives the green light to an expensive movie such as *Road Show*, the project instantly assumes a luster of infallibility. All the studio bureaucrats who the week before were still carping about dialogue changes and budget revisions suddenly line up like a cheering section. "I can tell you without qualification that *Road Show* will be next year's blockbuster," Frank Yablans intoned to a marketing meeting in March, instructing his troops to spread the word to exhibitors and anyone else who would listen. Freddie Fields, meanwhile, was telling trade columnists that *Road Show* would single-handedly revive the great tradition of the western.

But even as the trumpets were blaring, even as the accounting department started processing the big paychecks, problems were starting to fester.

The most important problem lay in Martin Ritt's growing skittishness. There were several things gnawing at the feisty sixty-three-year-old director. For one thing, despite their presumed enthusiasm for the project, Freddie Fields's D-girls were swamping him with last-minute script suggestions. "Call 'em off," Ritt growled to Fields. "I'm trying to make a fucking movie."

Casting battles were also beginning to get to Ritt. At the studio's urging, he had reluctantly accepted Cher for the role of Opal, Spangler's sexy wife, but now Jack Nicholson was resisting. He'd been spending time with Debra Winger lately, and informed Ritt that, in his opinion, she'd bring more to the role than Cher. Donna Dubrow and other aides on the film were not surprised. Whenever they'd gone to Nicholson's house for meetings lately, Winger, swathed in black spandex, seemed to be in evidence.

Apart from battles over script, budget, and cast, Ritt's overriding concern related to something else entirely—Frank Yablans. As an "old pro" who had once been blacklisted, Ritt understood the power dynamics of filmmaking. He also understood that Frank Yablans had not selected Ritt, but inherited him. Years earlier, when Yablans had first come to Paramount, he'd inherited another Ritt picture, called *The Molly Maguires*. Yablans hadn't liked the picture, and, in Ritt's mind, had done a halfhearted job of distributing it. Indeed, Yablans and Ritt had again tried to work together in 1981 on *Monsignor,* but hadn't got along at all. Ritt finally pulled out of the project, which Yablans went on to make with Frank Perry.

And now, in the midst of all the tensions on *Road Show,* here he was coming up against Yablans yet again. Would he be more supportive this time, Ritt wondered, or would it be a repeat of past performances?

There was, indeed, one way of finding out. Ritt's agent contacted the studio with an urgent message. After consultation with his doctor, Ritt had decided that perhaps *Road Show* might be too strenuous a picture for him, what with cattle drives and stampedes, all shot in the heat of summer. Ritt, after all, was a man in his mid-sixties who'd had health problems in the past.

It was, at best, a curious communication. To everyone who had talked with Ritt in recent days, he'd seemed robust and energetic. What was behind this notification, therefore? Had he lost his enthusiasm for the project? Did he want to delay the start of shooting? Or was he merely taking the temperature of the studio?

To Freddie Fields and Donna Dubrow, all this was cause for grave concern. "Let's tell Marty we love him and we need him," Dubrow argued passionately. "We can even push back the start date if he wants."

Yablans, however, saw it differently. It might be all for the best, he declared. Maybe the studio should replace Ritt with a younger director, one whose style and tempo might be more suitable for today's audience. Perhaps a contemporary western needs a contemporary director.

"We could lose the package," Fields cautioned. "You know how these things go."

"The world wouldn't stop turning," Yablans replied.

"Wait a minute," I said. "I thought you loved this script. That you thought it was a classic."

Yablans looked at me, puzzled. "It's okay," he said. "With the right director and the right cast, it's okay."

"'It's okay'!" I mumbled. "'Okay' isn't good enough for a picture that's going to cost us twenty million dollars." I glared at Fields, who sat there, twitching. I realized that I had never directly discussed *Road Show* with Yablans, who'd been spending most of his time in Europe lately, or doing his dog-and-pony show for junk-bond investors. Instead, I'd depended on Freddie Fields's report of Yablans's enthusiasm.

"We've got to move quickly here," Fields was saying nervously. "There are pay-or-play deals riding on this one. Major stars..."

"So get out your directors' list, guys," Yablans urged. "Let's see who's available."

Donna Dubrow was distraught when she learned that the studio had decided to accept Ritt's "withdrawal." Nicholson and Hutton, on the other hand, expressed their willingness to accept a replacement, provided he was a director of equal stature.

An urgent meeting of production executives was called to assemble a list of available replacements. Names of "hot" young directors ricocheted back and forth across the conference room table. John Badham, perhaps—he'd just finished *WarGames* for the studio. Or Peter Weir, who'd done a fine job on *The Year of Living Dangerously*. Seated at the head of the table, Freddie Fields didn't seem to be hearing the names. He had a far-off look in his eyes, as though he were pondering some higher truth. Finally, there was a momentary gap in the conversation.

"Richard Brooks," Fields said.

There was a hush. "Who?"

"Our director on *Road Show*—Richard Brooks," Fields repeated.

Richard Brooks! We all knew Fields and Brooks were friends. Five years earlier, Fields had produced *Looking for Mr. Goodbar*, which Brooks had directed superbly. In the intervening five years, however, Brooks's only film had been an unintelligible satire appropriately titled *Wrong Is Right*.

"I thought we were looking for a hip young director," someone at the table said. "Brooks must be older than Ritt."

"He's seventy-one," Fields replied, "but he's a kid at heart. Remember *The Professionals?*"

"That was 1966," I said.

"Brooks will turn *Road Show* into *Red River*," Freddie Fields intoned, obviously transfixed by his suggestion.

Over the next few days, Freddie Fields launched into a whirlwind of meetings to implement his new blueprint. At a breakfast meeting, he radiated satisfaction as he reported the results. Richard Brooks had agreed to take over *Road Show*, he said. There were the usual stipulations, of course—he wanted final cut and total artistic control. No executive would be allowed to read his shooting script except for Fields, Yablans, and me—no comments from D-girls this time. There were other Brooksian conditions, as well. When MGM screened the film, for example, no name would be allowed on the invitation list without his approval.

"Sounds good to me," Yablans said, when Fields had finished.

"I don't understand one thing—does he agree to shoot the present script?" I asked.

"He thinks the script is in pretty good shape," Fields answered. "He'll either do the rewrite or bring in a writer to do it."

"And Nicholson approves him?" Yablans asked.

"You know Jack—he had to make a pitch for his pals. Bob Rafelson, Hal Ashby, you know the list. But he said he'd approve Brooks."

"Good work," Yablans reiterated.

Road Show, it seemed, was back on track. Or was it? Analyzing Fields's progress report, I was still puzzled. In granting Brooks creative control of the film, for example, how had he squared this with Nicholson, whose contract also gave *him* these controls? Had he confronted this issue, or merely blurred it over?

Second, with summer approaching, how would Brooks find time to do his rewrite of the script? He still had to complete his casting, scout locations, hire the rest of his crew, and attend to all the other myriad details of preproduction. This would not allow much time for writing. Theoretically, he could bring in another writer, as Fields had suggested, but Brooks, I knew, was one of the few genuine American auteurs. He really wrote all of his films, as well as directing them. It was hard to imagine anyone as single-minded as Richard Brooks delegating the writing job to someone else.

It was not long before my questions were answered. By mid-June, Richard Brooks was ensconced in an office on the lot—an office that, at his request, was far removed from *Road Show*'s producer or other personnel. Indeed, Brooks didn't even want to be in the same building with them. Since his new office did not have a private bathroom, Fields ordered studio workers to construct one, even if it meant working around the clock.

Brooks's presence on the lot was a vivid one. A ruddy-faced man with an errant shock of white hair, Brooks would appear in his office each day, dressed in baggy sweats or soiled chino trousers. He would pace and fret and scribble script notes. At the studio commissary, slumped over his meal, he posed a vivid contrast to the slickly groomed, Armani-clad younger directors. Brooks embodied a throwback to the old mavericks—the Peckinpahs and Hustons—who were artistic soldiers of fortune rather than crafty corporatists.

He understood this, too. The "hot" directors in town were forty years his junior, and so were most of the development executives. They all saw him as an oddball anachronism who had somehow managed to creep out from the studio vaults.

Indeed, while the young would-be Spielbergs and Lucases were grinding out their MTV-paced cop movies and action-adventure sequels, Brooks, during his career, had reveled in making outrageous choices. He'd shoot a commercial movie like *The Professionals*, but then he'd come back with *The Brothers Karamazov* or *Lord Jim*. He'd rehabilitate himself with *In Cold Blood*, or *Bite the Bullet*, but would then be off again with *Elmer Gantry*.

Brooks was a man who gloried in his unpredictability. And he looked the part, with his darting, erratic eyes, expansive gestures, and disconnected patterns of speech. He would arrive at a meeting in midsentence, and often end it in midparagraph, his thoughts tumbling over one another in unstructured patches of dialogue.

Stalking down the hall one day, he saw me emerging from the elevator and started walking alongside. As usual, he was in the middle of a thought.

"...premise all wrong. Spangler wouldn't be the one to start a harebrained cattle drive. Makes no damned sense at all. By the time he'd get the cattle to market, they'd be so tough and leathery, no one would buy 'em anyway.... Maybe the old man could suggest the drive.... The old Jed guy who got written out.... And Spangler is an old oil rigger who returns to his ranch and ..."

Brooks kept rambling until we reached my office at the end of the hall, then he stopped suddenly and faced me.

"You're supposed to be a writer, aren't you? Books and stuff?"

"That's right."

"So what are you doing in a joint like this? This is no place for a serious person. You got kids in college or something—is that it? Alimony or something?"

"All of the above."

He followed me into my office and slumped onto a couch. "The thing about this movie is, when is it going to get written? I'm supposed to be prepping this goddam movie without a script. Now Freddie's solution is to hire a writer, and I'm supposed to work with him. Do you know of a writer who might be up for that?"

"There are a couple of guys I could introduce you to. You might enjoy working with them."

" 'Working with'—that's the part I don't get. I've never done this 'working with' crap. I write my own scripts."

"But if you have to start shooting in eight weeks ..."

"Get me a goddam writer," Brooks snapped, getting to his feet. "And then maybe someone will explain to me how to 'work' with a writer. I mean, what do I do while he writes, hold his ...?"

He started toward the door, then suddenly wheeled to face me again. "This one's gonna be a tough son of a bitch, does everyone realize that?"

"I think so. Explain one thing, will you?"

"What?"

"Have you really committed to do this movie?"

Richard peered at me, eyes twinkling mischievously.

"As I told Freddie, I'll direct it if I believe I can do a good job. If I can lick the script and get the production in shape..."

"In other words, you haven't made a deal."

"I don't believe in making deals. I believe in making movies." And with that, Brooks was out of my office.

I reported this conversation to Freddie Fields, who seemed unconcerned. "I know Richard like I know my mother," Fields said. "He'll do the movie. Just find him a writer."

In keeping with this dictum, I introduced Brooks to Denne Petitclerc, a grizzled, battle-hardened veteran of the movie wars. Petitclerc, I felt, could cope with these unusual conditions. He had worked tactfully with some of the industry's most exasperating people, such as Steve McQueen and George C. Scott. He'd also written a superb script for a film I had produced entitled *Islands in the Stream*.

Having read the Getchell draft of *Road Show*, Petitclerc said he was troubled by the curious absence of conflict. Once Spangler decides to defy the venal truckers and launch his cattle drive, the story seems to dissipate rather than build, Petitclerc reported. A tentative romantic triangle between Spangler, Leo, and Opal never develops into anything.

Indeed, nothing seems to develop!

When Petitclerc posed his analysis of the script to Brooks, he listened carefully and said he agreed. After tossing ideas back and forth for several hours, a working plan was agreed to. Petitclerc would start his rewrite, consistent with their discussions. Brooks, meanwhile, would go to Kansas to scout the actual locations and hopefully come up with some fresh solutions to the story problems.

"I'm not good at dealing with things in the abstract," Brooks said. "I have to get a sense of real people and places." And, having said that, he got an even better idea: He would also invite his two leads, Nicholson and Hutton, to join him on his jaunt through Kansas. Having waited so long for the picture to start, they might be energized by the trip and get into their characters.

The actors readily agreed, and they all took off. Once during the trek, Brooks phoned to say it was going well. The only setback thus far, he said, was that Jack Nicholson almost got arrested for mooning other motorists on the turnpike.

Upon returning from the trip, however, Brooks quickly fell into a dark mood. "He's worried," Donna Dubrow reported. "He won't tell me what's wrong, but he looks miserable, and he's popping glycerine or some kind of a pill for angina pains. He's worried, and therefore I'm worried."

A week later, Petitclerc turned in a stack of revised pages, but Brooks would not return his phone calls to disclose his reaction to them. An aide reported seeing clumps of pages atop Brooks's desk with epithets like "garbage" and "trash" scrawled in the margins.

Brooks himself burst into my office one day to explain, in his usual disconnected way, what was bothering him. "It's the goddam story," he said, pacing the room, "the whole premise. It starts from there."

"What starts from there?"

"If a rancher like Spangler felt he was being fleeced by truckers, he'd go out and rent his own goddam trucks, that's what he'd do. I realized that driving around Kansas, talking to people. And he sure as hell wouldn't start a goddam cattle drive, because he couldn't get the goddam cattle across the goddam turnpikes, and even if he could, the goddam bridges wouldn't hold up under a thundering herd."

Brooks stopped in his tracks. "You know what I think?"

"What?"

"No one involved in this movie ever went to Kansas, that's what I think. There are a hundred things in this script that wouldn't be there if anyone had visited Kansas. Well, let me tell you something. I've visited Kansas!"

Having said that, Brooks exited my office.

If Brooks's frustration level was mounting, so was Nicholson's. Having been attached to the project for almost a year, Nicholson was scheduled to start receiving weekly compensation on July 15, thereby triggering his $3.5 million pay-or-play deal. In view of the script problems, the date was now pushed back to August 15, and Nicholson sensed further delays were in the offing. He dreaded the prospect of filming *Road Show* in the fall, when the weather might turn cold and wet.

Still smarting from the cavalier manner in which Debra Winger had been vetoed for the Opal role, Nicholson phoned Fields to advocate Julie Christie for the part. Fields sounded vaguely encouraging, but now Nicholson picked up a rumor that Fields was, in reality, considering Mary Steenburgen, who was not on Nicholson's approved list. Whatever happened to my creative controls? Nicholson stormed. And, for that matter, whatever happened to the script?

Sandy Bresler, Nicholson's agent, had told Nicholson about his several conversations with Freddie Fields, during which Fields had assured him that Richard Brooks's rewrite of *Road Show* was "an Academy Award script."

That's great, Nicholson responded. If the script's going to win an Oscar, why can't I read it?

"Soon," Fields assured him, neglecting to mention, of course, that no such script existed.

The continued delays, meanwhile, were starting to affect the production in other ways, as well. The $18.5 million budget, approved by the executive committee, now looked dubious in view of the later start date. Moreover, Brooks, in his meetings with the budget people, had started describing complex new scenes, involving added stunts and extras.

The possibility of a runaway budget on *Road Show* was a source of panic at the studio. Other films that were now in preparation also were coming in at figures higher than anticipated. *2010*, the sequel to *2001: A Space Odyssey*, was vaulting toward a $28 million projected cost. *Teachers* and *Red Dawn* seemed headed for a combined cost of $30 million. If *Road Show* began to get out of control, there would be hell to pay.

"Everybody's procrastinating, while I'm left twisting in the wind," Yablans barked angrily just before once again getting on a plane for Europe. "I want this thing brought to a head."

Indeed, *Road Show* was about to come to a head, but in a far different way than Yablans envisioned.

On the evening of July 25, 1983, Richard Brooks was admitted to Cedars-Sinai Medical Center and placed in intensive care. Brooks, having suffered from angina, was now complaining of severe chest pains and numbness in his arm. As an angiogram was being administered, Brooks suddenly suffered a mild heart attack.

Freddie Fields, as president of MGM, was notified promptly of Brooks's setback, and told that further tests would be needed to determine the severity of his condition. Brooks was not in a life-threatening situation—that much was clear. On the other hand, it was equally clear that Richard Brooks would be in no shape to start a movie that month, or indeed that year.

Freddie Fields was stunned. He had lost his director. The project would now have to come to a halt. Or would it?

The morning after Brooks's hospitalization, Fields met with Mary Steenburgen and her agent, Martha Luttrell of ICM, to discuss the role of Opal. Neither knew anything of Brooks's illness, of course. Luttrell informed Fields that Steenburgen had been offered a leading role in Robert Redford's next film. In that case, Fields replied, he would make Steenburgen a firm offer to appear in *Road Show* for a fee of $750,000 plus 10 percent of the profits. Her start date, he said, would be August 23.

Surprised at the swift pace of events, Steenburgen said she'd prefer to meet with her director before committing to the film. Fields said that was impossible; Richard Brooks was on location.

Faced with a take-it-or-leave-it choice, Mary Steenburgen agreed to accept the role without the meeting.

Having accomplished his mission, Fields found Donna Dubrow sitting in his reception area in a state of high agitation. Dubrow reported she had been trying unsuccessfully to reach her director and sensed something was wrong.

"Brooks is at home with a bad cold," Fields told her. "You shouldn't be disturbing him."

Toward the end of this discussion, I arrived in the reception area, and followed Fields back into his office, shutting the door behind me. Fields grabbed a cigarette, started to light it, then remembered he had given up smoking and put it down. "I'm kind of busy, kiddo," he said.

"What's going on with Brooks?" I asked.

"A little cold."

"Hey, Freddie—it's me, remember? Your distinguished senior vice president? . . ."

"Look, I've got a lot to do. . . ."

"Let me make it easy for you. He's in intensive care. You know it and I know it. Does anyone else around here know it?"

Fields looked pale. He reached for another cigarette, this time lighting it and taking a drag.

"How did you find out?"

"Hey, I put in my ten years on *The New York Times*, remember? Reporters have their sources." Actually, I'd been informed of Brooks's condition by the medical partner of the doctor treating Brooks, but I decided not to invoke any names.

"Look, we've got a lot of hysterical people around here. People like Donna Dubrow."

"Why did you just close the Steenburgen deal?"

"We've got a picture to make, kiddo. . . ."

"How? We've got no script, remember? You're not going to give *me* that bullshit speech about Brooks having written an Academy Award script, are you?"

Fields took another nervous puff of his cigarette. "We'll push the picture back a few weeks. . . ."

"Look, Freddie, you know and I know we never really had a deal for Brooks to direct this picture to begin with. Now do you want to explain what's going on?"

Fields just sat there, smoking.

"Does Yablans know any of this?"

"No."

"I suggest you tell him. Like now."

"I'll tell him."

I got up and left the room. I felt both defeated and alienated. I had just joined a new company, only to discover it was enmeshed in more covert activity than the CIA!

Within twenty-four hours, the lid of secrecy was blown.

Mary Steenburgen demanded to know why she'd been signed for a nonexistent film, then lied to about the condition of the director. Jack Nicholson and Tim Hutton wanted to know who was going to direct their movie and when.

At the studio, meanwhile, I became aware of a series of closed-door meetings called to discuss the insurance implications of the fiasco. In view of Brooks's illness, the studio's insurance would clearly cover some of the damages. The question was, to what extent? If Brooks's heart attack had occurred after August 1, or within twenty-eight days of the scheduled start of the film, the policy would cover up to $10 million of the studio costs, but if Brooks fell ill before that date, the claim would be limited to the $500,000 in preproduction coverage.

The studio, it was clear, had backed itself in a corner, and the dilemma was worsening with each passing day. To pay off Nicholson and Hutton without getting a film out of them would be an enormous corporate embarrassment. But the prospect of making *Road Show* under these adversarial conditions was equally intimidating.

During the first week in August, Fields tried a new tack with Nicholson. While the studio still believed firmly in *Road Show*, he told him, perhaps a substitute film could be found. MGM/UA, for example, had become interested in a project called *Kingdom*, which dealt with sexual intrigues among evangelical preachers in the South. It could be a terrific Nicholson vehicle.

Nicholson flew into a rage. He reminded Fields that he'd taken himself off the market for a full year in order to do *Road Show*, and, by God, he intended to do it. "These cocksuckers at this studio are trying to screw me," he roared. Then, realizing who he was talking to, he added, "And you're one of the cocksuckers."

Ever the smooth agent, Fields tried to calm Nicholson down.

The studio would present him with a new list of directors for *Road Show* within forty-eight hours, he assured him. Then he could make his choice, and the production would be back in gear.

What Nicholson could not know was that, even as he was hearing these reassurances, the production office was sending out instructions to sell off the cattle that had been purchased to appear in *Road Show*, and also to fire the production manager. The brakes, it was clear, were being firmly applied.

A pall had now fallen over the studio. The once-amusing banter among executives had disappeared. People spoke in guarded terms, as though fearing that any remark, however trivial, might somehow be misinterpreted.

The war of nerves with Jack Nicholson now intensified. MGM/UA submitted the name of Bob Clark, the director of *Porky's*, as the new director of *Road Show*. Nicholson hastily turned him down and suggested instead Hal Ashby. The studio passed on the grounds of rumored substance abuse, and came back with Rob Lieberman, a commercials director. Nicholson now countered with Bob Rafelson, who had been fired from *Brubaker*, his most recent film, for striking a production executive. The studio came back with Stuart Rosenberg, the man who'd replaced Rafelson on *Brubaker* after that incident.

The process was getting nowhere. Each side felt the other's suggestions were mischievous. A production meeting was called to assess further alternatives.

Even before everyone was in their seat, Freddie Fields casually confided his latest brainstorm. Why not stop the game-playing, he proposed, and hire a director who could turn *Road Show* into the great film it was destined to become? That director, he said, was Michael Cimino.

Yablans, who'd arrived just in time to hear this proposal, stood staring at Fields as though he were a mental patient. Only three years earlier, of course, Cimino had directed *Heaven's Gate*, a $35 million fiasco that had obliterated an entire regime at United Artists and triggered the sale of the company. Now that UA was part of MGM, it seemed a bizarre suggestion.

"Are you fucking *crazy*?" Frank Yablans raged. "Are you out of your mind, Freddie? Can you see me, sitting here like a total idiot, explaining to the executive committee why Michael Cimino is being brought back to the company to direct another western?"

For the next two weeks, fresh accusations caromed back and forth between the studio and the actors. Where there had once been a steady, if discordant, dialogue, now there were two armed camps.

On September 1, the studio finally dropped its expected bomb. It formally notified the actors that *Road Show* had officially been abandoned because of Richard Brooks's disability. Hence, the actors' pay-or-play commitments did not apply because of a force majeure situation. The elaborately worded contracts, drawn up and refined at such vast legal expense, were not worth the paper they were written on. Except, of course, to the attorneys who had charged the fees.

The response of the actors, not surprisingly, was to file suit. The project that Donna Dubrow had nurtured so carefully had now vaporized in a mushroom cloud of litigation. Where once there had been hopes and fantasies and pay-or-play deals, there would now be threats, elaborate deceits, and still more legal fees.

Once *Road Show* was consigned to the courts, it took years for the disputes to work themselves out. Nicholson and Steenburgen ultimately settled their suits, rather than await the sluggish machinations of the legal system. As a sort of consolation prize, Nicholson also was assigned ownership of several films he had made for the studio in years gone by, such as Antonioni's *The Passenger*. (Better paydays lay ahead: In 1989 Nicholson cleared some $50 million from his gross participation in *Batman*).

The lone performer determined to take his case all the way was Tim Hutton, who, during the disputes with the studio, had seemed the most passive and accepting. In February 1989, Hutton was rewarded for his tenacity. A jury of seven women and five men in Los Angeles Superior Court awarded him some $2.5 million in compensatory damages and $7.5 million in punitive damages. Hutton and his persuasive attorney, James P. Tierney, had paraded a succession of witnesses, including Brooks, Ritt, Dubrow, and Nicholson, to convince the jury that the studio had committed fraud in failing to honor its contracts and produce the motion picture. The studio's two prime witnesses, Yablans and Rothman, failed utterly in their effort to persuade jurors that the studio had acted in good faith.

Ironically, however, it wasn't MGM/UA that had to foot the bill (which was marginally reduced in a 1989 settlement). Rather, it was Ted Turner, the Atlanta cable-TV entrepreneur. In his eagerness to close a deal in 1986 to acquire the MGM library, for which he paid over $1 billion, Turner also took over certain other liabilities—among them, the studio's lawsuits. Hence, while the three actors finally got the satisfaction of getting their money, they got it from the wrong source.

In the weeks following the collapse of the project, *Road Show* became an unmentionable topic. It was like being at the Kremlin after the fall of a powerful leader. Scripts quickly disappeared from the shelves, photos from the walls. *Road Show* had become a nonevent.

Several questions about the project still remained unresolved in my own mind, but no one was eager to deal with them. Why, for example, had Freddie Fields been so eager to lock in Mary Steenburgen at a time when the film was obviously teetering? Or, possibly, was he merely following orders tied in with the complex insurance machinations?

Apart from these, there were even more basic questions. Had Frank Yablans really wanted to make *Road Show* to begin with? Or, for that matter, could the studio even have afforded to make it had all the elements come together? Given the commitments to such expensive films as *2010* and *Red Dawn*, perhaps the ever-mysterious executive committee had already secretly turned against it.

Even while Richard Brooks was visiting locations, Yablans had admitted that he had started a new search for fully financed projects. "I don't want any more big pictures unless someone is ready to put up big money," he'd told me on the phone from Europe. With this objective in mind, he had started a round of meetings with such producers as Dino De Laurentiis and Tarak Ben Amar, both of whom made it a practice to fund their projects.

In late August, Yablans and I sat across from one another in the studio commissary to discuss a variety of thorny issues, these among them. It was eight-thirty in the morning, and the vast room seemed eerie at this early hour. Yablans had asked the commissary manager to open his room for breakfast meetings once a week. Coffee and muffins were customarily served to the production or marketing staffs, or to anyone else who'd been invited. But on this particular morning, the meeting consisted solely of Yablans and me. And the only sounds in the room, besides our voices, were the footsteps of the lone waitress who sleepily served us.

Yablans had opened our discussion with his customary direct-ness. "If something's eating at you, just get it out on the table."

What was "eating at me," I explained, was the pervasive dishonesty that was creeping into the studio's dealings with the creative community. "We're starting to lie to our filmmakers," I said. "And we're starting to lie to one another."

"You're still riled up about *Road Show*," Yablans shot back, thereby mentioning the unmentionable.

"It's certainly a vivid example," I said. "Freddie lied to me. The studio lied to everyone else."

"I was gone during that whole incident," Yablans said. "Things went on that should not have gone on."

"It's not the only example," I said. "The studio lied to Stuart Rosenberg about *Running Man.*" A veteran director, Rosenberg had a pay-or-play deal to make a thriller starring Mel Gibson when the studio switched the star to another project. Instead of settling with Rosenberg, the director was informed by business affairs that, as a result of a heart bypass operation three years earlier, he was "uninsurable."

"That was a tactical mistake," Yablans replied stonily. "The legal wizards were trying to be cute."

"The *WarGames* deal," I added, pointing to an incident that had also just flared up in which the studio was suddenly trying to pull out of a deal with its co-financier.

"Why are you suddenly on your high horse? Who do you think you are, Ralph Nader?" Yablans was grinning.

"Look, Frank, I'm not here to give moral sermons. The business runs on credibility. Once a studio loses its credibility, it's in deep shit."

Yablans sipped his coffee thoughtfully and said nothing.

"I was brought in here to find important projects for the studio," I continued. "Every time this company screws up, my job becomes less tenable."

I was getting through to him now, or so it seemed. The two of us had often talked in the past about the difficulties of attracting major talent to the studio, given its turbulent recent history.

"Look," Yablans said, leaning across the table, "you're making a valid point, but there's such a thing as the corporate white lie. Companies have to tell white lies as a matter of self-protection ..."

"There's a distinction between white lies and the stuff that's been going down around here...."

"...And I have to be the final arbiter on questions like that. You owe your primary loyalty to me, and I'll deal with this on an issue-by-issue basis. If you feel we're screwing up, you bring the incident to me, and I will make the determination."

"That's fair," I replied, "provided I agree with your determinations. 'Cause if we keep going down the road we're on now . . . well, this isn't a place where I want to work under those conditions."

"There you are, on your high horse again."

"You can call it that. Or you can just say I don't want to sit by while we self-destruct."

"We're not self-destructing, we're just getting rolling," Yablans flared.

"I know. And I hope we keep rolling happily ever after. I want it as bad as you do, Frank."

He stared across at me for a beat, then reached across the table to shake hands. "Okay, we understand each other, right, pal?"

"Right," I responded, doubting, even as I said it, that that was indeed the case.

CHAPTER FOUR

■

THE PREVIEW

1983

ON a warm spring evening in Phoenix, the desert air, even at 8:00 P.M., smelled vaguely parched, as though someone had released it from a giant microwave. Outside the movie theater, the crowd emerged slowly from the assembled RVs and pickups, moving with measured strides toward the box office. Both the vehicles and the people looked as if they'd been out in the sun too long. On the popcorn line inside the lobby, the clerk had to keep yelling "next" to move along the sleepy-looking customers.

None of the paying customers took any notice of the limousines parked to one side of the theater, or of the echelons of tense-looking executives in suits and ties hovering at the edges of the lobby. In contrast to the moviegoers, who looked as though they might get lost on the way to their seats, the tight-lipped suit-and-tie functionaries seemed steeled for a hostage swap or some crisis of like magnitude.

There was indeed a lot riding on the results of this late April evening, at least for them. The just-completed film *WarGames*, was about to be previewed before an audience for the first time, and expectations were high. Only a couple of studio officials had actually seen the finished film, and they'd steadfastly refused to talk about it, but from the looks and whispers, one could sense this was not a normal preview. Unlike the other films that had emerged from the Begelman years at MGM/UA, *WarGames* had the aura of a winner. A hit film owes its success to a chance convergence of craft and timeliness, and the people who guided *WarGames* along its tortuous path apparently had seized their moment.

One thing was certain. It had been a long time since MGM/UA had had a hit. A very long time. And if *WarGames* was to click, the timing could not have been more propitious, what with a new regime taking office, and vast new sums of money being pumped into the studio to support its ambitious plans.

Kirk Kerkorian and his advisers, after all, were Vegas people. If *WarGames* scored, they would surely be inspired to up the ante.

Typically, Kerkorian decided not to show up for the preview, nor did Frank Rothman. Yablans was on hand, however, along with Freddie Fields; Leonard Goldberg, the executive producer, and John Badham, who had been brought in as director early in the shooting schedule, after the first director had been fired.

And scattered about the theater were a motley mix of distribution and marketing executives, all of them looking vaguely discomfited. Their nervousness derived not so much from the occasion as from alarm over their own personal fortunes. For in these early days of the new Yablans regime, rumors of a "clean sweep" were running rampant. Indeed, two or three of the "replacements" had been invited to the preview, standing around at the periphery, hoping not to make eye contact with those men whose jobs they would be filling.

As with most such previews, the studio had taken over a conventional theater, but had substituted its own film into the time slot of the regularly scheduled feature. Ads proclaiming a "major studio preview" had been placed in newspapers and on radio stations to help assure a good turnout. At the end of the screening, cards would be distributed to as many filmgoers as possible to elicit their reactions. For the director and his editor, however, the real indicators would not lie in the data from the cards, but rather in the "sounds" from the audience during the screening itself. They would listen for listlessness, for laughter, for the gasps of surprise. And during the moments of jeopardy in the story, they would, most of all, listen for that most gratifying of sounds—rapt silence, that wonderful silence when an audience is totally caught up in a film to the point where not even the chomping of popcorn can be heard in the auditorium.

Now, the theater had darkened, and the late arrivals scurried to their seats. Included among them were several "spies" from the big exhibitor chains—men whose job it was to infiltrate previews such as this and brief their head offices on the results. Nothing stays a secret for long in the film business, and by the next morning, the outcome of this supposedly closed "sneak" would be broadcast around the industry.

Yablans sank into a seat at the back of the theater. Seated across the aisle, I noticed the director wipe the perspiration from his face and murmur a quick prayer. The audience fell silent.

And suddenly the movie was up there, in all its nakedness. Nothing really mattered now except what flickered across the screen. No amount of hype could transmogrify that modest strip of film into something grander or more imposing than what now flashed across the front of the theater.

Would it work? The audience watched passively. The executives sat and hoped.

That *WarGames* could ever have reached this stage in itself had once seemed unlikely. Like so many projects, this, too, seemed destined for a fate similar to that of *Road Show*.

In the beginning, five years earlier, *WarGames* had not been one project, but rather two. A struggling young writer named Lawrence Lasker had written a piece called *The Genius*, about a dying seer who was searching for a protégé to whom he could pass on his wisdom. Lasker's onetime Yale classmate Walter Parkes had been writing yet another scenario dealing with a young genius who was searching for recognition. The two decided to combine their failed efforts into a new story, which would deal with a teenage computer prodigy who inadvertently taps into top-secret Pentagon codes, thus triggering nuclear confrontation.

This story, both recognized, would have a much better chance for commercial success, since it combined two time-honored genres: It was a wish-fulfillment youth comedy merged adeptly into a service comedy. How could it fail?

Their optimism was shared by a young D-girl named Lisa Weinstein, who was working for the production team of Leonard Goldberg and Jerry Weintraub at Universal Pictures. At Weinstein's urging, the script was optioned, and Martin Brest, a young director whose first film, *Going in Style*, had been well received, was brought in to supervise its further development.

Lasker and Parkes were thrilled. After years of wandering in the

Hollywood wilderness, they suddenly had high-powered producers in their corner, along with a director and a studio.

Their exuberance was short-lived. Goldberg and Weintraub, it seemed, were in the process of terminating their brief collaboration. While Goldberg would retain control of *WarGames*, he shared Martin Brest's belief that a more experienced writer was needed to bring the script to fruition. Walon Green, who'd written *The Wild Bunch*, was hired to perform the needed surgery, and his rewrite was duly handed over to Universal.

The studio felt the story wasn't strong enough to justify its projected cost—$14 million. It was therefore condemned to the netherworld of "turnaround," which meant it was now up to the producer to find a new buyer and, if successful, to reimburse Universal for its development costs.

For most projects, turnaround constitutes a death knell. But *WarGames* had picked up its supporters—too many, in fact. The project suddenly found itself entangled in a complex web of nepotistic interrelationships.

David Chasman, an executive working for David Begelman at MGM, was one of those who liked the script. He'd first learned about it from his long-term companion, Toni Howard, an agent who was also Leonard Goldberg's sister-in-law. Another new admirer was Paula Weinstein, an executive at United Artists, whose sister, Lisa, had first found the project for Goldberg. Indeed, Lisa was now living with Martin Brest, who was still connected with *WarGames* as its director.

Given this wellspring of enthusiasm, Begelman now optioned the material for MGM, only to discover that Kerkorian had decided to move him over to become chairman of UA. Begelman's former agency partner, Freddie Fields, was brought in to head MGM. Begelman naturally assumed he would take *WarGames* with him, but Fields, to everyone's surprise, was resisting. *WarGames* was a good project, he argued; it technically had been optioned by MGM and should stay there.

The entire issue became instantly moot, however, when Frank Rothman, the new chief executive officer of MGM/UA, the parent company, announced an important policy change. Henceforth, said Rothman, there would be a lid of $10 million on all films to be made by both studios. The lid, he said, wasn't his idea. It had been imposed by the banks, which had been daunted by the dismal openings of Begelman's expensive slate of films.

To Rothman, a litigator by training, the new policy posed no special threat to *WarGames*, whose budget was now $12.5 million.

Martin Brest, the director, would simply have to make the necessary adjustments, hacking away a scene here or there. Freddie Fields had assured Rothman the film could be done for $7.5 million. Begelman disagreed; so did Brest.

While the budget debate continued, Begelman and Goldberg decided to take some emergency steps to save their project. Goldberg had become friendly with a multimillionaire coin dealer named Bruce McNall who, together with the Hunt brothers, Nelson and Bunker, decided to invest $2.5 million in the project in return for a small piece of the gross after recoupment. Begelman also closed a deal with a British company, EMI, to put up an additional $5 million advance against all foreign rights.

Begelman had pulled off a remarkable entrepreneureal coup. The money was now in place to make *WarGames* at its original $12.5 million budget.

But just as *WarGames* was now in, Begelman was about to be let out. Frank Rothman had rewarded his efforts with dismissal from the company. *WarGames* would proceed at UA under the aegis of Paula Weinstein.

WarGames seemed to have a charmed life. Everyone, with the exception of Begelman, was now getting his just desserts. Lasker and Parkes were brought back to set their script right once again. Matthew Broderick and Ally Sheedy were signed to star. Lisa Weinstein was accorded co-producer credit with Leonard Goldberg. And the director was still her live-in, Martin Brest.

Within days, the temperature would change drastically yet again. As he watched dailies each afternoon Freddie Fields was becoming alarmed about the caliber of work. Though he had never before been a production head and could boast very limited experience evaluating rushes, Fields felt that Brest's work was plodding and unimaginative. At the end of each day's screening, Paula and Lisa Weinstein would turn to Fields, aglow with enthusiasm for the material they had just witnessed, but Fields would sit in the back row, glowering.

John Kohn, the head of production for UA's new British partner, EMI, was also watching the dailies and, unlike Fields, made it a point to visit the set each day. When Fields expressed his concerns, Kohn told him to calm down. "The work isn't great, but it's not terrible," Kohn said. "There's no reason to fire the guy."

Kohn had uttered his remark half-seriously, but even as the words left his lips, he could see that Fields was not smiling. He was actually thinking of firing director Martin Brest!

A crisis meeting was called in Fields's office. In attendance were

Fields, Paula Weinstein, Anthea Sylbert, who was a production
vice president, and several others. As the current president of
United Artists, Paula Weinstein technically was Fields's co-equal
(he was president of MGM). But from the moment the meeting
started, it was clear that Fields did not accept this parity. Martin
Brest had to be replaced as director of *WarGames*, Fields declared.
The only issue under discussion was who would replace him.

Weinstein and Sylbert were beside themselves. Brest's work was
perfectly acceptable, Weinstein argued passionately, and when Sylbert rose to her defense, Fields interrupted, "Shut your mouth or
I'll kick your ass out of my office."

Sylbert did not flinch. "I've argued with the best of them," she
declared, "and I've never been talked to that abusively, even by a
disgruntled lover." As Fields looked on, openmouthed, Sylbert
stalked from the room.

Paula Weinstein hurried down the hall to Frank Rothman's office
to plead the case for Marty Brest, but to no avail. When a client
is dissatisfied with his lawyer, Rothman said, he simply changes
lawyers, and the trial goes on. And now, the studio, in the same
vein, had decided to change the director, who was just a hired
hand. To Rothman, the whole thing was being blown out of
proportion.

Late that afternoon, as he observed the shooting, John Kohn
received a call from Fields. Since he happened to be on the set,
Fields asked, would he mind slipping Brest the bad news?

Kohn was bewildered. Technically, he was just a co-financier,
not UA's head of production, and he didn't feel Brest deserved to
be canned. Nor did Leonard Goldberg, the executive producer.
Nonetheless, Kohn took Brest aside and told him he was through.

If Kohn felt a bit awkward at having been assigned this task,
he would feel even angrier several months later, when MGM/UA
would take the formal legal position that Kohn's company, EMI,
had never been involved in the project to begin with.

The debate over Brest's successor was resolved expeditiously.
Freddie Fields proposed Stewart Raffill, an obscure British director
whose only known credits were *The Sea Gypsies* and *Across the
Great Divide*. Kohn advocated John Badham, who was best known
for *Saturday Night Fever*, but who'd more recently directed one of
the unsuccessful films of the Begelman era, *Whose Life Is It Anyway?* Goldberg supported Badham, and he won the day.

Within two weeks, *WarGames* was filming again. Oddly enough,
the interruptions and controversies now seemed to be working
for the picture rather than against it. There was a special energy

on the set—a sense of high adventure. Here they were, Goldberg, Badham, Lasker, Parkes, and the others, succeeding where all others had failed, improvising as they went along. With Frank Yablans now assuming power at MGM/UA, Freddie Fields had more urgent bureaucratic issues to deal with. Yablans himself was also preoccupied by the demands of his office. The two dissenting Weinstein sisters, meanwhile, had been banished. Lisa had departed with Marty Brest. And Paula had declined to come to work, contending that her contract had specifically stated that she would report to David Begelman, not to Freddie Fields, who had suddenly become her new boss. (She subsequently lost that argument in arbitration.)

Paradoxically, *WarGames*, which had in the past been wrenched by corporate power struggles, was now wallowing in the freedom created by the power vacuum. There was no one to second-guess creative decisions, no one to pass judgment on the dailies. *WarGames* had been liberated!

The screening had ended now, and, oddly, the filmgoers seemed glued to their seats for a few beats, as though pondering their own reaction. Then, amid a slight scattering of applause, the audience rose and headed for the exits, picking up their cards along the way. Many simply headed out into the night; others paused to scrawl their responses on the questionnaires.

The assembled executives, meanwhile, waited tensely in the lobby. There were abortive attempts at levity, a few nervous jokes, but they were quickly quashed. A team of clerks had taken refuge in the theater manager's office to tabulate the questionnaires as they came in. Finally, Frank Yablans, who'd been pacing the lobby, could contain himself no longer. Trailed by two executives, he rushed into the manager's office and grabbed preview cards out of the hands of startled aides. With Freddie Fields now at his side, Yablans started riffling through the cards feverishly, a man possessed, flinging them to the ground when he had finished. Even as the tabulators scrambled all over the floor to reassemble their cards, Yablans suddenly looked over at Fields, a beatific smile on his face. "They love it," he said, his voice conveying a sense of utter incredulity. "They fucking love it."

Half an hour later, with the formally tabulated results still filtering in, Yablans summoned Badham, Goldberg, and others to an impromptu conference outside the theater lobby. The filmmakers knew by now that the results were superb. Even the MGM marketing people, a stolidly noncommittal lot, had conveyed their enthusiasm. But if John Badham expected any plaudits, he was quickly snapped back to reality. "The picture has potential," Yablans began, "but it needs work. I mean, the musical score—give me a break. There are maybe six pieces we can take out of the picture, just for starters...."

"But I like the score," Badham protested.

"Do you want a blockbuster or not, pal?" Yablans countered, and then proceeded to elaborate his other changes. Badham and Goldberg exchanged a quick look of forbearance. The adventure, they knew, had not yet ended.

Though Frank Rothman had only known Frank Yablans for a short time, he'd already observed his ability to project a wide range of moods. He'd seen him angry and calm, cheerful and depressed—sometimes with only a moment's transition. But now, in his office, this was the first time he'd ever seen him downright excited.

And the cause of his excitement was *WarGames*. The film, he effused, was a surefire winner. It had jeopardy, passion, humor. It also had a high degree of technological sophistication, Yablans added, and that could be both good news and bad. The upscale kids in the suburban malls would love the detail about computers. But the advertising campaign would have to be designed so as not to discourage minority audiences.

"And I'll guarantee you one thing about *WarGames*," Yablans added. "It'll be a huge hit overseas. Our foreign-distribution guys will have an orgasm when they see it."

The pipe almost fell out of Rothman's mouth. He gave Yablans a blank stare. Yablans stared back at him. "Did I say something wrong? I mean, suddenly it got very quiet in here."

"We don't have the picture overseas," Rothman said meekly. "There have been ... uh ... discussions with EMI. We had to get our costs below ten million dollars...."

"What business are we in—foreign aid? How could we give away foreign!"

Rothman took a deep breath. "We'll give the situation some study," he told Yablans.

It didn't turn out to be that simple. The contract, like most contracts in the entertainment industry, had been batted back and forth between MGM and EMI attorneys, but had not yet been signed by either party. EMI took the position that a basic understanding had been reached and that both parties were legally bound. MGM had even asked John Kohn to fire Marty Brest. MGM took the position that no deal had ever been consummated.

In due course, depositions were taken and legal positions formally staked out. A key bone of contention was a meeting between Freddie Fields and Gunther Schiff, the attorney for EMI, at which the deal had been closed in principal, according to Schiff. He'd even sent a letter to Fields confirming the understanding—a letter, Fields maintained in his deposition, that he'd never received. When the EMI attorneys produced a copy of the letter from Fields's files, Fields conceded he'd received the letter, but had never got around to reading it.

Rothman and Yablans were the next executives scheduled for depositions, but MGM decided the dispute had gone far enough. A settlement was reached with EMI guaranteeing the British company its $5 million from *WarGames*.

Meanwhile, John Badham had dutifully completed the changes in the music that Yablans had insisted on, and the film was ready for its release.

To herald the film's opening, Yablans presided over a special party at the studio. A select group of celebrities and industry executives rolled onto the lot to see the film in the studio theater. A lavish buffet dinner was set up in the commissary. A beaming Frank Yablans, standing alongside Frank Rothman, greeted guests, who ranged from Gregory Peck to Neil Diamond to the heads of rival studios, all of them extending their compliments on the film they had just seen. Observing it all, Leonard Goldberg now realized the ultimate paradox: that this embattled movie, which had twisted in the wind for six years at three different studios, had been brutalized and abandoned, rewritten and redirected, was now, in the official eyes of Hollywood, the first Yablans film at the new MGM. And that was exactly the message Frank Yablans wanted to project.

"It's all turning around now," Yablans told a circle of new friends. "This is the beginning."

CHAPTER FIVE

■

THE BOSS
1973

W HEN Jim Aubrey was fired in the fall of 1973, Kirk Kerkorian
wasted no time installing himself as the new chief executive officer
of Metro-Goldwyn-Mayer. The move surprised some observers
who'd assumed that Kerkorian had wanted to maintain his phan-
tomlike status. But those inside MGM were well aware that "the
boss" had long bristled over the degree of autonomy exercised by
Aubrey. Aubrey's obstinacy about United Artists had been the last
straw.

Executives at Kerkorian's other companies understood the
ground rules. They might hold imposing titles like president or
chairman, but in the end they were mere adjutants who might be .
summoned, on the boss's fleeting impulse, to far-off places for
middle-of-the-night meetings, just like aides to Howard Hughes.

That's the way Kerkorian wanted things run. As though to em-
phasize this point, Kerkorian now announced that his new president and chief operating officer at the studio would be Frank
Rosenfelt, who had previously served as its general counsel. Rosenfelt seemed ideally suited for his role. A small, nondescript man
who became almost "mousy" in the presence of stronger person-

alities, Rosenfelt had always followed orders. In Frank Rosenfelt's eyes, he was the lawyer and Kerkorian was his client. It was as simple as that.

Rosenfelt, like other Kerkorian aides, understood the built-in contradictions of Kerkorian's management style. Kerkorian wanted to be the boss, but was uninterested in day-to-day operations. He wanted everyone to know it was *his* company, which was run according to *his* decisions, yet declined to appear at stockholder meetings or press conferences.

These contradictions carried over to his personal life, as well. He was a modest man, yet he lived in opulent surroundings. He hated Hollywood parties, yet coveted the company of stars like Cary Grant and Roger Moore. He would go out of his way to be courteous in social milieus, yet pursued a ruthless business code.

The New York Times once began an article about Kerkorian by asking, "Can an honest and ambitious American boy start out in the Civilian Conservation Corp and wind up with nearly $200 million—and everybody still be his friend? Yes, if he's Kirk Kerkorian...."

The need to appear "the good guy" was a compelling drive in Kerkorian's life. If there was a crisis at one of his companies, or an executive to be chastised or dismissed, invariably one of Kerkorian's functionaries would perform the dirty deed, taking the responsibility onto himself. Kerkorian was never "the heavy;" it was always some semi-anonymous aide.

Kerkorian maintained the same nonconfrontational style in his social dealings. Having been with him at several social occasions, big and small, I never heard him respond discourteously to a question, no matter how inane. Nor have I heard him give a direct response on any issue that might involve controversy, political or economic. He was at all times stoic and noncommittal; at once personable and utterly impersonal. One prominent Hollywood executive who spent weeks with Kerkorian, locked in complex night-and-day negotiations, could not recall a single personal anecdote or allusion during the entire interlude. "He is the nicest nonperson I've ever not known," he observed.

At one small dinner party in Malibu, Kerkorian was seated next to an extremely shrill matron, who assaulted him with the "hottest" gossip involving well-known Hollywood personalities. Kerkorian tried to listen, but the expression on his broad, leathery face was frozen. Finally, he could contain himself no longer. In midsentence, he interrupted, "Ma'am, since I've never heard of a single person you've mentioned, I wonder if I could tell you instead about the time I ran out of fuel in an old C-47 on the way from Hawaii to San Francisco."

While the lady looked at him in utter disbelief, he continued, "It was back in the late forties, and you never could really tell how much fuel you had in those days. I'd thought I'd filled the tanks, but, you know, the way those planes sat, nose in the air, resting on their rear wheels, the tanks looked full, but there was all this room at the uphill end. I found that out the hard way when the engines started sputtering after fifteen hours, and there was no land anywhere in sight...."

While Kerkorian was happily reminiscing about his days as a daring young aviator, the others around the table realized that he was, at last, in his element. He concluded his story in about three minutes, then lapsed back into silence for the remainder of the evening.

"There are, in the end, only two subjects that interest Kirk," one old friend observed. "They are planes and money. He will tell airplane stories. He will talk about convertible debentures. And if he's had a few drinks, he may talk about Vegas, but that's the entire inventory."

Kerkorian's carefully cultivated benign presence belies a rough, roistering youth and years of struggle and disappointment. Kerkorian's family roots go back to that portion of Armenia that is now Turkey, a part of the world where some 1.5 million Armenians were killed by Turks during World War I. His grandfather joined other Armenians who had migrated in the 1880's to the San Joaquin Valley of California, where he bought a small farm and sent for his son, Caspar, who arrived in the United States at the age of seventeen. Caspar's bride, Sushon, preferred to take an American name, Lilly, and the two started a family.

A big, handsome man with a handlebar mustache and a fierce temper, Caspar was a born promoter with an appetite for adventure. An inability to read or write left him desperately vulnerable to loan sharks, however. Intrigued by the raisin business, he bought first one farm, then another, but the bankers squeezed him out in the minirecessions of the early 1920s, and Caspar was forced to move his family to the pavements of East Los Angeles. There, Caspar continued to find new ventures—a chain of fruit stands, a watermelon-trucking business—but success eluded him.

Even as the family moved into smaller and more rickety homes, it remained insular and tight-knit. Armenian was the language spoken at home, which did not help the school performance of the four children. Kirk—his real first name is Kerkor—was deemed a troublemaker at an early age, and was consigned to a school for problem children. He finally talked his way into trade school where he was able to study auto repair. The totality of his high school education consisted of three months at Metropolitan High School.

When Kerkorian dropped out of school, the Depression was taking a terrible toll. His only chance at employment lay in a New Deal program called the Civilian Conservation Corps, which dressed poor kids up in World War I uniforms and marched them off to the country to cut fire trails and dig trenches. Kirk persuaded his parents to lie about his age, and soon he was in the wilds of Sequoia National Park, doing backbreaking labor for thirty dollars a month, most of which he sent back to his parents. While many of the city-bred kids ran away from the camps, Kerkorian stuck it out. It was, after all, his first paying job. And it marked an escape from the tight-knit Armenian community into which he had been locked.

After his CCC tour of duty ended, Kerkorian struggled to find a job. For a time, he cleaned engines at a used-car lot. He even worked as an occasional laborer at the MGM studio, where he was paid the grand sum of forty cents an hour. The lot held no magic for him; it was just another job.

Though a spindly 5 feet 11 inches and 130 pounds, Kerkorian was rock-hard from his CCC work. Now and then, when he needed a paycheck, he would do some fighting at the so-called amateur boxing arenas. His purses would come to a few bucks, but he won all but four of his thirty-three fights. He might have turned pro except for a newfound passion—flying.

Flying fever hit him in 1939 when a friend, Richard Lentine, took him up in a small plane from minuscule Alhambra Airport. Soon Kirk was doing the unthinkable—reenrolling in a night school math course in Burbank so he could learn to plot wind vectors. Instinct told him that, after all the odd jobs and wasted opportunities, flying held the key to his future. Here was something he could master and build upon so that he would not drift, like his father, from one scheme to the next.

Kerkorian became a flight instructor at a propitious time. With World War II looming, the need for pilots was desperate. Kerkorian managed to persuade a former schoolteacher to fake a letter stating that he had graduated from high school and, armed with this bogus credential, became a lieutenant in the Air Academy. Given this sudden respectability, he proposed to a girl from his old neighborhood whom he'd been dating for two years. Her name was Hilda Schmidt, and they were married on January 24, 1942.

Rather than pursue the more conventional wartime assignments, Kerkorian opted for the maverick tours of duty, such as ferrying transports across the North Atlantic. Before the war was over he'd become a captain for the RAF Transport Command, flying to India and Africa, functioning more like a soldier of fortune than a conventional serviceman. There were hairy escapes, crash landings—but also one thousand dollars a month pay, the first real money he'd ever earned. Kerkorian was often flying planes that only Lindbergh and a few other daredevils had ever flown.

With the end of the war came even greater opportunity. The landscape was virtually littered with old planes—and customers who wanted to buy them. Kerkorian had flown nearly all of them, and now he was buying twin-engined Cessnas and Lodestars, delivering them to Rio or Hawaii. It was not work for the fainthearted. Kerkorian would often find himself in some distant place, guiding some groaning old aircraft down the runway, wondering if it would really get off the ground.

The passion for buying and selling aircraft was to remain with him throughout his career. Thirty years later, when he was worth hundreds of millions of dollars, Kerkorian flew two bankers to Europe in his private 707. In Madrid, Adnan Khashoggi, the Saudi financier, admired the plane and offered to buy it. Kerkorian closed a deal on the spot, leaving his party without transportation home.

But in 1947, Kerkorian decided to impose some order in his life, purchasing a tiny charter service for some sixty thousand dollars. The charter's first plane was a single-engine Fairchild, its principal destination was Las Vegas, and his customers were gamblers who were too impatient to wait for the scheduled airlines, or kids bent on getting married in a hurry. As Kerkorian kept expanding, he cultivated the friendship of Walter Sharp, who managed the Montebello branch of the Bank of America, and who steadfastly kept extending him credit. Sharp ultimately was rewarded with lifelong membership in Kerkorian's inner circle.

By now, Kerkorian was making $100,000 a year, but his gypsy habits had taken their toll on his personal life. In 1951, his first wife filed for divorce. Kerkorian took it hard. More and more, he was becoming a creature of Las Vegas. Though still a man of modest means by Vegas standards, he was winning or losing fifty thousand dollars a night. He was dating showgirls, studying the operations of the casinos. On occasion, he even encountered another Vegas habitué—Howard Hughes. Kerkorian admired Hughes, and understood his devotion to airplanes, girls, and gambling. Kerkorian even tested his mettle by trying to sell Hughes a

Constellation for $1.6 million, but every time he thought he had closed the deal, Hughes would reopen negotiations. The enigmatic Hughes, Kerkorian concluded, had taken it upon himself to administer his "rites of passage."

In 1954, Kerkorian took another stab at domestic stability. He married a tall blond showgirl named Jean Hardy, who danced at the Thunderbird. At the time of their marriage, he was thirty-seven and she was twenty-three.

By the early 1960's, Kerkorian's charter service had become Trans International Airlines, flying DC-8s to a wider list of locations, including Hawaii. Initially, his most loyal clientele were members of the Armenian community, but soon he had added important U.S. military air-transport contracts. Kerkorian had brought into the business a tough old flying buddy named Fred Benninger, who had been working for the Flying Tiger Line. Benninger, like Walter Sharp, was to become part of the permanent entourage.

As business picked up, Kerkorian's penchant for financial maneuvering exercised a stronger hold. He closed a deal to sell Trans International for $1 million, then changed his mind and bought it back at a small loss, deciding, instead, to take it public. It was the first "supplemental airline" to sell stock to the public, and the shares went nowhere for many months before finally rising in a revived bull market.

By 1968, the expansion-minded Transamerica Corporation was eagerly courting Kerkorian's charter line, and the numbers kept going higher and higher. Finally, Kerkorian decided to sell. It was a fortuitous deal, for Kerkorian emerged briefly as Transamerica's biggest stockholder. Within a year, he was to sell his stock for $104 million. Kerkorian by now was definitely in the big leagues. And it was time to return to his original agenda—Las Vegas.

To Kerkorian, the lure of Las Vegas was intense and visceral. It was, in his mind, the ultimate boom town. One could make millions overnight just by buying the right piece of land at the right time. It was a matter of knowing the key players, and Kerkorian had already come to know many of them. It was a town of tough guys, but Kerkorian was as tough as any of them. His two daughters, Tracy, born in 1959, and Linda, born six years later, spent their time in the safe confines of Los Angeles with his wife, Jean. But Vegas was *his* town.

He had survived his "Vegas initiation" in 1950, dropping fifty thousand dollars on his ill-fated venture at the Dunes. He had also learned how to control his personal gambling problem. That was not to say he no longer bet, but his approach was disciplined and businesslike. He would go into a casino and place three bets. They might be huge or they might be small, but they never exceeded three in number. Then, whether he had won or lost, he would force himself to quit. "The longer you stay, the more the odds work against you," he explained to one of his production chiefs, who had accompanied him to a casino and was gambling recklessly—at least in the eyes of The Boss. "The key is to avoid getting sucked in. Three passes and I'm out."

A casino in Monte Carlo once denied Kerkorian's request for credit, but he quietly persisted in his request. The casino finally granted him a line of $50,000. Kerkorian marched to a roulette table, bet the entire sum, and won. He wheeled and left the casino, never to return.

By the mid-sixties, Kerkorian was also starting to do a lot better in Las Vegas in terms of his personal investments. Some vacant land that he owned was acquired as the site for a new hotel, and its owners offered to pay Kerkorian a small piece of the casino's earnings as partial payment. The hotel turned out to be Caesar's Palace, and Kerkorian finally sold his cut in 1968 for $5 million.

Now, he was ready for more. The Flamingo had had a checkered past, but it marked a promising first step for him. In the days when Bugsy Siegel presided over it, there were only 97 rooms, but now the place had been spruced up and expanded to 767. It wasn't exactly a "showpiece," but it would be Kerkorian's "training ground" for bigger and better things.

After the Flamingo, Kerkorian's dream was to build a brand new thirty-story hotel called the International. It would be shaped like a giant triangle and would boast the largest casino in the world, with thirty-two blackjack tables and twelve craps tables. It would have 1,512 rooms and would, unlike others on the Strip, be designed specifically for the convention trade.

News of Kerkorian's grandiose plans immediately caused a firestorm of protest from an unexpected source—the ever-mysterious Howard Hughes. Kerkorian's two hotels together would rival the combined 3,178 rooms of Hughes's structures. To meet this challenge, Hughes issued a hasty announcement of plans to build a Super Sands hotel, boasting four thousand rooms. When this announcement failed to halt Kerkorian's plans, Hughes tried another, more unorthodox tack. He sought to convince Kerkorian that the government's underground nuclear tests, which were scheduled to be set off some seventy-five miles from Las Vegas, would pose a threat to Kerkorian's venture and, indeed, to the entire city.

The underground tests had become an obsession with Hughes

in recent months, and he'd tried, by his typically bizarre means, to warn Washington of their potential destructiveness. Having taken refuge in a Las Vegas hotel suite, never venturing out into the world, Hughes was convinced that he would be blown to smithereens by the detonations, and no amount of scientific data could dissuade him.

Hughes assigned to Robert Maheu, his principal lieutenant, the task of winning Kerkorian to his side. Maheu, who occasionally played tennis with Kerkorian, tried to make his case as best he could, but Kerkorian obviously thought it was ludicrous. What puzzled Kerkorian, however, were Hughes's true motivations. Did Hughes really want him to join in this hopeless fight against the tests? Or did Hughes, in his deranged state, simply believe he could scare Kerkorian out of building the International?

In either instance, Kerkorian informed Maheu to carry back word that the International was moving forward.

The opening of the International in 1969 was Kerkorian's finest hour. His new friend Cary Grant was in attendance; indeed, he actually stood up in public (a rarity in itself) to thank Kerkorian as "the guy who made this spectacular hotel possible." Barbra Streisand then rose to sing some songs. Kerkorian had arrived.

Or so it seemed. Kerkorian would lose the International eventually, only to recapture it in the form of the MGM Grand, which would itself become the site of a major tragedy. He would also have to sell off much of MGM, only to regain it and relose it.

Kerkorian would, in fact, never achieve anything resembling the financial stability of other corporate builders—men like Henry Luce of Time Inc. or Lew Wasserman of MCA. A key reason, of course, was that Kerkorian never saw himself as a "builder," but rather as a "trader." The only acquisition that he would zealously cling to over the years would be the MGM trademark—not the studio, not its pictures, or traditions, but its treasured logo, which seemed to carry its own special value in his mind.

Despite the surface turbulence in his business life, Kerkorian carefully carved out a private life that, while idiosyncratic, nonetheless insulated him from the outside frenzy. His homes kept changing, and they were frequently rented, not owned, but they were always comfortable and private. From time to time, he had places in Las Vegas and Palm Springs. He rented various celebrity homes in Los Angeles—Harold Robbins's place at one time, Eva Gabor's at another. He also maintained a twenty-three-acre spread high above Benedict Canyon in Beverly Hills. Its main feature was a cherished tennis court that nestled at the bottom of a hill. Atop a half-mile driveway, which looked like a freeway off-ramp, sat a large, rambling ranch-style house and two smaller ones. One of these smaller houses was actually "annexed" by Kerkorian after he had acquired the original property. This house had been owned by a onetime MGM starlet, Yvette Mimieux, who maintained a friendship with Kerkorian over the course of many years. Indeed, Mimieux, a forceful and intelligent woman of considerable beauty, continued to live in her house after its "annexation." Kerkorian, meanwhile, maintained a separate residence in Bel Air with his wife and children. Kerkorian was ultimately divorced from his second wife, Jean, in 1985—the settlement reportedly totaled $200 million—but maintained a close relationship with his two daughters, Tracy and Linda, who were memorialized in the name of Kerkorian's holding company: Tracinda.

CHAPTER SIX

■

THE SLATE
1983

With the onset of the summer of 1983, Frank Yablans felt a vise tightening around him. He had become irascible with colleagues, testy with friends. Bouts of discomfort stemming from diverticulitis, a long-standing intestinal disorder, grew more frequent.

He understood the source of his malaise. Crucial decisions were at hand—a time of reckoning.

Half a year had gone by since Yablans had become studio chief. The months had been so frenetic, so packed with negotiation and maneuvering, that they had now become a blur. There had been moments of triumph, as with *WarGames;* of disaster, as with *Road Show.* But at no time could Yablans remember sitting down by himself, pencil in hand, and carefully, cautiously listing the films that he would shepherd into production. What had happened instead was that a constellation of projects had taken shape around him—projects to which he now found himself committed, and which, he knew, would determine his destiny.

And it made him acutely uncomfortable. It was as though he had awakened one morning to the realization that his fate was no longer in his own hands, but in the hands of an eclectic band of filmmakers over whom he would essentially have little control.

Frank Rothman and others had tried to reassure him that the fate of his regime would not be irrevocably tied to the performance of the first three or so films, but he knew that was sophistry. He had seen what had happened to Begelman at MGM/UA and to studio chiefs at other companies.

Yablans wished now he'd been less impulsive about his "picks." Perhaps *Road Show* would have been a safer bet than *Red Dawn*. Maybe he should have held off on *Pope of Greenwich Village* until a stronger cast could be assembled—a Pacino or De Niro, for example, instead of Mickey Rourke and Eric Roberts. Yablans knew he had a tendency to be quick-triggered in his judgments. There were so many intangibles that went into the arcane process of "picking pictures" that it defied logic. He remembered David Picker, who had served as studio chief at four companies, reflecting one day that if he'd flipped a coin rather than tried to marshal his arguments rationally, he would probably have come out ahead.

Yablans found himself carping at his staff. "Why isn't anyone bringing me a Stallone picture or a Clint Eastwood picture?" he would bark. "Why am I always being given these arty-farty projects?" But it was all rhetoric: the rhetoric of frustration.

Yablans and I were walking toward the commissary one day when we passed John Foreman, a producer and former MGM executive whose deal Yablans had just terminated. Foreman, who didn't know as yet that he was about to be thrown off the lot, greeted us effusively. Yablans nodded a stiff greeting, then turned to me. "Think of all the John Foremans in this town, all the guys knocking their heads against the wall. And here I am—I can make any picture I want. Anything! I'm the little kid who got lost in the candy store!"

Yablans was not smiling at his metaphor, for it defined his dilemma. The candy store was too vast, the choices too overwhelming. He had done his best to make good decisions, but were they good enough?

It was not only a question of choosing projects; then came the further decisions on script and casting. Every project posed its own universe of complicated options. And none caused him more consternation than *Red Dawn*.

The script, originally entitled *Ten Soldiers*, was a poignant throwback to *Lord of the Flies*. Written in film school by a young Texan, Kevin Reynolds, the story was set in the near-future when a combined force of Russians and Cubans invade the southwestern

United States. Ten high school students manage to escape and take refuge in the hills surrounding their small town.

Initially, the kids derive a perverse enjoyment from their plight. It's a lark, a vacation from school and parental discipline. They learn to live off the land and care for themselves.

Then the story darkens. The youngsters discover that many adults from their town have been imprisoned, others killed. As in *Lord of the Flies*, the tougher, mean-spirited kids now take control, molding the once-benign band into a juvenile guerrilla force. When a tough Russian officer is assigned to find and destroy the ragtag guerrillas, the story becomes a descent into hell—a touching parable about the brutalization of the innocent.

An alert, street-smart writer-producer named Barry Beckerman was among the first to read Reynolds's script. To Beckerman, *Ten Soldiers* had the potential to become a taut, tough "art" picture made on a modest budget that could possibly break out to find a wider audience. He took it to his father, an industry veteran named Sidney Beckerman, who wrote out a check for five thousand dollars to option the script. In signing the deal, Kevin Reynolds timorously explained that he aspired to be a film director, and that he would like to be considered as a candidate to direct *Ten Soldiers*. In making his plea, Reynolds knew his chances were remote; Beckerman heard him out with the distracted, faraway look of someone who is going through the motions.

Indeed, the Beckermans were already showing the project to other directors, with little success. Walter Hill flirted briefly with the script, but decided against it. Other directors found it too downbeat or controversial. Sidney Beckerman also submitted it to his good friend David Begelman, then head of UA, who turned it down. Begelman made it clear he was interested in big, glamorous movie-star vehicles, not grim little parables of the Cold War.

With their option time running out, the Beckermans decided to take another stab at MGM/UA now that Yablans had come to power. To their surprise, the project was instantly accepted. At roughly the same time, Steven Spielberg had decided to take an interest in young Reynolds's career, orchestrating a deal whereby Reynolds would direct a small film entitled *Fandango* at Universal.

Given the fact that both Reynolds and his script were suddenly "hot properties," the Beckermans hoped they could capitalize on his momentum and get a quick start date for *Ten Soldiers*. The studio, however, was having difficulty assessing the project. Everyone agreed as to its potential, but potential for what?

Kevin Reynolds took time off from *Fandango* to make a persuasive case for his original conception, but another notion was already forming in Frank Yablans's mind. *Ten Soldiers* was too good to become another *Lord of the Flies.* Instead, it could become another *First Blood*—another *Rambo.*

MGM/UA desperately needed a hot action movie for the summer of 1984, he argued. *Ten Soldiers* could be that film. And the ideal director would not be Kevin Reynolds, with his "arty" affectations. Rather, it would be John Milius, the swaggering, gun-toting director of *Conan the Barbarian* and *Dillinger.*

The idea sent shock waves down the corridors. A good-natured but off-the-wall character, the forty-year-old Milius was widely known in the industry for his fascination with weaponry and his advocacy of right-wing causes. Milius unabashedly loved war movies. He was the sort of man who could lovingly describe the proficiency of a Gatling gun with the good-natured smile of a man discussing his pet terrier. He knew he was outrageous; he clearly relished that role.

Though most of his colleagues opposed the Milius idea, Frank Yablans was not in the mood for prolonged debate. The studio needed pictures, he insisted. It needed commercial pictures.

"You keep telling me it will become a different movie with Milius directing!" Yablans exploded at a breakfast meeting. "I say, bullshit. The script is there. Milius will shoot the script."

And John Milius himself seemed to support Yablans's theory. "I like the script," he asserted. Then, staring at Yablans, he added, "Besides, I am a feudal person. I see myself as a knight who vows to serve the wishes of his king."

Yablans beamed. "You have come to the right place, squire," Yablans replied.

In an eleventh-hour effort to save Kevin Reynolds's cause, I decided to visit Steven Spielberg, who had "sponsored" Reynolds's picture *Fandango.* Spielberg received me at his specially designed Santa-Fe-modern palazzo at Universal Studios. Cordial and scrupulously tactful, Spielberg said he would gladly show me the as-yet uncompleted *Fandango.* Listening to him discuss the project, however, I could detect he was less than thrilled with it. It wasn't as though he were knocking it—Spielberg would never "knock" a colleague. But reading between the lines of his faint praise, I could surmise that Steven Spielberg was not in a mood to do battle on behalf of young Reynolds.

And without the support of a superstar director like Spielberg, the effort to save Reynolds, or even Reynolds's conception of the film, was futile.

John Milius had won the day. There was widespread disappointment along the studio corridors, but, as Milius yet again reiterated,
he would simply shoot the script. How different could it be?

In signing his deal, Milius supplied an initial clue. The deal
called for payment of $1.25 million for Milius's directing services,
plus an additional request. As in his two previous deals, Milius
would also require the studio to buy him a gun of his choice. An
exotic gun.

With Milius's demands met, the signal was given for all the
studio's support systems to kick into action. The screenplay would
be budgeted. Locations must be found. The roles must be cast.
There was no time to waste if the film was to be ready for release
the following summer.

Now that Milius was able to focus full time on the project, certain
ideas also suggested themselves about the script.

There was, for example, the issue of the invasion itself. Reynolds
had focused his attention on character and nuance, rather than on
Cold War strategy, but Milius prided himself in being something
of a military historian. An elaborate scenario would have to be
developed to explain Russian intervention in the Western
Hemisphere.

Hearing of Milius's concern, Yablans had a brainstorm. General
Alexander Haig, the recently resigned secretary of state, had just
become a member of the MGM/UA board of directors. Surely, the
State Department had developed its own scenarios about possible
Russian incursions, and Alexander Haig might be willing to impart
them.

John Milius was in hog heaven. Not only would he be directing
a movie about the military, but he'd even have his own distinguished military adviser.

Haig himself was more than receptive to the idea. Milius flew to
Washington, where he was received by Haig in the august surroundings of the Hudson Institute, a conservative think tank.
There, in the oak-paneled library, surrounded by maps, charts, and
computer readouts of State Department analyses, Milius and Haig
evolved an elaborate backstory, detailing the dominolike collapse
of Western Europe. The Green party had swept to victory in West
Germany, neutralist regimes had taken control of France and Brit-
ain, NATO was dissolved, etc. A combined Russian-Cuban force,
with the help of the sympathetic Mexican government, invades at
Vera Cruz with the aim of splitting the United States in half. The
invasion strategy, Haig advised, had actually been "stolen" from
Hitler's high command—that was the way they had hoped to in-

vade the United States—but it would serve the Soviet cause just as well.

The Milius-Haig notion was to introduce this backstory as quickly as possible at the beginning of the movie to add poignance to the plight of the young protagonists. It would all be accomplished with deft, economical strokes; the intent was not to politicize the film.

But when Milius briefed Yablans of his sessions with General Haig, Yablans saw no need to downplay the political subtext. "This movie," Yablans enthused, "could be one of the biggest hits in history in the European market. The Europeans always talk about how America has never experienced the nightmare of occupation. Well, now they can line up for the privilege of seeing us suffer."

Prolonged exposure to Haig and Yablans was starting to make even John Milius a bit nervous. Wandering into my office one day, he confided his concern that the studio was maneuvering him into "a flag-waving, jingoistic movie." Both Yablans and Haig, he said, were convinced that the country was moving "to the right," and both felt that a film like this could ride this ideological wave.

Milius saw me grinning. "What the fuck are you smiling about?"

"Come on, Milius, you're a connoisseur of irony," I said. "Here we have the Great Milius, the scourge of Hollywood's professional liberals, complaining about a right-wing conspiracy."

Milius allowed himself a pained smile. "All right, it's funny, I admit it. But it's also a pain in the ass. I want to make a movie about the futility of war. And I have a nervous feeling that Yablans and Haig are jabbering away on their hot line about a different movie."

"You'll be directing it," I said.

"But what happens if they decide to recut it?" Milius shrugged helplessly, then left the office.

With Yablans and Haig offering their continued input, Milius began his script revisions. Emphasis on the political backstory at the start of the film in turn deemphasized the relationships between the kids themselves. Milius had also been urged to add some scenes in which the kids infiltrate back into town and witness the imprisonment and brainwashing of their parents. All this further heightens their sense of rage.

For practical reasons, Milius had decided to make his characters older. In the Reynolds draft, the kids were in their early teens, reinforcing the *Lord of the Flies* motif. Milius wanted them to be seniors in high school. The trouble with casting younger kids, he reasoned, was that there would have to be social workers and tutors on the set. There would also be restrictions governing the length of the workday. Milius had his eye on Patrick Swayze, who was in his early thirties, and Charlie Sheen, who was in his mid-twenties.

Again, Yablans agreed. The presence of older kids, he argued, could permit the introduction of much more violence into the film without bringing down the wrath of the critics.

Apart from worrying about the politics of the film, Milius also had one other grave concern: That was the schedule.

Because of the complexity of the project, he did not see how it was possible to start shooting until the following spring. Yablans was apoplectic. "This is my hit summer picture!" he shouted. "Without this, do you know what I got for next summer? *Bubkes*, that's what I've got!"

Milius patiently led Yablans through the logistics. Construction of the weaponry alone, he pointed out, would take months. Since the action was set in the near-future, the Russians would have exotic new armaments at their disposal, and this meant designing and building new tanks and choppers.

Let them work overtime, Yablans shot back. "We're talking round-the-clock overtime," Milius protested.

Yablans put his arm on Milius's shoulder. "Let me spell it out for you," he said. "I don't give a fuck what it costs. I've got to have *Red Dawn* for summer . . ."

"*Red Dawn?* . . ."

"That's the new name of your film, John," Yablans announced. "It's hot. It's a winner."

Milius tried to assimilate this new information. He could live with the new title for his film, but he wasn't sure he could live with the start date. A summer release meant shooting all winter, in rain and snow, and that, in turn, meant possible production delays. Milius had decided to shoot the film in the mountains of New Mexico, and winters could be harsh in that locale. With all his "macho" mannerisms, Milius was really a "soft" southern California kid who liked the sun and the beach. These new demands filled him with apprehension, both in terms of "creature comforts" and budgetary considerations.

What had started as a "small picture" was suddenly becoming a very expensive and dicey project, Milius realized. He wondered if Frank Yablans, as well, realized that.

While *Red Dawn* was being hastily mobilized for the following summer, progress on other projects was also proceeding apace.

Casting was being completed on *Teachers*, on *Until September*, a love story to shoot in Paris, and on *The Aviator*, a period "survival picture," starring Christopher Reeve, to shoot in Yugoslavia. Mel Gibson was set to star opposite Diane Keaton in a period film tentatively entitled *Mrs. Soffel*. Negotiations were moving forward on the next Bond and *Rocky* sequels. And Peter Hyams was nearing completion of his first draft of *2010*, although that project, per his instructions, remained cloaked in secrecy.

To everyone's amazement and relief, a coherent production schedule was somehow taking shape. On the surface, it appeared to be a rather balanced program at that. There were action films, love stories, period pictures, contemporary dramas.

The two categories not represented were comedies and youth-oriented pictures—paradoxically, the two genres that dominated the production schedules of the other major studios. This omission was disturbing to Frank Yablans, and to marketing executives as well. Audience studies had reinforced the notion that film-going was a youthful habit, not a middle-aged one. And kids loved comedy.

In view of all this, the decision to go with Robert Altman as director of *O.C. & Stiggs* seemed less outrageous than when Freddie Fields had first broached it. In Altman's eyes, the film was not only a "youth comedy," it was the ultimate send-up of "youth comedies."

The curmudgeonly Altman had survived his stormy meeting with Yablans with his morale intact. He understood Yablans wanted him to make a commercial movie—that was to be expected. At the same time, Altman had his own notions about the style and content of *O.C. & Stiggs*, and had no intention of tipping his hand as to what they entailed.

With this in mind, Altman structured the project as a nonunion film that would be made on a convenient arm's-length arrangement with the studio. The ostensible purpose of this was to save money. Altman's fifty-four-day schedule would cost only $6.4 million. But there were fringe benefits: The arrangement would facilitate greater freedom from studio scrutiny.

Based on a picaresque yarn that had originally run in the *National Lampoon*, *O.C. & Stiggs* was a loosely structured, nihilistic, mean-spirited, and occasionally very funny portrait of growing up in the Sunbelt.

The script, written by Tod Carroll and Ted Mann, focused on the misadventures of two nonconformist teenagers in Phoenix, Arizona, who were in a state of unconscious rebellion against the rampant materialism that surrounded them. This materialism was embodied in a family called the Schwabs, headed by a uniquely obnoxious insurance tycoon. O.C. and his friend Stiggs were obsessed with the mission of reducing the Schwabs's sumptuous household to a state of disarray.

In his rewrite, Altman sought to sharpen the film's satiric edge, and also to enhance its visual possibilities. New scenes were added showing the boys frolicking in a surfing machine in the middle of the desert, rafting down to Mexico, etc. In shaping his characters, Altman sought to depict a certain self-awareness in his two lead characters. The protagonists in his youth comedy acted the way they did in partial reaction to the fact that they themselves had seen too many youth comedies. This was Altman's complex aim, at least.

Upon reading his rewrite, several members of the production staff expressed their concern that Altman had sacrificed the likability of his principal characters. The debates among the production executives were spirited:

"The characters have lost their empathy."

"Did you ever read *The Graduate?* You could have said the same about that."

"The structure's a mess. Where's the character arc?"

"This is a picaresque story, and you're trying to conventionalize it."

"Conventional movies make money."

The debates raged on. And meanwhile, Altman kept reshaping the film in accordance with his own vision.

Having cast two newcomers, Dan Jenkins and Neil Barry, as his leads, Altman assured the studio, "The characters will be downright lovable. I guarantee it."

"Bob Altman smells a hit," Freddie Fields added reassuringly. "This picture will mark his comeback. Wait and see."

Even as Robert Altman was reinventing *O.C. & Stiggs*, another important film on MGM's agenda, *The Pope of Greenwich Village*, was running aground. The studio's original plan was to start shooting *Pope* in early summer to have it ready for Christmas release. But now, with the film in preproduction, the viability of the entire project was threatened.

Though *Pope* was modest in scope—its projected cost was under $9 million—the project ranked high on the studio's priority list. When he first read the screenplay, Frank Yablans had declared that "*Pope* is the best-written script of its kind I've ever read." Though Yablans was clearly indulging in hyperbole, *Pope* had acquired a "cult" status in the three years since it was first written. Al Pacino and Robert De Niro at one time had expressed an interest in the leads, but scheduling problems had prevented this from happening. A few public "readings" of the script had been staged in New York by prominent actors—an honor rarely accorded a movie script. Many felt that Vincent Patrick, the writer, had uniquely captured the flavor of New York's Little Italy. *The Pope of Greenwich Village* seemed both vivid and real.

Even MGM's notoriously skeptical story department seemed impressed by Patrick's revised draft. "This is a streamlined action comedy," the story editor commented at the conclusion to the synopsis.

What could go wrong with a relatively inexpensive "streamlined action comedy" set in Little Italy? At MGM, a great deal.

To begin with, the studio was suffering a loss of confidence in Ron Maxwell, the young director who was scheduled to direct *Pope*. The thirty-six-year-old Maxwell had directed *Little Darlings* at Paramount and *Kidco*, which Frank Yablans produced at Fox, and Yablans felt he had a good grasp of the project. Despite this, Maxwell was exhibiting a talent for creating problems for himself.

Having chosen actress Ann Reinking to play the lead female role of Diane, Maxwell then abruptly decided she was wrong for the part, thus bringing down a hail of criticism from her powerful agent, ICM's Sam Cohn, and her then-companion, investment banker Herbert Allen, Jr., both of them king-makers in the entertainment industry.

Nor was he faring better with his co-stars. Eric Roberts, who played Paulie, was "not cutting it," Maxwell confided after the first two days of rehearsals. Mickey Rourke, who was cast as Charlie, on the other hand, was convinced that Ron Maxwell wasn't cutting it, either. "He's got no class," Rourke remonstrated in his characteristic semiwhisper.

Frank Yablans, who'd first advocated Maxwell on the strength of his solid work on *Kidco*, now, too, had second thoughts. He'd heard that Fox hated *Kidco* and might not even accord it a theatrical release.

By the end of August, two weeks before the scheduled start of production, a decision was reached at the studio to replace Maxwell with another director. There was divided opinion about his possible replacement, however. As the designated "project supervisor" on *Pope*, I advocated that Stuart Rosenberg be brought in as the new director. Rosenberg, whose best-known film was *Cool Hand Luke*, had stepped in for Bob Rafelson on *Brubaker*, the Robert

Redford film, and had done an excellent job. Besides, Rosenberg had an outstanding commitment of $750,000 at MGM because of the last-minute cancellation of his projected Mel Gibson film—a commitment that seemed headed for litigation.

Freddie Fields had a more daring idea—Michael Cimino. "We know in advance what kind of movie we'll get from Rosenberg," Fields argued. "Cimino will give us a surprise." The question, of course, was whether it would be a good surprise or a bad surprise.

Fields only recently had been shot down when he'd suggested that Cimino take over *Road Show*, but that did not discourage him from giving it another try. *Road Show*, after all, had conjured up the nightmare of *Heaven's Gate*. *Pope*, on the other hand, was a more confined picture—the sort even Cimino could bring in at a price. But could he?

Freddie Fields was persuaded that Cimino had undergone a total personality change in the four years since *Heaven's Gate*. He had given Cimino the script. Cimino had liked it, and was prepared to fly to New York, examine the budget and the locations, and then give his final answer.

"How about Joann Carelli?" I asked. "Is she coming to New York, too?" Carelli, the abrasive, tough-talking producer of *Heaven's Gate*, had been Cimino's "protector" on that film, effectively sealing him off from studio executives who tried to bring the film under control. The sheer mention of her name still produced tremors among surviving UA personnel.

"I told Carelli, 'You have been the most destructive force in Michael Cimino's career,'" Fields replied. "That's what I told her."

"Then she's not coming? . . ."

"It hasn't been worked out yet, kiddo."

The following day, Fields arrived in New York with Cimino, but not with Carelli, and Cimino immediately began his rounds, meeting with cast and crew. Wherever he went, the forty-year-old director was meticulously polite, even deferential. He was clearly determined to refute his reputation as a swaggering autocrat.

Freddie Fields beamed as he watched Cimino at work. "Michael has come of age," he kept repeating. Indeed, Cimino's every action seemed studied and wary. Despite the warm, dank weather in Manhattan, Cimino always looked as though his clothes had been newly pressed, his hair newly coiffed, his face newly shaved, his nails newly manicured. He was the Italian Prince, mixing smoothly, easily, among the great unwashed.

Cimino's agent, Sue Mengers, watched the situation with open skepticism. "Freddie's acting as though Michael were his client, rather than his director," Mengers warned. "He's taking him to dinner, wining and dining him. He's doing it all wrong."

Cimino himself seemed to relish the hospitality. He was staying with Fields at his penthouse apartment on West 57th Street. The only thing that seemed to disturb his equanimity was the constant questioning from the media. "The press is always gunning for me," he complained, eyes darting nervously, his hand running through his large swath of black hair. "I'm like Target Number One."

Fields tried to ease his fears, but the pressure was unrelenting. Was Michael Cimino really taking over as director of *Pope?* Was everything forgiven on *Heaven's Gate?*

Even as Michael Cimino was completing his spadework in New York, Stuart Rosenberg was simmering with anger in Beverly Hills. A thoughtful, professorial man who held a Ph.D. in Celtic Litera-ture, Rosenberg had been preparing a thriller called *Running Man* at the studio, and had elicited a commitment from Mel Gibson to star in the film. Before he could implement these plans, however, he was dealt two lethal blows. First, the studio informed him that it had chosen not to make *Running Man*, despite the fact that Rosenberg had a $750,000 pay-or-play commitment. As for Gibson, he would instead do another studio film, *Mrs. Soffel*, opposite Diane Keaton.

Further, the studio announced that it would not honor Rosen-berg's pay-or-play commitment, since he could not physically di-rect the film by reason of bad health. As evidence, the studio noted that Rosenberg had had triple-bypass surgery in 1981.

Rosenberg insisted this was nonsense, that he was indeed in excellent health now, but MGM had dispatched a doctor to examine him in the presence of Rosenberg's personal physician. Rosenberg could tell the examination was not going well when the MGM doctor probed his ear and exclaimed, "Oh my God . . ."

"What's wrong?" Rosenberg asked.

"Wax. Lots of it," said the studio doctor.

It was not a surprise to Rosenberg, therefore, when the studio informed him that he had failed the examination. Rosenberg im-mediately paid a visit to Bert Fields, a veteran Hollywood litigator whose reputation rested on the sheer ferocity of his onslaughts against offending studios.

Even as he was mobilizing his lawsuit, Stuart Rosenberg now received a phone call from New York. It was Freddie Fields on the line, and his message was straightforward. The studio was sending him a script called *The Pope of Greenwich Village*, Fields said coolly. If he liked it, then he should promptly get on a plane for New York to start preproduction. The picture would start shooting in a week.

Rosenberg couldn't believe his ears. "I have two problems with what you're telling me," he replied. "First, according to your studio, I am not in good health, not insurable, all that sort of stuff."

"Read the script," said Fields, dodging the issue.

"I'd heard Michael Cimino was going to do the picture," Rosenberg persisted.

Fields responded with a laugh Rosenberg thought was somewhat forced. "Michael came to New York as an adviser, that's all," Fields said. "He's Italian, you know. Knows Little Italy."

"I realize that," Rosenberg said.

"He did it as a personal favor. An adviser."

"I see."

The next night, Stuart Rosenberg was on a plane to New York. He arrived in the middle of a furious rainstorm, which caused the diversion of his plane from Kennedy to Newark. Rosenberg hefted his several bags (he had packed for the duration of the picture) into a cab, and an hour later, arrived at Freddie Fields's apartment house, per Fields's instructions. It was after midnight and still pouring, and no doorman was on duty. Rosenberg was soaking wet with rain and perspiration after toting his luggage onto the automatic elevator and then up to Fields's penthouse.

Even as he rang the doorbell, dripping wet, Rosenberg pondered the irony of the situation. Here was the studio that had declared him physically unfit now putting him through this stress test! And he would have but one week to prepare a complex movie! What could these people be thinking? Rosenberg wondered.

The door to Fields's penthouse opened. Standing there, smiling warmly, was none other than Michael Cimino. As Fields poured drinks, Cimino helped Rosenberg with his bags and offered him a towel to dry off. Then the three men sat down to begin what would be an all-night meeting.

Cimino explained candidly that he had decided not to accept the studio's offer to direct *Pope* because he couldn't contend with the eight-week shooting schedule and the restrictive budget. He'd only directed two films before *Heaven's Gate*, he said, and didn't feel he had the experience to shoot a big-city movie under such rigorous conditions. Having thoroughly scrutinized the project, however, he would be happy to turn over his notes to Rosenberg.

"Michael's work has been invaluable," Fields chimed in. "He's been a terrific consultant."

During the course of the next six hours, Cimino went through his extraordinarily copious notes, which he had inscribed in miniscule handwriting on every page of the script. Even as he talked, Rosenberg clearly comprehended Cimino's dilemma. Cimino was the ultimate perfectionist! There was not a single detail of the production that he hadn't worried to death.

One key scene, for example, was scheduled to be shot under an elevated train in the Bronx, with trains rolling by every three minutes. "I can't shoot with trains banging along on top of me," Cimino complained. "I'd have to loop the whole scene." Rosenberg, by contrast, liked this sort of location, because it created a heightened sense of reality.

When the meeting finally ended, an exhausted Rosenberg thanked Cimino for his input and, at first light, trudged toward his hotel. It had stopped raining. The dawn air smelled fresh and clean. He took a deep breath and realized he was glad to be in New York again, shooting a movie.

As Rosenberg launched into his tight preproduction agenda, he found that his initial analysis of Cimino had been correct. To Cimino, any situation he couldn't totally control was not acceptable. Rosenberg, by contrast, though twenty years older, had a much more flexible philosophy about the details of filmmaking.

Cimino, for example, had been affronted that Mickey Rourke had been allowed to buy his own wardrobe for the picture—flashy Little Italy–type clothes that Cimino found unacceptable. Rosenberg, by contrast, felt that the actor had made shrewd choices. Cimino had warned Rosenberg that the sound crew was suspect. Upon investigation, however, Rosenberg had learned that they had done two Woody Allen pictures and had solid credentials.

Of greater concern to Rosenberg, however, was the condition of the screenplay. Despite all the praise that had been heaped on it for its witty writing and shrewdly drawn characters, Rosenberg felt the story lacked an effective resolution.

At the studio, Rosenberg's critique was respectfully considered. It was true, the production staff agreed, that no one had ever figured out a satisfactory ending for *Pope*. On the other hand, with the film starting in less than a week, it seemed late in the game to try to find one.

Indeed, in the sea of memoranda that had flowed from one desk to another on *Pope*, not one executive had ever brought up the matter of the ending before this. One memo proposed more scenes be devised outside of Little Italy to broaden the appeal of the movie. Another said the script "felt dated" and needed to be hipper. Still another proposed building up the character of Diane (ultimately played by Daryl Hannah). One memo criticized the two protagonists for using the word "nigger"—only heavies should use this expression.

To Stuart Rosenberg, however, Vincent Patrick had written a novelistic script that movie audiences might find ultimately unsatisfying. And while he didn't himself have the luxury of time to suggest a possible rewrite, he would nonetheless meet with Patrick to exchange ideas.

In the script, Paulie and Charlie are two small-time losers who, with the help of a professional safecracker, pull a heist that they believe will be foolproof. When they break into the safe, hoping to find $50,000, they inadvertently come upon $150,000, which the local mafioso had stashed away for police-payoff money. Having thus stumbled into a hornet's nest, the safecracker is killed, and Charlie and Paulie are pressured to turn against each other. In the end, Paulie poisons the local Mafia boss, the boys are reunited, and they flee town after making a winning bet at the racetrack.

In Rosenberg's view, the ending was unsatisfying because the boys had not changed in any way. The suggestion was that Charlie and Paulie had luckily survived their ordeal, but would surely get themselves into another impossible mess in the future.

The response to Rosenberg's criticisms was unencouraging. Vincent Patrick advised that he did not have any fresh ideas for a new ending—indeed, he rather liked it the way it was. The introduction of a new writer, Eric Roth, was proposed by Rosenberg, but Freddie Fields felt Roth was wrong for the job. Instead, why not hire Michael Cimino to do a rewrite? He was available for only $150,000! Rosenberg thanked Fields for his suggestion, but said discreetly that Cimino had already made his contribution to the project.

At summer's end, Stuart Rosenberg started principal photography on *The Pope of Greenwich Village* with the initial ending intact. Given the pressures of mounting the picture, concerns about the story were quickly forgotten.

CHAPTER SEVEN

■

MARKING TIME
1973

THE resignation of Jim Aubrey in 1973 left Dan Melnick in both the best of times and the worst of times. He was now rid of the man who had become a lightning rod for filmmaker disaffection. Hopefully, it would now be possible to redefine the studio as a support mechanism for the filmmaker, not as an enemy.

In his brief tenure at MGM, Melnick had already observed several hits slip from the studio's grasp, in part because of the hostile atmosphere. After losing *Jaws*, Melnick had ardently pursued *The Sting*, a script by a young writer named David Ward, brought to him by the husband-and-wife producing team of Julia and Michael Phillips and their partner, actor Tony Bill. As an inducement to close the deal quickly, Melnick had offered the producers a fifty-thousand-dollar bonus if they and their attorneys would work through the night with MGM to hammer out details of the deal. Despite this bold tactic, the project quickly became embroiled in an intense flurry of offers and counteroffers. By week's end, *The Sting* belonged to Universal Pictures, with Robert Redford and Paul Newman committed to the starring roles. In Melnick's mind, if he'd had a full-fledged studio behind him—a studio with a commitment to an ongoing program of films—he might have buttoned up the deal.

In trying to create a more positive atmosphere at MGM, Melnick was also keenly aware of his vulnerability. He was, after all, a "lame duck" studio chief. Aubrey had appointed him, not Kerkorian. Melnick had no notion of Kerkorian's opinion of him, if any, nor could he figure out where he stood with Frank Rosenfelt, the new president of MGM. Would this nondescript attorney want his own input on production? Would he suddenly turn up with his own "wish list" of filmmakers and stars?

There was another problem, as well: how to deal with the dizzying array of product Aubrey had left in his wake. The ever-troubled *Pat Garrett and Billy the Kid* was still in its final throes of postproduction. Yet another sequel to *Shaft*, this one called *Shaft in Africa*, was winding up. So was a curious sci-fi thriller called *Soylent Green*, starring Edward G. Robinson, who died during post-production. In this grisly film, the New York of the future was depicted as a polluted, overpopulated place in which the hero (Charlton Heston) discovers that the staple food for the masses is made from human corpses.

Also in the works was another offbeat western with the unlikely title *The Man Who Loved Cat Dancing*, which starred Burt Reynolds and Sarah Miles. The project was distinguished mainly by the lurid publicity stemming from the unexplained death on location of Sarah Miles's male secretary.

A sudden and unexpected telephone call eradicated these worries, however. Alan Hirschfield, the chairman of Columbia Pictures, wanted Melnick to move over to Columbia as the head of production under David Begelman. An ambitious program was under way to revive the fortunes of that ailing company, and refinance its $220 million debt. It would be a great opportunity. Melnick had known both Hirschfield and Begelman for many years, and knew he could work well with them. They, like Melnick, were "New York" people, who understood each other's taste and sense of humor.

Melnick said a quick yes. The problems of MGM would be behind him. The next day, he told his decision to Frank Rosenfelt, who accepted it with equanimity. Rosenfelt would be free to pick his own production chief, rather than inheriting Aubrey's. Melnick felt a keen sense of relief.

It was cut short, however, by a visit from Rosenfelt the following morning. "We have a little problem," the diminutive lawyer informed him. "Kirk is very upset. So upset, in fact, that he's flying back from the Mediterranean to talk you out of leaving."

"But I already accepted the Columbia job," Melnick protested.

"Kirk wants to see you," Rosenfelt repeated portentously.

A tanned but tense-looking Kerkorian pulled up at the Thalberg Building the following day, and Melnick was summoned to his office.

His message was terse, as usual. "Solow wasn't right for the job," Kerkorian said. "Aubrey wasn't right for the job. You are right for the job. If you don't stay on, I'm going to shut this place down. It's as simple as that. Think it over."

For the next twenty-four hours, Melnick, his mind reeling, pondered his decision. He paced the lot, from one end to the other. The size had been drastically reduced, the work force cut back, but it was still MGM, and it was still humming with activity. If he took the Columbia job, and if Kerkorian followed through on his threat, what would happen to this place and to these people? It was as though Melnick himself were pulling the plug. That is, unless Kerkorian had been bluffing.

The following day, Melnick made his phone call to Hirschfield, declining the Columbia job. He would make his stand at MGM.

It had been Jim Aubrey's prediction that once MGM had sold its distribution company, the studio would simply be "marking time," and his prediction turned out to be largely correct. Between 1973 and 1980, the studio operated like a small, undercapitalized independent-production company, turning out between four and seven films a year, and keeping budgets in the $3 million to $5 million category.

While declining to sell the studio, despite an occasional offer, Kirk Kerkorian made it abundantly clear that he still looked upon the movie business as an unwanted stepchild. By mid-1974, the MGM Grand was boasting that it had become "the most profitable hotel in the world," but these profits were quickly channeled to Reno, where yet another MGM Grand would be constructed. The money would not go back to the studio after which the hotel had been named.

In 1974, on the occasion of MGM's fiftieth anniversary, Frank Rosenfelt remarked, "Contrary to recent public speculation, the roar of Leo the Lion will not be reduced to a weak meow." In point of fact, the "meow" had not only become weak, it was almost extinct. An anonymous sort of man by nature, Rosenfelt felt impelled to make his studio anonymous, as well. His main interest was in cutting costs; his main pleasure, studio officials observed, seemed to come from sifting through expense accounts and returning them with excisions.

One friend of the forty-three-year-old Melnick recalls running into him at a restaurant in a state of utter exasperation. "Do you know a doctor who could tell me how to fake a nervous breakdown?" Melnick asked him. Thinking it was a joke, the friend laughed, only to see Melnick staring at him with great seriousness. "If I could fake a nervous breakdown, maybe that would be a graceful way of easing out," Melnick muttered.

"The only way Melnick could get anywhere with Rosenfelt was by giving him an ultimatum," one colleague at the time observed. "He would say, 'If I can't make this, I'm leaving,' and then he had a fighting chance."

These tactics helped Melnick pull off some modest successes, including *Hearts of the West* starring Jeff Bridges, and *The Sunshine Boys* starring Walter Matthau and George Burns.

Paradoxically, his two most successful films were released after his resignation in 1977. They were *Network*, Paddy Chayefsky's stinging satire of television, and *The Goodbye Girl*, a touching comedy-romance that Neil Simon had written as a vehicle for his new wife, Marsha Mason.

Melnick had figured that the respectable reception accorded these films, combined with the surprise success of *That's Entertainment*, would prompt Kerkorian to step up his support for the studio. Indeed, Kerkorian himself seemed briefly caught up in the festivities surrounding the opening of *That's Entertainment*. The studio flew a contingent of its stars from yesteryear first to the opening in New York, then on to Cannes, where the film opened the festival. At Cannes, the studio threw an enormous "American dinner party" featuring New York steak, baked potato, corn on the cob, and apple pie, as the likes of Astaire, Kelly, Grant, and Weismuller stood at the ready for picture-taking and interviews.

Kerkorian delighted in the occasion. He even donated his yacht for some of the festivities. But he wouldn't change his mind about the studio.

"Kirk connects on an emotional level to Vegas," Melnick told a friend at the time. "He simply cannot make that connection to Hollywood."

Given the limited resources at his disposal, Melnick found the frustrations of his job mounting. Not only did Rosenfelt represent an inhibiting obstacle, but now Kerkorian's friend Greg Bautzer had started pressuring him about projects. He'd call from the south of France and report that he and Kerkorian had just had a meeting with a producer. "Kirk and I want you to button up the deal," he'd state.

There were other frustrations, as well.

Projects that interested Melnick, like *The Deep* and *Close Encounters of the Third Kind* escaped his grasp, ending up at the more aggressive Columbia Pictures. More and more, he had come to regret his own decision to reject Alan Hirschfield's invitation to join that company.

At the end of 1977, Hirschfield repeated the offer. This time, Melnick did not wait around for another Kerkorian pep talk. He packed his briefcase and was gone from Culver City in record time.

Now, Frank Rosenfelt finally had his long-awaited chance to pick his own man—hopefully, someone who understood his style better than the volatile Melnick.

His choice was Richard Shepherd, a low-key, even-tempered man who, for the last three years, had been a senior production executive at Warner Bros. Shepherd had recently been passed over for the top spot at Warner, and thus had let it be known he was open to offers.

In style and bearing, Shepherd seemed more the sort one would encounter at an exclusive men's club rather than at a Hollywood studio. He had the tweedy good looks of a corporate attorney, and conducted his affairs with a measured civility.

Hence, while other studio executives would schedule "pitches" at ten-minute intervals, hustling their visitors in and out, Shepherd's schedule would accommodate leisurely, hourlong sessions. A loquacious man himself, Shepherd would occasionally embark on an intricate anecdote that might require fifteen or twenty minutes to unfold; his visitors might fidget, but Shepherd would not take notice. A good meeting should entail good conversation, he felt. It was all part of the camaraderie of the business.

Shepherd, too, had the advantage of linking up to the MGM past. His wife, Judy, was a granddaughter of the fabled Louis B. Mayer. Judy's father, William Goetz, had married Mayer's daughter, Edith, and had gone on to become a powerful producer in his own right during Hollywood's golden era.

As a young man, Shepherd, too, seemed destined for a brilliant producing career, having co-produced the estimable *Breakfast at Tiffany's*, but veered off into the agency business, becoming a partner at powerful Creative Management Associates. At CMA, his calm, judicious manner helped smooth over the controversies generated by his volatile colleagues Freddie Fields and David Begelman. It was always Shepherd saying, "David, you can't do that," or "Freddie, we can't get away with that," recalls one colleague. While Fields and Begelman "signed" the clients and romanced the "buyers," Shepherd sculpted the deals and helped steer the business affairs of the company.

Now, at MGM, Shepherd saw a similar need for restraint. Without the ability to market and distribute its own pictures, MGM was in a tenuous position. Though Rosenfelt, the good company man, defended the UA deal that Kerkorian had negotiated, it was nonetheless apparent to him that the films UA had financed were receiving preferential treatment over those from MGM.

The UA executives, after all, had a powerful emotional stake in the success of their films, and hence would assign the prime release dates and the bountiful advertising budgets accordingly. If MGM was not happy with an ad budget, its executives would have to go "hat in hand" to UA to beg for more.

It was, by definition, a discomfiting situation. But since Kerkorian had designed the deal, Rosenfelt was not of a mind to revive the issue with "the boss."

Indeed, word had gone out that Kerkorian was not interested in discussing any MGM business any longer, other than having Rosenfelt run down the "bottom line" numbers with him. His appearances on the lot were becoming rarer, as well.

Shepherd was surprised one day to get a call from Kerkorian about a film shooting on the lot called *Coma*, a medical thriller that starred Michael Douglas and Genevieve Bujold. "A friend told me about that movie," Kerkorian said. "Sounds interesting."

"I think it's very promising," said a perplexed Shepherd. "It just started shooting last week."

"Well, I wonder if it would be all right to visit the set," Kerkorian said.

Shepherd almost dropped the phone. Here was the man who owned the studio asking permission, as though he were a tourist from the Midwest. But why *Coma?* So far as he knew, Kerkorian had never before visited any MGM film set; why would he choose this set, with corpses dangling from the ceiling?

"It's your shop," Shepherd offered finally. "You are welcome to visit any place you want."

"Then I should just walk by the stage . . . ?"

"I'd be glad to arrange to have someone meet you. . . ."

"No...no," Kerkorian replied quickly. "I wouldn't want to cause a fuss...."

Shepherd had a sudden flash. "Are you planning to take anyone with you? Any children, for example?"

"No," Kerkorian said. "Would that require special permission?"

"It's just that the set—well, I assume you know that this particular set is full of corpses and other medical specimens. It's downright grisly, is what it is."

"Oh," Kerkorian said. There was a moment's pause. And that was the last Shepherd ever heard about it.

Despite the fact that he was lodged in this never-never land, Shepherd nonetheless managed to bring together a modest agenda of low- and medium-budget films. In 1978, the year the MGM Grand opened in Reno, the year *Annie Hall* and *Saturday Night Fever* and *Close Encounters of the Third Kind* brought lines to the theaters, MGM released but four films. They were *International Velvet*, a lame sequel to the old Elizabeth Taylor film; *The Champ*, a remake, starring Jon Voight and Ricky Schroder, of the old Oscar-winning Wallace Beery film; *Brass Target*, a low-budget war thriller that misfired; and *Voices*, a love story shot in New Jersey, starring Amy Irving and Michael Ontkean. *Coma*, released the year earlier, was a modest success, but the company's effort to step up to a bigger film in *The Formula*, starring George C. Scott and Marlon Brando, produced disappointing results.

By 1979, the only films emanating from the studio were *Hero at Large*, starring John Ritter, *Why Would I Lie?*, with Treat Williams, and *Sunday Lovers*, a French pickup. MGM was slowly, but inevitably, grinding to a halt.

What Dick Shepherd could not know was that even as he was struggling to cope with the modest funds available to him, Kerkorian, in his usual secretive way, was putting together a more grandiose agenda—one that would sweep Shepherd from office.

While MGM was drifting aimlessly through the 1970's, Kerkorian's Las Vegas activities were once again setting the stage for another face-off with the federal regulatory agencies. The opening of the MGM Grand in Las Vegas, at the end of 1973, had been followed two years later by the acquisition of the Cal-Neva Lodge at Lake Tahoe, which in turn was followed in two years by completion of the MGM Grand in Reno.

As was his custom, Kerkorian had started construction before completing his financing package—a practice that might prove unnerving to many hotelmen but seemed oddly stimulating to Kerkorian.

To help finance these ventures, Kerkorian had engineered huge dividend payouts from MGM in 1973 and 1975—the first dividends in four years from the wobbly film company. Kerkorian himself had netted $11.1 million from these special dividends, which had helped him meet the payments on his bank loans.

Kerkorian's allies pointed out that he took only $50,000 in annual salary from MGM as a "consultant," and very little in executive perks. He even paid a self-imposed nightly rate when he stayed at the MGM New York or London apartments.

The SEC nonetheless cried "foul," contending that Kerkorian was effectively operating MGM as though it were a privately held company, even though 49.9 percent of the stock was owned by stockholders. In its complaint, the SEC pointed out that Kerkorian should have made full disclosure to directors and stockholders as to the status of his bank indebtedness.

The Wall Street Journal, in reporting the incident, cited the conclusion of a federal investigator, who had probed Kerkorian's operations. The investigator said that while he'd found Kerkorian to be extremely shrewd, "I wouldn't want to put *my* money with him. He looks out for Kirk. I don't think his sense of public responsibility is what it might be."

In 1976, Kerkorian put his latest cash crunch behind him by selling his stake in Western Airlines for $30 million. Since both of the MGM Grands were profitable, plans were now moving ahead to build a casino in Atlantic City.

The Atlantic City casino, like those in Las Vegas and Reno, would confound Kerkorian's critics, his aides promised. The Las Vegas hotel was built at the wrong time, critics said, but it prospered. The Reno hotel was too big for the town—but it, too, prospered, to a smaller degree.

And the Atlantic City hotel and casino would be bigger still, but would be nearly two miles away from the Boardwalk, where the competitors had staked out their turf. It will change the face of the town, Kerkorian promised.

Instead, this was one Kerkorian scheme that would never get off the drawing boards.

CHAPTER EIGHT

■

WAR
1983

A stern, owlish man, always impeccably clad in his uniform of blue serge, black glasses teetering at the end of his nose, Lindsley Parsons, Jr., could easily pass for a high school principal, or perhaps a small-town minister. But Parsons, like his father before him, and like his son, Lindsley III, pursued a more rarefied profession. Parsons was one of an elite circle of executives charged with the responsibility of supervising the physical production of movies turned out by the major Hollywood studios. His mandate at MGM/UA was to see to it that its films were delivered on budget and on schedule.

It was a hazardous calling. His office in the Thalberg Building crackled with the unglamorous, nose-grinding, moment-by-moment tensions of moviemaking. While the "artistes" in neighboring offices were holding their lofty discussions about the intangibles of story structure, Parsons's world was rooted in reality. An assistant director had been fired after an argument with his producer. The permit to shoot at a key location had been suddenly canceled. A director had taken a week to shoot a scene scheduled for a morning.

Each film, Parsons knew, posed its own mine field of potential traps and traumas, and even a veteran production man like himself occasionally could be caught by surprise. Parsons's predecessor, George Justin, had been a case in point. Justin's career dated back to *On the Waterfront*, the great Marlon Brando film on which Justin served as production manager in 1954. At MGM/UA, one of the films Justin was supervising was a dreary sci-fi epic entitled *Ice Pirates*. After the books had been closed on the project in 1983, a grim discovery was made: One million dollars more had been spent on the film than was in the budget, and no one could account for the money.

Frank Rothman, the former litigator who now served as the studio's chief executive officer, leaped into the fray. He would make *Ice Pirates* an example of the studio's militant cost-consciousness. In an atmosphere resembling a criminal investigation, Rothman summoned witness after witness to his office to testify about the malfeasance.

The results of his inquisition were anticlimactic. No money had been stolen, no conspiracy unearthed. An elderly production manager, it turned out, had carelessly stashed handfuls of invoices in his desk drawer and forgotten about them—bills totaling $1 million, which were later paid. And none of the accountants or estimators, with all their high-powered computers, had discovered the discrepancies until the picture was audited.

George Justin, as the studio's production overseer, took the blame, and was summarily dismissed. With major new productions gearing up, the time had come to install a tough new production man, Rothman declared. And that man was Lin Parsons.

Lin Parsons had been there before. He'd first served in that job back in 1964 when MGM was still turning out its grandiose *Doctor Zhivago*-like epics. After a couple of years toiling on Jim Aubrey's squalid slate of films, Parsons, in 1974, had moved on to the more bountiful pastures of Paramount. In the late summer of 1983, however, Yablans and Rothman convinced Parsons, now fifty-two, that the studio had once again committed itself to pictures of size and substance. The company, he was told, had formulated a new policy: No budget overages would be countenanced, no surprises tolerated.

Lin Parsons was by no means intimidated by this mandate. He emphatically endorsed the notion that filmmakers, once they have signed a budget, should be held accountable to it. What concerned him, however, was the fact that each of the major films the studio was now putting into production seemed to be a potential tinder box. And Frank Rothman clearly did not have the sophistication to realize that. *Red Dawn* was being rushed before the cameras without proper "prep time" in order to meet its release date. *Mrs. Soffel,* a period piece to be shot in snow, was being directed by a young Australian, Gillian Armstrong, who'd had no previous experience in making projects of this size and complexity. And, finally, *2010* embodied the type of film that seasoned production men most dread—large-scale special-effects films. Its director, Peter Hyams, was the sort of headstrong filmmaker who had to do everything his own way.

The other pictures on the studio's schedule were relatively straightforward projects that were in the hands of old pros like Stuart Rosenberg, Arthur Hiller, and Robert Altman. Those would not be headaches. But Parsons wondered if Rothman, or even Yablans, for that matter, had any idea of the risks they faced on those "big ones." If they were so intent on running a tight ship, why start with three projects that were fraught with danger?

It was mystifying. Mystifying, but also challenging.

The atmosphere surrounding a motion-picture undergoes a remarkable transformation with the approach of principal photography. In the initial stages, when key crew members are assembled and overall plans formulated, a production office exudes a sense of camaraderie. Old friends and colleagues, who've worked together in years past, reconvene once again to exchange war stories. There is an excitement about the task ahead.

As the start date approaches, the mood stiffens. Suddenly, there are deadlines to be met, budgets to be conformed to. And there is also turf to be protected, as each key department strives to protect its own precious fiefdom.

In the waning days of October 1983, the production offices of *Red Dawn* resembled the war zone depicted in the screenplay. It seemed as though everything that could go wrong with a picture was now going wrong.

Despite John Milius's felicitous dialogues with General Alexander Haig, the Department of Defense was now adamantly refusing to extend any cooperation whatsoever to the production. They wouldn't even allow some jets to do an innocent "flyby." Having read the script, the Pentagon brass insisted that a Russian-Cuban infiltration such as that concocted by Milius and Al Haig could never possibly take place. Since the story suggested a weakness in the American military establishment, the Pentagon's posture would be one of total noncooperation.

While General Haig was shocked, Milius was undaunted by this rejection. If the Pentagon didn't want to lend its equipment, then he'd just have to be a little more creative and build his own.

The price tag on that creativity, however, was now soaring with each passing week. Milius wanted to create state-of-the-art Russian tanks, for example, that would bristle with exotic and menacing weaponry as they pursued the youthful guerrilla band into the mountains. The "tanks" were actually aged personnel carriers that had been drastically altered. Because of all the structural changes, such as artificial turrets, the vehicles tended to tip forward during test runs, as well as overheat and spew oil. When the subcontractors were accused of delivering faulty goods, they pointed out that the vehicles had been sitting in surplus yards since World War II, and inevitably would be subject to mechanical failures.

The futuristic Russian choppers Milius had conjured up were just as chancy. When FAA inspectors took a look at them, they decided to permit their use only on the proviso that they not fly over people—a limitation that created grave logistical problems.

With each revision of the script, meanwhile, Milius's requirements grew more abstruse. The cost of ammunition alone was running $200,000 over budget because of the addition of new battle scenes. There were three separate scenes in which the Russian invaders lined up local citizens to be shot. Long columns of Americans were also to be killed in the final scene of the film. None of these scenes, of course, had appeared in the original Reynolds script.

With the film still in preproduction and its budget steadily expanding, Parsons and his associates dutifully broke the bad news to management: What had once been conceived of as an $11 million project would now cost well over $15 million. And given Milius's appetite for battle scenes, combined with the possibility of bad weather, there was reason to project that the budget could soar even higher.

Not all of the increase could be put at Milius's feet, Parsons stressed. In the rush to start the picture, all sorts of costs were escalating. Location expenses were $700,000 over budget, for example, because of exorbitant rentals. Inevitably, the sites had been selected at the last minute, when there was no time for negotiation. Contractors were working around the clock to meet their deadlines, which necessitated enormous overtime pay.

Parsons expected that all this information would be assimilated by Yablans and Rothman in a calm, collected manner, and that appropriate cutbacks would be ordered. It was not too late, for example, to instruct Milius to lower the body count and reduce the scope of combat scenes.

What Parsons encountered instead was modified hysteria. "I don't understand this. . . . I just don't understand this!" Frank Rothman screamed in rage. His customary lawyerlike pallor turned to bright crimson.

"You people have lost control of this picture," Yablans fumed to his production staff, black eyes burrowing into Lin Parsons. "This whole fucking mess is unacceptable."

Parsons and his aides led Rothman and Yablans through each item of the budget, patiently explaining the cause of each overage. Expert witnesses were brought in to fill out the picture. Elliot Schick, the veteran production manager, explained that he had been hired on *Red Dawn* only eleven weeks prior to the scheduled start of shooting; *Tora! Tora! Tora!*, another war picture requiring exotic hardware, had hired its production manager a full year ahead of shooting.

All this detail was clearly starting to bore Frank Rothman. In the end, what really bothered him was one grim reality: that with the film costing in excess of $15 million, he would now have to go before the executive committee yet again to win their approval— a prospect he clearly did not relish.

If Rothman were to take on the executive committee, Yablans knew he had to take on John Milius. The two had not been getting along of late. Milius had wanted to hire Robert Blake for a leading role in the film, but Yablans had vetoed him. Now, Powers Boothe had been selected for the role, and Yablans wasn't enthusiastic about him, either.

With Milius, as with most directors, Yablans knew, everything came down to the process of trade-offs. "Forget the Yak base," Yablans urged, referring to one location. "It's too expensive."

"It's a war picture, remember?" Milius countered.

"You've got enough people and equipment down there to start World War Three," Yablans said. "My ass is on the line."

"So's mine," Milius replied. "And I have a fatter ass than you."

Yablans fought hard, but he knew Milius held the cards. The studio had already committed millions to the film. To replace the director would entail a delay of weeks and an expenditure of millions more. While Milius had compromised on a few locations and eliminated several action scenes, he was still going to shoot exactly the picture he wanted to shoot.

*   *   *

The viewing of "rushes" at a movie studio is, at best, an anesthetizing experience. The purpose of the exercise is for the studio chief, accompanied by whichever aides he may designate, to assess the work-in-progress, and then convey the appropriate critiques. The process may take from ten minutes to several hours each day, depending on the number of films in production.

Theoretically, it can prove illuminating to see how a director "visualizes" a particular scene, and how his principal actors perform it. In "dailies," as they are called, however, each scene is covered from many angles, and each angle encompasses many "takes." To the director and to his editor, each "take" is the subject of keen fascination, since they are essentially cutting the scene in their minds even as they watch the film, calculating exactly where they will apply their close-ups, etc. To the studio executive, however, the repetition of the various takes may lead to acute numbness.

While at some studios the head of production watches dailies alone, at MGM/UA it became the practice for the entire staff to attend. This served to fortify team spirit, Freddie Fields believed, and also was instructive to his younger D-girls, some of whom had never been on the set of a movie. Yablans, who attended dailies only sporadically, did not agree with this notion. He always seemed vaguely annoyed when he wandered into the screening room to find as many as fifteen silhouettes lined up in the darkness. His annoyance became acute when it became clear that the dailies were playing to a highly critical audience—an audience that was not inhibited about "talking back" to the screen.

It would be hard to pinpoint the precise moment when this relatively inexperienced "audience" at dailies began turning against the studio's own pictures, but somewhere during the long, labored sex scenes of *Until September*, things began to turn sour. Directed by Richard Marquand, *Until September* was intended to be an erotic love story about an American tour guide, played by Karen Allen, who becomes involved with a handsome (but married) Frenchman. The film sought to create a Parisian ambience that was stylish and sexy, but early on it became apparent that things were not working out. The chemistry between the two lovers, Karen Allen and a French actor named Thierry L'Hermitte, was misfiring. The Parisian backgrounds seemed blandly predictable. Even the wardrobe seemed gauche and ill-fitting. Freddie Fields, who had fostered the film, fired off angry telexes, demanding to know why the expensively designed clothes not only looked as though they'd come off the rack, but "it was the wrong damned rack," as he put it.

The sex scenes were the capper, however. They were graphic, plodding, pedestrian, overlighted, and excruciating in their anatomic detail. And as they were screened, reel after reel, the disembodied voices in the screening room became increasingly plaintive.

"If this is erotic, I'm having a sex change."

"For a handsome man, he's got a fat ass."

"That's 'cause the camera is always tight on it."

"How can they do it, take after take?"

" 'Cause they're getting paid."

"I'm not getting paid enough to have to watch it."

"Sex per se isn't sexy—doesn't the director understand that?"

"Shut up, it's a love story."

"What a turn-off. My husband's gonna have a cold bed tonight."

The incipient rebellion in dailies was triggered once again by a climactic scene in *Teachers,* during which JoBeth Williams was called upon to do a striptease in the hallway of a high school. The point of the scene was that Williams was so intent over winning her argument with Nick Nolte that she was willing to make a spectacle of herself.

To the female members of Freddie Fields's production staff, however, the scene was both sexist and asinine. They had fought it in script form. And now, during dailies, they continued to voice their opposition. Even as Williams stripped off her clothes in take after take, the disembodied voices could be heard:

"The scene will never play."

"In the very long shot, it's a possible...."

"Long shot, close-up—it's sexist bullshit."

"No woman, under any condition, would do what she..."

"...unless she had better tits, she'd never..."

The argument ended abruptly with the sound of first one, then two, then finally five people stomping out of the screening. Lin Parsons was nonplussed. "First time I've ever seen walkouts in dailies," he muttered.

By the time *Red Dawn* and the other major films started shooting, the list of people invited to attend dailies had been slimmed down, and the atmosphere had acquired new tension. Not only was Yablans in frequent attendance now, but also Rothman and, now and then, an anonymous representative from the executive committee. These, after all, were the films that would make or break the new regime. Playtime was over.

* * *

Red Dawn was not getting off to a smooth start. During the first week, John Milius decided to stage part of the "invasion," showing hundreds of parachutists descending on U.S. soil. The chutists were recruited from several sources—a Special Forces unit, a local "jump" club, and random volunteers who answered an ad in *Gung Ho*, a *Soldier of Fortune*–type magazine. A gusty wind had come up during the course of the jump, playing havoc with the chutists, who ended up in trees, hanging from telephone poles, etc. Though the Special Forces troops and the volunteers from the local sky-diving club quickly lined up for their second and third jumps, the would-be soldiers of fortune did not fare so well. A hard-drinking, tattooed, belligerent lot, several reported in with bruised or broken ankles, and others threatened darkly that they would bring the "unsafe conditions" to the attention of the authorities unless they were given more pay. Their demands were rejected.

As he viewed dailies, Frank Yablans directed a steady stream of questions at colleagues.

"Why is this a day scene? I thought this was going to be night."

"It's day-for-night," David Wardlow, the project executive on *Red Dawn*, responded from somewhere in the darkened screening room.

"But it looks like day. What's wrong with these people?"

"When it's printed down ..."

But Yablans was already onto his next worry: "Why does that Russian prisoner stand there holding a stick?"

"It was Milius's intention in this setup to suggest a painting by Frederic Remington," Wardlow responded.

"Will you explain to Mr. Milius that I'm paying him to shoot a movie, not an art gallery," Yablans said. "Son of a bitch is blowing up half of New Mexico, and now he's getting arty."

Meanwhile, the so-called soldier-of-fortune types who'd defected during the parachute jump had followed through on their threat to take their story to the press. The Associated Press ran a piece about the supposed rash of injuries, dramatizing the dangers incurred by the "volunteers."

In view of the recent *Twilight Zone* case, the story received considerable play, even though the alleged injuries were minor. Alarmed at the prospect of potential lawsuits, Rothman summoned Yablans to his office and instructed him that extra safety measures would have to be taken.

Yablans in turn assembled his production staff, and he was in a table-pounding mood. "John Milius may think he's General Patton," Yablans said, "but it's our ass on the line." Given the simulated combat that was scheduled, as well as the erratic weather, Yablans warned there could be further injuries, "even casualties," on the film.

As usual, the burden of response fell to Lin Parsons. A qualified expert was supervising each facet of the physical shooting, he explained, whether choppers or weaponry or whatever. Another supervisor—"the best powder man in the business"—was presiding over all special effects. If any problem was encountered, Parsons continued, that supervisor had instructions to place an immediate call to the studio.

Yablans was not pacified. "Isn't it true that this 'powder man' can be overruled by the director?"

"Technically, that is true," Parsons said, "but he can appeal directly to me, and the studio can overrule the director."

"That could be too goddamn late," Yablans countered. "By the time the studio gets involved, we could have someone blown away by those lunatics. I want to have someone on location who can overrule Milius. I want a safety czar—a retired general or something like that. I want a man who can walk on the set and order Milius to do it his way. That's the sort of person I want, and I want him this week."

There was a quick look of exasperation exchanged between Parsons and his aides. They knew that to place someone in this position would be inviting a chain reaction of insults and power plays on the set. Besides, a "general" would be totally baffled by the workings of a film set. But there was no point in arguing. What Yablans was clearly doing was laying down a legal defense for himself and Rothman in case any accident did occur on location. At least they—Yablans and Rothman—had instructed their employees to take appropriate preventive action.

In fact, there were no further injuries on the *Red Dawn* location. And no "safety czar" was dispatched to location.

But even as the debate over safety raged, the film company was confronting a new threat. Snow was falling in the mountains of New Mexico. The crew and youthful cast were suddenly up to their knees in drifts, and freezing. And the imitation Russian tanks, which had barely navigated the mud, sputtering and spewing oil, were now stalled in the snow. What had started out as a picture about invasion was now turning into a film about survival.

* * *

While the controversies surrounding *Red Dawn* were raising the decibel level of the studio, another, far larger, and more complex project was almost surreptitiously easing its way into production.

The movie *2010* would have been a massive project at any studio, but at gun-shy MGM/UA it constituted a truly momentous gamble. Nothing of this magnitude had been attempted since the pre-Kerkorian 1960's. And there was no way of skimping or cutting corners: To succeed, *2010* would have to be a historic high-tech extravaganza.

Peter Hyams, no stranger to hyperbole, remarked just prior to production, "If my film works, no director will ever again want to do a sci-fi film."

Going in, the cost of the movie was projected at $23.7 million, but as Lin Parsons and his aides warned, even the most educated guesswork did not apply to special-effects films. There were too many incalculables, too many unknowns. And if the production staff was nervous about *2010*, its discomfort was matched on the marketing side. Greg Morrison, the droll, heavyset advertising chief, openly called the project "a dumb idea." There was no marketing cachet, he pointed out, in attempting a sequel to a fifteen-year-old film that itself had not been a big hit. The Kubrick film had achieved a sort of underground immortality as the world's first "head picture." The air in movie theaters had been positively dense with marijuana smoke in 1968, as youthful moviegoers "turned on" to the universe.

But society had changed. These were now the Reagan years, and if *2010* was to succeed, Morrison and his colleagues warned, it would have to do so on its own merits. It would have to be a positively dazzling film.

Mindful of these realities, Hyams himself had initially been reluctant to take the job. Yablans had approached him with his usual directness: "I need a picture for the Christmas of 1984," he told him. "I need this from you. You have to do it for me."

The inducements he offered were considerable. The studio would pay him $1 million. Hyams would have total control over the project: He would write, direct, produce, and even serve as his own cinematographer, as Hyams preferred to do. And he would be permitted to labor in complete secrecy. Hyams would report only to Yablans, and only Yablans would read the script (Hyams later voluntarily circulated copies to Maisal and to me). No one would be allowed to visit the *2010* set without Hyams's explicit permission. And all crew members would have to wear ID badges consistent with the intense security.

The rationale for all this was ostensibly to surround the project with an aura of mystery and importance, but the secrecy also served Hyams's overall *modus operandi*. A furtive, zipped-up man, Hyams had always disliked the fishbowl atmosphere in which directors worked, with echelons of studio bureaucrats and others second-guessing and critiquing each step of the way. Now, he could seal himself off in his enormous office—Yablans had seen to it he had the biggest on the lot—and make a movie to suit himself.

One of his few points of contact with the outside world during preparation of his film was Arthur C. Clarke, the sixty-six-year-old sci-fi seer and author of the book *2010: Odyssey Two*. As a prolific writer and a scientist instrumental in the development of radar, communications satellites, and the like, Clarke was in a position to render great expertise. And since Clarke lived in the seclusion of Sri Lanka, and communicated with Hyams via computer linkup, he represented no threat to the director's rigidly enforced privacy.

Nor did Stanley Kubrick, who also communicated regularly with Hyams from the safe distance of England, offering his thoughts and wise counsel.

For Peter Hyams to be chatting via computer with these pundits in itself represented an impressive milestone. Only twelve years earlier, Hyams had been a young anchorman in Chicago when, at age twenty-eight, he'd decided that his future lay in film directing, not TV news. Having written a script called *T. R. Baskin*, Hyams went about the task of setting it up as his first directing stint. A tepid love story, *T. R. Baskin* was not greeted enthusiastically in Hollywood, but after some diligent spadework, Hyams succeeded in selling the piece to Paramount.

The film ultimately was made under the direction of Herbert Ross, and it was not a success.

Undaunted, Hyams went on to direct some television projects, then fought his way back to features once again. Over the years, his output of films had been steady, eclectic, and largely undistinguished. They included *Hanover Street*, a period love story; *Capricorn One*, a sci-fi adventure; and *Star Chamber*, the thriller that had been produced by Frank Yablans.

While establishing him as a diligent craftsman, Hyams's body of work had failed to betray a style or voice. Each film, though well crafted, left its audience entertained but oddly disengaged.

Star Chamber, his most recent film, was a case in point. The conceit of the film was that a secret band of distinguished jurists could become so outraged by the injustices of the system over which they presided that they would be driven to create an outlaw "kangaroo court" that meted out its own justice. Hyams's idea was an intriguing one—a sort of upper class *Death Wish*, with judges, instead of Charles Bronson, wreaking their revenge.

While the slickly made film contained its share of deftly executed chase scenes, it utterly failed to elicit the empathy of the audience for the maverick judges. What could have been a provocative and thoughtful film was in and out of the theaters with lightning dispatch.

Now, with *2010*, Hyams was working on the largest of all canvases—the cosmos. He was also picking up on some of the haunting, unanswered questions of *2001:* Who or what had transformed Dave Bowman into the Star Child? What cosmic purpose was served by the monoliths? Was Hal, the computer, truly malevolent, or did he, too, serve a higher scenario?

Toiling in his lonely isolation, Hyams himself came to represent a sort of mythic figure on the lot. He was at once remote and inaccessible, yet he held in his hands the destiny of those around him. At this fleeting moment, Hyams was indeed the most important person at MGM/UA.

As far as Lin Parsons was concerned, however, the issues of survival came down to a myriad of seemingly mundane points. The rigging, for example. In scenes showing the space travelers free-floating, the camera was picking up the wires that controlled the movements of the actors. They would be invisible for one take, but then everything would be on hold while technicians would have to work on them again.

Then, too, there was the issue of smoke. Hyams the cinematographer liked to pump a great deal of smoke onto his set for lighting effects. The smoke infiltrated every nook and cranny of the vast set with suffused light. On the other hand, the huge arc that synthesized the sun had also started unexpectedly creating its own smoke. The combined effect was to make it seem as if the space travelers were drifting through a permanent cosmic fog bank.

Given the technical problems, the work was going slowly; often a full day's work would comprise only two takes.

When questioned at a production meeting, Parsons pointed out that Peter Hyams was the "ultimate control freak." He was personally directing two full-fledged units on two different soundstages. Most directors normally permit a second unit director to do some of the "action" scenes, but not only was Hyams directing both, he was also doing the camera work. Hence, a small army of technicians would spend their days waiting as Hyams shuttled from one stage to the next, handcrafting his mammoth epic.

The result, Parsons estimated, was that the film would go about 20 percent over budget. And there was nothing he could do about it.

The cast, too, was impatient. Roy Scheider, who played the lead, would drop by my office to complain that Hyams was so involved with his technical obsessions that he was shortchanging the human elements of the film. A slender, rumpled man who prides himself on being a true-blue "New York actor," Scheider felt that his character had no color or subtlety. "I don't have dialogue, I just make speeches," he said plaintively. "And my speeches sound exactly like Peter Hyams."

The absence of sexual tension also bothered the actor. "Women," he said, "seem to occupy no place in his universe. Even the letters that my character writes to his family are all addressed to his sons, never to his wife."

Whatever reservations others may have had about *2010*, Frank Yablans, for one, did not share them. Visiting the set often, and carefully viewing dailies, he was utterly convinced that the studio had a hit on its hands. Indeed, even before the film had finished principal photography, Yablans had already started meeting with Irv Ivers, the studio's president of worldwide marketing, to map out an ambitious campaign. As befits a hit in the making, the campaign would ultimately involve an expenditure of some $16 million to "open" the film. This, combined with the film's aggregate final cost, which amounted to $27.3 million (including studio overhead) meant that the *2010* gamble had reached stratospheric heights of $43 million.

The soaring costs of *2010* and *Red Dawn* at the studio had one unexpected by-product: They provided a protective cover under which *Mrs. Soffel* managed to inch its way to the starting line.

Under normal circumstances, *Mrs. Soffel* was exactly the sort of project that would self-destruct in preproduction. Everything seemed to militate against it. Senior executives at the studio were in disagreement as to what the film was about, or how to market it. Nor could anyone even agree on a suitable name to replace the embarrassing working title.

The screenplay itself had an oddly *Rashomon*-like effect on people. Everyone seemed to stare at the identical pages, yet come away with an utterly divergent analysis of what they had seen. To Frank Yablans, *Mrs. Soffel* was a hot love story, deftly merged into a chase picture—two supposedly surefire genres. To Freddie Fields, however, it was *Bonnie and Clyde* revisited—two outcasts from society who find romance on the run.

To Gillian Armstrong, the thirty-three-year-old Australian charged with directing the film, *Mrs. Soffel* was none of the above: It was an erotic tragedy—a movie about a desperately repressed woman who is victimized by a desperately repressed society. Armstrong concluded that MGM, in selecting her to guide this film, had opted to make not a chase picture, but an art picture—a bittersweet and occasionally violent glimpse of turn-of-the-century America as sifted through the sensibilities of a tough-minded feminist director.

In so doing, the studio had made a courageous choice, Armstrong felt. And she in turn had tried to reward that choice by persuading two outstanding talents, Mel Gibson and Diane Keaton, to assume the leading roles. Their presence in the film would not guarantee a mass audience, she acknowledged, but at least would bring visibility to the project.

Set in the Pennsylvania countryside of 1901, the film was based on the true story of Kate Soffel, the wife of a prison warden who becomes entangled with two young brothers, Ed and Jack Biddle, who have just been convicted of murder. Kate visits the handsome young prisoners to dispense Bibles and Christian mercy, but she soon finds herself attracted to the charismatic Ed, played by Mel Gibson. Adeptly playing on her sense of compassion, Ed persuades her of their innocence. The only way they will escape execution, he says, is if she helps engineer their escape.

Not only does Mrs. Soffel spring them from jail, but she decides to abandon her sternly Puritanical husband and three children and run off with the brothers. In so doing, she becomes a folk heroine to the women of the community. To the men, however, she represents a threat to law and order, not to mention Christian rectitude. Setting forth in their vigilante-style posse, the men hope to bring the three to justice, perhaps dispensing some "instant justice" along the way.

The climax is uncompromising: Kate and the two brothers are tracked down in the snow and shot. Ed is killed, and Kate is condemned to prison.

Written by Ron Nyswaner, the screenplay was brought to MGM by a veteran producer named Edgar Scherick, who in turn had sparked the interest of Gillian Armstrong. It was an intriguing, if unlikely, choice. The feisty, free-spirited Armstrong had directed two small and unique Australian films, *My Brilliant Career*, a graceful period piece, and *Starstruck*, a raucous little rock-and-roll comedy. She had never worked in the United States, never made a big-budget film, and never coped with the bureaucratic intrigues of a Hollywood studio.

Presenting herself for her first studio meetings, Armstrong made no effort to disguise her attitudes or her intentions. Though she wore a "serious" gray cotton dress, there were strands of purple in her blond hair—a suggestion of a rebellious, "punk" approach to her craft.

In conversation, she was engaging, but cautiously distanced. Working in the United States represented a major change, she acknowledged, but her passion for *Mrs. Soffel* was such that she would gladly make the needed adjustments.

On the subject of budget, she was similarly wary. "My last film cost two million dollars," she advised, "but that does not mean that I can make *Mrs. Soffel* for that sort of money." She would meet with studio estimators, she said, and try to work out a budget. "I am," she cautioned, "a stickler for detail. I want to capture the detail of the period." Her listeners nodded approvingly, and with only a flicker of apprehension.

In landing her two stars, Armstrong clearly understood she had acquired "muscle" in terms of her future dealings with the studio. It was unusual for an obscure director to win commitments from two major stars, but she had pulled it off. Keaton had responded favorably to Armstrong's films, as well as the script. Gibson had been a tougher catch. For one thing, he'd been committed to another MGM/UA film, *Running Man*, but had cooled on the project. He preferred the notion of working with his fellow Aussie on a subject that ran counter to normal studio fare.

Only a week earlier, Gibson's agent, Ed Limoto, had turned up in Freddie Fields's office to announce the shift. "It's a 'no' on *Running Man*," Limoto blurted, "and it's a 'yes' on *Mrs. Whatchamacallit*."

Fields was delighted to have Gibson for the romantic lead in *Mrs. Soffel*, but he also wanted to negotiate yet another Gibson commitment in return for surrendering *Running Man*. Limoto was not buying it. "Everyone in town's chasing Mel. You should be grateful. He likes Gillian, he likes the role. Just find a new goddamn title, okay?"

Given the imposing cast, MGM/UA let it be known that it would proceed with *Mrs. Soffel*, provided the budget was acceptable. With that in mind, Armstrong and Lin Parsons got together for a marathon session to review her requirements.

When Parsons emerged from the meeting, he was visibly shaken.

Parsons came into my office and closed the door behind him. As always, he wore his blue suit and carried a neatly arrayed sheaf of papers and computer readouts.

"What sort of movie does the studio think it's making here?" Parsons asked.

I shrugged. "That's a matter of opinion. Freddie and Frank have it in their heads that this is a big commercial movie. You've spent time with Gillian, however..."

"They'd better be right," Parsons said. "Because it's going to cost what a big commercial movie costs."

"We're talking...?"

"At least thirteen million dollars," Parsons said.

I let out a soft whistle. The number that had always been bandied about the studio was closer to $10 million, and now it was already escalating into the teens.

Parsons began to tick off a list of Armstrong's demands. She wanted a schedule of at least seventy-two days to shoot her film (*Pope of Greenwich Village*, by contrast, was scheduled for forty-eight days). She was going to insist upon authentic wardrobe of the era for her large cast, plus period coaches and other props. And though Scherick had talked about making the entire film in the environs of Toronto, Armstrong was now proposing a major move to Pittsburgh, where an "authentic" old prison of the period was still standing. Built around 1900, the prison would add a vital dimension to the picture, she asserted.

When all the items on her "wish list" were added up, the total came to $13 million, but Parsons was not prepared to believe that, either. "We're sending off an inexperienced young director to shoot in the snow," he cautioned. "She's never worked under conditions like this. She doesn't have the technical background...." His voice trailed off, and he made a quick gesture of frustration.

"You're saying this picture could soar like *2010*."

"That's an understatement. I'm going to insert a big fat five-hundred-thousand-dollar cushion for starters. I don't know how far that will take us, but it's a token."

As a seasoned production man, Lin Parsons understood, of course, that a budget, like a screenplay, was basically a product of the imagination. It was predicated on a list of assumptions, which might or might not prove valid, depending on a wide range of factors, including the whim of the director. In theory, of course, a director could shoot only the material in the screenplay, as budgeted, but even that is subject to interpretation. On *Heaven's Gate*, for example, Michael Cimino spent two weeks shooting a scene that had been described in the script in half a sentence of presumably off-camera stage direction.

To Frank Rothman's lawyerlike mind, a budget constituted a quasi-legal document to be duly signed by the producer and director. To more knowledgeable film people, however, a budget was more like a social contract, embodying a given set of goals and objectives, and Lin Parsons was not prepared to be hung out to dry based on Gillian Armstrong's goals and objectives.

When the $13 million figure was conveyed to Fields and Yablans, there was a collective gulp. Fields argued that the addition of Mel Gibson to the cast had given the project some "spin." Yablans countered by demanding that Armstrong be brought back to cut the budget. "Let's kill the move to Pittsburgh," Yablans suggested.

"That prison is important to her," Parsons warned.

"We're giving this purple-haired bitch her big break," Yablans raged. "In return, she can cut the budget."

Fields and Parsons nodded their acquiescence and turned to leave. "And by the way," Yablans continued. "Since this picture's becoming a hot item, can't someone come up with a better name than *Mrs. Fucking Soffel?*"

By the end of the third week of principal photography, Lin Parsons's intuition had been borne out. *Mrs. Soffel* had been officially declared a "problem picture," falling further and further behind schedule. The company had moved to a new location, and after three days of shooting, only one day's work had been completed. Even more troubling was the fact that Gillian Armstrong was becoming more and more withdrawn, communicating only with her small Australian coterie on the film, which included her cinematographer, Russell Boyd, and her live-in boyfriend. She declined to discuss her "shot list" with her producer, Scherick, nor would she draw on the resources and experience of her veteran department heads—art director, stunt coordinator, or whoever.

Apart from the production and communication problems, there was yet another, graver concern: The material itself wasn't working. Photographed in dark, brooding hues, the scenes seemed curiously mannered and impersonal, as though Armstrong had decided to shoot her "period" film from a "period" perspective. And, in my view, at least, she was making some dangerous choices. Would anybody care about these cold and distanced characters, acting out their tragic roles? The issue of empathy was important in *Mrs. Soffel*, it seemed to me, because of the sudden twist of the narrative.

The "point of view" of the audience was the Keaton character—a woman who was prepared to desert her husband and three young children to run off with an accused murderer.

Watching dailies, I could imagine a Thalberg or Mayer protesting wildly, and with good reason. The romantic attraction between Kate Soffel and Ed Biddle was not being delivered on film. The Mel Gibson character seemed coldly manipulative, and the Keaton character came across as cloyingly submissive.

My worries were shared by David Wardlow and Lin Parsons, but not by Freddie Fields. In Fields's view, Mel Gibson's charisma would carry the film. He had seen it happen on his previous movie, *The Year of Living Dangerously*, and it would happen again on *Mrs. Soffel*. Artistically, he assured me, there was nothing to worry about.

Yablans, meanwhile, had been taking heat from his executive committee and from Frank Rothman about the production overages on *Mrs. Soffel*. He had not been watching dailies, and did not want to hear a debate about artistic concerns. He wanted to get this picture under control before it detonated another corporate crisis.

"I cannot tolerate what is happening on this film," Yablans stormed, at a hastily called meeting in his office. "Something has to be done!"

Yablans listened impatiently as the usual range of options was bandied back and forth: The producer could be fired, the cinematographer replaced, a full-time studio "overseer" could be assigned to the film. Perhaps—the most drastic solution—Gillian Armstrong would have to go.

As usually happens in these war-room confrontations, all of these proposals were tabled in favor of a more benign option: A senior executive of the studio would have to be dispatched to location to assess the situation. That senior executive, it was concluded, would be me, and I was to leave immediately.

A production executive visiting the location of a troubled movie feels about as welcome as a traveler on a package tour of downtown Beirut. To cast and crew, he is a harbinger of doom, his every movement watched with suspicion. It is assumed that to justify his visit, he will pick some sacrificial lamb who will be summarily dismissed from the film—an assistant director or the production manager, perhaps. He will then return to the studio, having demonstrated his seriousness of purpose.

This cynical scenario is usually borne out, to be sure. Like papal visitations, quick location trips tend to be heavy on symbolism and short on substance. If a film is going wildly over budget, or if the content is blatantly mediocre, then a quick visit by a production executive cannot be expected to alter the course of events. The only valid option is to shut down the picture altogether and eat the losses. Actions of this magnitude are rarely taken, however, for one very good reason: If a head of production shuts down a film, he is tacitly admitting his bad judgment in green-lighting the project to begin with. On the other hand, if a movie is allowed to run its course and then, after release, is deemed a failure, the filmmaker becomes the person at fault—the studio executive becomes the innocent victim of others' incompetence.

There are circumstances under which a friendly unannounced visit to location can yield positive results. I remember dropping in on Hal Ashby in San Francisco, circa 1970, during the third week of *Harold and Maude*. The company was shooting in a stately old mansion in Burlingame, and the work was exceptional but slow. Very slow. At the lunch break, I guided the director, Hal Ashby, into the baronial library of the mansion. Since Ashby knew that I had been responsible for the project's quick approval at Paramount, he was pleased that I had unexpectedly materialized, but still wary.

ASHBY: How's the work look to you? I'm feeling good about it.

BART: I think it looks great. The problem is, there's not enough of it.

ASHBY: Well, we may be running a little behind, but...

BART: A little?! Hal, you get one day's work every two days.

ASHBY: The problem is, lining up our shots in the confines of these rooms...

BART: I'm sure those are legitimate problems, but look around you, Hal. We could smoke a ham in here.

Ashby glanced around the smoke-filled mansion as several members of the cast and crew were puffing away on their joints. Ashby himself had started to take a joint from the pocket of his shirt, but tucked it away now.

ASHBY: (a sheepish grin) It's a mellow company.

BART: I like mellow. I'd like faster mellow. No one lights up till after work—that could help.

ASHBY: Maybe not till after lunch...

I took out a packet of one-way airline tickets from San Francisco to Los Angeles and handed them to Ashby.

BART: A suggestion, Hal. If any technician lights up on the set, just hand him his ticket back to L.A. No scenes, nothing...

ASHBY: (a thoughtful nod) I guess we've been slowing down a little lately.

BART: But stay mellow, Hal.

ASHBY: Very mellow.

After our "mellow" talk, the pace of shooting started picking up markedly. And the film kept getting better.

While the atmosphere in San Francisco was both mellow and hospitable, a palpable tension hung over the set of *The Godfather* during my visit to New York the following year. After a week's shooting, Marlon Brando's performance seemed flat, the lighting was oppressively dark, even the camera work seemed perfunctory. An edgy Francis Ford Coppola joined Albert Ruddy, the producer, and me in a drafty hallway where our conversation could not be overheard.

Coppola, as usual, was brutally candid. If I'd come to tell him the movie "looks like shit," I could save my breath, because he shared my opinion. He and Ruddy had heard rumors that Bob Evans, Paramount's executive vice president, was already making inquiries about replacing Coppola with Elia Kazan. That rumor was correct, I replied. Evans and I had had a big argument about the film, which ended with Evans promising me another week to try to pull things together. Now that we had the week's reprieve, the key was how best to use it.

Coppola was angry about his dilemma. The principal reason for his disarray, he felt, was that Evans had instructed him to keep shooting screen tests of actors at a time when Coppola wanted to be prepping his picture. Evans had been particularly skeptical about the choice of Al Pacino as Michael—"that midget Pacino," he called him—and had insisted on looking at several other actors, including Dean Stockwell, before bending to Coppola's opinion. As a result of the delays over casting, Coppola had not had time even to "walk" some of his key locations.

Now, the most important task was to buoy up Brando.

In his excruciating effort to master the facial and physical nuances of a Mafia don, Brando had been blowing his lines with astonishing consistency. And those lines he managed to deliver were so slurred as to be virtually incomprehensible.

The solution, we all felt, was a banal and obvious one—cue cards. If politicians could use them, why not Marlon Brando?

Coppola favored the idea, but Ruddy looked worried. "How do we go up to Marlon Brando and say, 'Pardon me, Marlon, you may be the greatest living screen actor, but now we're giving you cue cards.'"

"We don't ask him, we just do it," Coppola decided.

Starting the next morning, the cue cards appeared. Brando never mentioned their presence, nor did he blow any more lines.

To be sure, the problems involving *Harold and Maude* and *The Godfather* lent themselves to possible solutions because of a pervasive spirit of amity. Whatever the short-term strains and disagreements, there was still a sense that we were basically on the same side. But as my car neared the location of *Mrs. Soffel*, I reflected on the subtle changes in atmosphere. These were the eighties of Reagan America, after all, not the sixties. There were no "mellow" movie sets anymore. The costs of filmmaking had soared, and the sides had been clearly drawn. To Gillian Armstrong, I was the enemy—the representative of the "suits." Our meetings would be all about confrontation, not accommodation.

Glancing at my watch, I realized we had been on the road for three hours since leaving my hotel in downtown Toronto. I had been told that the location was a two-hour ride. The Canadian driver assigned to me had made a few peculiar turns, and it seemed as though we'd doubled back on ourselves.

"How much longer do you figure?" I asked finally.

"Hope to be there within half an hour." His tone seemed a bit nervous.

"Did someone instruct you to deliberately get us lost? That's a question, by the way, not an accusation."

The driver, a red-haired man with a slight Irish brogue, looked back at me. "Funny you should mention that."

"How so?"

"Well, I'd overheard some discussion...I mean, there was talk..."

"...about getting me lost!"

"Suppose I shouldn't have told you that."

"It's okay. I'm prepared for anything."

"But that didn't happen, anyway. I mean, I managed to get us lost without anyone telling me to. Sorry about that."

"Do you know where you're going now?"

"I do, yessir, I do.... That is, I think I do."

Half an hour later, as we drove along a lonely rural road through the frozen countryside, I finally caught sight of the maze of mismatched trucks and Winnebagos that always signals the presence of a movie company. Pulling closer, I could see the drivers and some of the crew standing around, warming their hands over portable heaters and open fires.

As I stepped out of the car and stretched, I was startled by the numbing coldness. Somehow, the brilliance of the noon sun made the cold seem even more insidious. I thanked the driver for getting me there, albeit behind schedule, and started trudging toward the ramshackle schoolhouse where, according to the shooting schedule, today's scene was being shot. The rustic old structure looked very turn-of-the-century—a perfect setting for the scene in question.

The trouble, however, was that the scene was not being shot. Nothing was. The camera, lights, cable, and all the other paraphernalia of filming were at the ready inside the schoolhouse, but the only person in evidence was a very harried-looking man who seemed to be studying the ceiling.

The harried-looking man, I discovered, was Russell Boyd, Armstrong's handpicked Australian cinematographer. He had been working since daybreak to light the schoolroom to the satisfaction of his director, but without success. According to Armstrong's design, the only source of light for the scene, which was supposed to take place at night, would be moonlight filtering through slits in the ceiling. It would be moody and vaguely menacing. Whenever Armstrong had been brought in to examine Boyd's work, however, she had shaken her head disapprovingly. There was too much light one time, too little the next, and so forth.

"You know Gillian," Boyd explained, with an embarrassed shrug. "Always the perfectionist."

Edgar Scherick, the producer, had joined me now, and he did not look happy. Mindful of the fact that the company had been falling further and further behind, he had hoped for a solid day's work. Instead, it was almost lunchtime, and the familiar cry, "Roll cameras," had not as yet been heard. The actors were vegetating in their respective trailers, reading or napping or doing whatever actors do during the interminable periods of waiting when they are on location.

"Another day in heaven," Scherick said, glowering.

"Correct me if I'm wrong," I said, taking him aside, "but as I understand it, we went to considerable trouble to bring this cinematographer all the way from Australia because Gillian had worked with him before and had great confidence in his work."

"You got it right so far," Scherick said.

"And still, it takes him over four hours to light a simple interior?"

Scherick nodded gravely. "It gets more interesting. As a result of the delay, we won't be able to finish the scene. Tomorrow we have to move to the next location, or we'll lose that, as well."

"So how do you finish?"

"We'll have to build the interior of the schoolhouse on a sound-stage. Costs money, costs time, but that's what we're left with."

I had known Scherick for only a brief period of time, but I had heard stories of his towering rages, his screaming tantrums directed at underlings. A gray-haired, grandfatherly figure, Scherick, to my observation, seemed the model of restraint. During his earlier career in television, the Harvard-educated Scherick had created *Wide World of Sports*, and been head of programming for the ABC network. Besides producing some distinguished features, he had also become one of the major suppliers of long-form TV—movies-of-the-week, miniseries, and the like.

Now in his mid-sixties, his ample experience notwithstanding, Edgar Scherick was clearly being taxed to the limit by *Mrs. Soffel*. He was not yelling and screaming. He was beyond that. His mood seemed to be one of smoldering helplessness.

On the one hand, Scherick wanted to defend his director against the onslaughts of the studio. Armstrong was working well with her cast, he assured me. Gibson and Keaton were supportive of her. Slowly, painfully, she was getting her movie on film. Any notion of possibly replacing her was absolutely out of the question.

And yet, there were the realities to deal with. The frustrations of this morning were grimly representative. There'd been too many mornings when the cast and crew would be waiting around while an ill-prepared director changed her mind about a camera angle or felt that a detail of the wardrobe was inappropriate. She was not so much a director leading her film company; she was, instead, a painter who, standing in splendid isolation on a hilltop, decided to rearray her palette.

Out of the corner of my eye, I could see her now, emerging from the schoolhouse with Boyd, exchanging a few quiet words, vapor billowing from their mouths. Now, she turned and started off, then caught sight of me and stood still as I walked over.

"Hello, Peter, welcome to sunny Canada."

"Good to see you, Gillian."

"Bit slow getting started today, I'm afraid. Tough setup."

As the two of us started to talk, I noticed the others in the company pulling away from us. It was either that they respected our privacy, or perhaps did not care to hear the potential unpleasantries that might be exchanged.

"Look, Peter, I know why you're here. You want me to go faster, of course...."

"It would be an understatement to say this film is causing consternation at the studio."

"Surely, you all must understand that I'm doing my best. It's a complex film. And there's the weather...."

"You haven't even got your first shot today, and that's not due to the weather. And I don't see anything complex about the schoolroom."

"This scene represents a key emotional confrontation between the two characters...."

"If a cinematographer cannot light a schoolroom in four hours, there are three possible reasons. He's an incompetent. The director has demanded an effect that is impossible to achieve. Or one or both of you keep changing your minds. Any other possibilities?"

"I think you've exhausted the lot. Do you have any suggestions?"

"A very simple one. Let's get our first shot before lunch."

Without responding, Gillian coolly turned and walked toward her A.D. Within ten minutes, the actors were on the set and the cameras were rolling.

The work continued at a brisk clip for the remainder of the day. Gillian and I did not have cause for further discussion.

At rushes, however, Gillian seemed both tired and cross. The process of watching dailies on location always constitutes an ordeal for filmmakers, already exhausted from their eighteen-hour days, but it also provides a source of satisfaction and reassurance. All the scurrying and vamping and desperate improvising of the previous day, they now see, has actually resulted in some material that is coherent, even sleekly professional—an illusion perfectly realized.

But the film she saw this evening was far from satisfying to Gillian Armstrong's stern gaze. The scene involved a moving POV (point of view) shot of a cluster of farmers waving good-bye to Gibson and Keaton as they rode off on their sleigh. Armstrong had decided to try for this shot at the last minute, and the crew had worked hard to pull it together. The delicate sleigh, authentic to its period, had to be handled carefully. The camera itself had been mounted on the back of a pickup truck.

To the unschooled eye, the scene looked fine, but Armstrong caught something she didn't like at all—a wisp of some kind behind the sleigh.

"That wisp," she called out, "what is it?"

"It looks like blowing snow, Jill," Russell Boyd responded.

"No, it looks like exhaust to me. Exhaust from the pickup truck. Why didn't we have a real camera car instead of a pickup truck?"

"Because you decided to do the shot at the last minute, and we don't have a camera car on standby every day," David Nicksay, the line producer, replied.

"We do when we shoot in Australia," Armstrong said.

"You don't have snow in Australia," Boyd said.

"I don't like the shot," Armstrong reiterated. "I think we should do it over as soon as we can."

There were muffled groans in the room. And that was the end of the conversation.

The following day, it was business as usual on the set. Armstrong had changed her mind about the first shot of the day, and the crew was hard at work implementing her revised instructions. There was a look of stoic acceptance among them. This was clearly going to be "one of those pictures," a gaffer said, warming his hands over a blazing oil drum. And the cast, too, remained stalwart—at least that was the impression they were careful to convey.

"We all knew this was going to be a tough picture," Mel Gibson explained, flashing back and forth between his normal Australian-shaded accent and the Middle-American twang that he'd carefully cultivated for the film. "Jill's doing her best to get it right." Though he was a man of ordinary size and build, Gibson, like many movie stars, somehow projected a larger-than-life presence. Part of it was his voice, a resonating baritone; and there was his gaze, fierce and unyielding—the ultimate "don't-fuck-around-with-me" movie-star stare.

Gibson was not simply enunciating support for his director, he was also working hard on her behalf, even to the point of incurring personal danger. In one scene, he was called upon to hurl himself atop a fire in his prison cell, and Gibson, typically, did not permit the intervention of a stuntman. He coated his body with gel and performed the stunt himself.

Nor did he flinch when his director demanded take after take. In one scene, Gibson and Diane Keaton were called upon to kiss passionately through the prison bars, and the myriad takes from myriad angles had left both performers exhausted. Keaton, sipping tea and applying Blistex to her parched lips, was obviously frustrated by her director's obstinacy, but she, too, was being the good trouper. "Thank God you're the world's best kisser," she whispered to her co-star between takes.

Though the cast was displaying its support, the strain was beginning to show. Each week, the crew complained, Armstrong would fixate on a different individual as the source of her difficulties—her assistant director had been her latest target, and had been abruptly fired. The crew was beginning to drag its feet.

Even Mel Gibson had begun to show the effects. By the time the shoot was over, some fifty thousand dollars had been spent to repair damage inflicted on his rented house in Toronto as a result of the actor's after-hours tantrums.

Before my departure for Los Angeles, Armstrong and I had arranged to have a brief final chat, standing atop a frozen hillside, surrounded by a seemingly infinite moonscape of rocky, snow-covered vistas. This was the backdrop of the film's final chase scenes, involving horses and sleighs and other intricate logistics. Sipping her coffee, Armstrong was clearly concerned about the upcoming scenes.

"I do not envy you the next couple of weeks," I told her. "This is combat duty."

There was a trace of a smile on her face. "Just tell them back in Hollywood that it's not all laughs out here."

The smile was quickly replaced by a taut, flinty glance. "Now that you've seen what we're up against, tell them to butt out so we can get our work done."

"I don't think it's going to be that easy," I replied, softly. "There is a mania about budget at MGM. It isn't Frank Yablans—it's the politics of the place. When a director goes over budget, it's viewed as a defiance of authority. That's the way it is."

"I'm doing the best work I can," she said.

"The reality is, if you keep losing days, the back end of your schedule is going to get shaved. You know that as well as I."

"You mean they're going to take away Pittsburgh?" Her expression hardened as she pondered the possibility of losing her favorite location. "If the studio cuts Pittsburgh, I walk off the picture. Everyone should know that."

"Jill, I'm not making threats, I'm just posing possibilities. I want you to have Pittsburgh. That's the point of the conversation."

She shook her head and studied a far-off vista. "There are times," she said slowly, "when I wish I'd stayed home in Australia."

That evening, on the plane back to Los Angeles, I found myself sipping my third vodka and trying to analyze my own sense of futility. Gillian Armstrong was a tough case, but there had been tougher. Though fiercely adversarial, she was, nonetheless, a dedicated filmmaker. In her own faltering, procrastinating way, she was reaching for her artistic vision. The movie was alive in her own mind and imagination. She could hear it, see it.

If it turned out to be a big hit, wouldn't that be the happiest surprise of all?

* * *

I had been back in Los Angeles for barely forty-eight hours before the next flare-up over *Mrs. Soffel* took place. The intercom had summoned me to Yablans's office. Fields and Parsons were already in attendance, as was Ileen Maisel, Yablans's assistant. As I entered the room, I heard the voice of Edgar Scherick booming over the speaker phone. Gillian would complete only half the scheduled work that day, he was explaining, trying not to sound defensive. The rest of the scene would be bumped to the end of the schedule. Unless, of course, the studio had a better idea.

Yablans looked around the room, hoping someone would come up with a brainstorm.

"Do we need the scene?" the ever-practical Parsons inquired. "Maybe we can just drop it from the schedule. We're piling up too many fragments of leftover scenes."

"It's crucial to the story," Scherick replied.

"We're just starting a meeting," Yablans said, in his clipped, flat voice that usually portended trouble. "We'll get back to you."

He punched a button, then rose from his desk and started pacing. "Every one of our pictures is over budget. Every goddamn one. *Red Dawn, 2010, Mrs. Soffel*—and I'm getting the shit kicked out of me. And what are we doing about it?" Yablans wheeled on me. "You were up there, Bart. What is your recommendation?"

"I talked to Ed Scherick earlier," Freddie Fields cut in. "He said Gillian had been terribly hampered by her A.D. There's a terrific kid in Australia who is available, and we're flying him over..."

"I asked Bart," Yablans shot back. "He was there, remember?"

All eyes were focused on me. "I'm afraid I don't have any magic solutions. I am persuaded Gillian is working as hard as she can, given the problems with which we are all familiar. Her cast is behind her. If we impose further pressures, they could prove counterproductive."

Yablans glared at me. "Three days on location, and suddenly you're her goddamn champion."

"I'm not her champion, Frank. She is who she is. I'm not happy with the way the film is turning out...."

"Then what the fuck are we going to do about her?"

"We're not going to change her," I said. "We hired her. We can always fire her. If something has to be done, that's the only realistic option."

Freddie Fields moved in fast. "I don't want to hear talk like that. She's getting great stuff on film. That's what matters."

"What matters is that I'm getting the shit kicked out of me," Yablans reiterated.

"Great stuff on film," Fields reiterated. "Have you seen dailies, Frank?"

"I fell behind because of my last trip," Yablans replied. He looked around the room, then added, "I've got to do something. I'm gonna take away Pittsburgh."

"That's not a solution," I said.

"It's her prize location," Fields added.

"Fuck her. I'm canceling Pittsburgh."

The meeting ended on that note. That afternoon, Yablans canceled the move to Pittsburgh. The next morning, Gillian Armstrong phoned him from location and delivered a passionate plea to restore the location. Yablans reversed himself, and Pittsburgh was back on the schedule.

Gillian Armstrong finally completed her film, just as the snows melted in the spring of 1984. She had fought her battles, and won nearly all of them. It had taken her eighty-three days, or eleven days over the original schedule. And even as the last day of principal photography was commemorated, Frank Yablans put out the word: Let's find a new name for *Mrs. Soffel*.

The Boss, Kirk Kerkorian, relaxes at a restaurant.

Herb Solow (first row, center) and Jim Aubrey (on his left) pose with
the entire MGM executive corps on the steps of the Thalberg building
in 1970.

Herb Solow exchanges a few words with his star, Frank Sinatra, on the set of Dirty Dingus Magee *in 1970.*

Director David Lean (left) escorts Herb Solow down through the set of Ryan's Daughter *in 1970.*

Producer Martin Ransohoff, who helped create Jim Aubrey's luster at CBS, was the victim of his cost-cutting at MGM.

Dan Melnick tried to cope with the stringent financial controls at MGM, but ultimately fled to the greener pastures of Columbia.

Frank Rosenfelt (left), Kerkorian's faithful lieutenant, poses at a reception with the then studio chief, Richard Shepherd, and actress Faye Dunaway.

David Begelman thought MGM could be his "second chance" after the Columbia debacle, but he quickly discovered his mistake.

A recently deposed Richard Shepherd (right) briefs his former colleague and the new MGM chief, Freddie Fields.

Frank Yablans, whose executive panache was admired by Kerkorian until the Boss saw the first slate of films

Frank Rothman (left), the onetime litigator who became Kerkorian's close adviser, chats with the author after a studio screening.

Jerry Weintraub, far right, the short-lived president of UA, peers over the shoulder of his friend, George Bush, as the president chats with stars Dan Aykroyd and Kim Basinger.

Broadcaster Ted Turner initially seemed to have fallen victim to Kerkorian's hard bargaining, but analysts soon realized that it was Turner who had made a shrewd deal.

Peter Guber, who tried to buy a piece of MGM and later became chief of Columbia, visits the author on the set of Youngblood *in Toronto.*

Alan Ladd, Jr., exchanges a laugh with Mel Brooks shortly before Spaceballs *went into production.*

Lee Rich seemed to have stabilized the MGM/UA empire, but he too was swiftly swept from office as a result of Kerkorian's negotiations to sell the company.

CHAPTER NINE

■

THE EMPIRE BUILDER
1978

As the 1970's wound down, Kirk Kerkorian's long-dormant appetite for the movie business unexpectedly began to show new signs of life. Kerkorian had realized his dream in 1978 of opening "the world's largest casino" at his new MGM Grand in Reno. But the Reno complex was not showing the instant success achieved by his Las Vegas operation, and Kerkorian seemed ready to turn his attention elsewhere. The sale of Kerkorian's remaining 17 percent stake in Western Airlines had left him with some $30.6 million to play with.

At age sixty-two, Kerkorian was restless again. He found himself looking on from the sidelines as rival movie companies were amassing huge profits. The advent of *Star Wars* in 1977 had ushered in the new era of the superhit—the era of *E.T.* and *Raiders of the Lost Ark*. Yet MGM had scaled down to its lowest level of production in the studio's history.

Even Kerkorian's most timid advisers were suddenly touting the new movie boom to him. His "caretaker" president, Frank Rosenfelt, was trying to educate his boss to the new economics of filmmaking. "When we cut back, it was an all-or-nothing business," he told Kerkorian. "Today, with video, cable, etc., the downside risk of making a film is limited, and the upside potential is going through the roof."

Herbert Allen, Jr., the powerful investment banker who had been so influential in engineering the comeback of Columbia Pictures in 1973, was surprised at lunch one day to hear the reticent Kerkorian suddenly expressing regret over his Draconian cutbacks in MGM's operations.

The time had come to take the offensive, Kerkorian now told his inner circle. What this meant, they assumed, would be an upsurge of activity at MGM. They were wrong.

An MGM buildup would take time, and Kerkorian had always preferred instant gratification. His plan was to launch a raid on Columbia Pictures.

Kerkorian's disclosure that he had taken a $42 million position in Columbia sent a shock wave through Hollywood. Given Kerkorian's undistinguished leadership at MGM, no one was anxious to see him replicate that performance at Columbia. The Justice Department was equally troubled, but for another reason. Any combination of two major distributors, even one with MGM's pathetic market share, could spell a lessening in competition. Given this threat, the government filed suit to block the takeover.

Kerkorian was furious that he was yet again stymied by a federal agency. Taking his case to court, he produced an agreement in which he pledged not to increase his stake in Columbia for a period of three years. He also paraded out a group of witnesses to argue that he was not a corporate raider, but rather a passive investor. Even Herbert Allen, a Columbia director, came forth to testify that Kirk Kerkorian was "an honest man." If Kerkorian said he merely wanted to invest in Columbia, then Allen believed him.

In the face of all this, a U.S. federal judge, A. Andrew Hauk, ruled against the Justice Department. Kerkorian's stock acquisition could proceed on schedule.

Both the judge and Herbert Allen would soon have second thoughts. Six months after signing his pledge not to acquire more stock, Kerkorian suddenly announced that "events have transpired which warrant termination" of that agreement. Without bothering to explain these "events," Kerkorian announced his intention to take over the company.

Columbia's management was outraged. "We will not let him proceed with the acquisition of any more shares," proclaimed Francis T. Vincent, Jr., Columbia's president, in filing a new lawsuit.

Kerkorian countersued, charging that Columbia was, in fact,

secretly ruled, not by its board of directors, but by two men who had "usurped" control. These two were none other than Herbert Allen, who had testified on Kerkorian's behalf, and Allen's close friend Ray Stark, who had produced some of Columbia's most important movies—*Funny Girl, The Way We Were,* and *The Electric Horseman.* According to Kerkorian, Allen and Stark had been manipulating Columbia into making deals that were highly favorable to Stark.

Now, it was Ray Stark's turn to detonate. Stung by these charges, the combative Stark dispatched a letter to Kerkorian, leaking copies to the press. The letter revealed that he and Kerkorian had held several secret meetings, during which Kerkorian had solicited Stark's advice on a variety of subjects. Since he knew Kerkorian to be "a private man," Stark said he had never disclosed the meetings—a decision he now regretted. "I was naive in trusting you and believing what you and your associates advised me you stood for," Stark declared. He went on to deny Kerkorian's charge that he and Allen represented a "shadow government" at Columbia. "Through the years, Columbia management turned down many of my projects that were subsequently made elsewhere.... My dear friend, Kirk Douglas, no longer talks to me because Columbia did not undertake a project about which I was extremely enthused and recommended very highly to the Columbia management." Stark's broadside concluded by pointing out that he "had been privileged to know Howard Hughes," and had found him to be much more straightforward than Kerkorian.

If Stark's assault was designed to irritate Kerkorian, it was just a warm-up for the events that would soon overtake him. On November 21, 1980, Kerkorian was locked away in a contentious, no-holds-barred meeting with Columbia directors in New York City, and had left strict instructions that they were not to be interrupted.

When the meeting finally broke up, the exhausted directors saw Kerkorian turn ashen as he read his phone messages. They carried the news that the Las Vegas MGM Grand was engulfed in flames and that casualties were mounting. By the time he had reached Las Vegas, the fire had caused some eighty-four deaths and six hundred injuries.

Kerkorian's antagonists at Columbia were quick to exploit his misfortune. Columbia had discovered it owned ten shares of stock in the MGM Grand—enough to justify a stockholder suit. In its action, the studio claimed the hotel was "unsafe," that its sprinkler system was inoperative and its insurance "woefully inadequate." The hotel had been built by a method known as "fast tracking," the suit argued, alluding to the practice of commencing construction prior to the receipt of appropriate permits. Since Kerkorian had used the assets of the company "for personal benefit and profit, in violation of his fiduciary duties," Kerkorian's plans to open yet another casino in Atlantic City had been "seriously jeopardized."

Not surprisingly, Kerkorian's attorney, Stephen Silbert, denounced the suit, warning that "Columbia will prove to be very embarrassed for its action today."

If Columbia was, in fact, embarrassed, there were no surface signs of it. The fire had eroded Kerkorian's desire for further combat. The battle for Columbia was over.

Kerkorian had something to show for his effort, however. He had realized a cool $60 million profit from his takeover attempt. And with that money in hand, he would now turn his attention back to long-neglected MGM.

In January 1980, David Begelman was desperately trying to pull his life back together after enduring a tumultuous, almost Wagnerian, cycle of events. The once proud and imperious production chief at Columbia Pictures had stood numbly in court, hearing a judge impose sentence for felony grand theft.

Begelman knew he had no one to blame but himself. In a bizarre chain reaction of self-destructive dealings, Begelman had committed three acts of forgery and embezzlement, which had yielded him a total of seventy thousand dollars—a meager sum for a man who had made millions.

He had forged signatures and cashed checks, and had made little effort to cover his tracks. One was the celebrated check for ten thousand dollars made out to the actor Cliff Robertson. Another check had been made out to Pierre Groleau, ostensibly to cover payment for marketing consultation services. Groleau proved not to be a marketing consultant at all, but rather the maître d' at Begelman's favorite restaurant, Ma Maison. Begelman had cashed that check, too.

By the time events had run their course, not only had Begelman lost his place of power, he'd also brought down his friend and ally Alan Hirschfield, who had been fired as Columbia's president and chief executive officer.

Begelman's crimes could easily have landed him in jail, but Judge Thomas C. Murphy of Burbank Municipal Court had opted instead for a five-thousand-dollar fine and three years' probation. Only a year later, on June 27, 1979, the same judge reduced Begelman's crime from a felony to a misdemeanor. When Begelman then entered a not-guilty plea to the reduced charges, the judge revoked the remaining two years of probation.

The reason for this leniency, the judge explained, was that he had been impressed by Begelman's public service documentary, entitled *Angel Death*, which dealt with the dangers of the drug PCP. The documentary, while financed by Begelman, had actually been made by a young filmmaker named John Cosgrove, but the judge nonetheless felt it demonstrated Begelman's attitude of contrition. As a result of therapy, Begelman contended, he now "understood the motivation that led me to commit the acts for which I have atoned."

The deputy district attorney was not impressed. Decisions like this one, he said, made it "very tough to explain to someone that the justice system treats everyone equally."

For David Begelman, it was now time to get on with his life. The prospect of returning to the agency business held no attraction for him.

Despite his forgery conviction, he knew his friends at Columbia would help set him up as a producer. Even while awaiting final disposition of his case, he and his former agency partner, Freddie Fields, had produced a Biblical spoof at Columbia entitled *Wholly Moses*. Though that had proven an unmitigated disaster, the company recently had paid $9.5 million for the rights to the hit musical *Annie*, and Begelman had been promised the producing credit.

The problem was that Begelman didn't really see himself as a producer, either. He was an executive, a studio chief. He even dressed and spoke like a studio chief. He walked into a restaurant like a studio chief. A chameleonlike individual with great natural charm, Begelman had, perhaps unknowingly, assimilated the imperial mannerisms of a head of state—at least, a corporate state. From his always-polished Rolls to his tailor-made suits, Begelman embodied a regal style.

He had always had an instinctive yearning to become a "class act." As a poor boy from the Bronx, he'd had as one of his early role models a colorful New York agent named Billy Goodheart, who would always pull up in a limousine in front of the tailor shop owned by Begelman's father. Begelman admired Billy Goodheart's style—the way he dressed, the way he moved around town. Most of all, he appreciated Billy Goodheart's offer to help young David get a job in the agency business when he had finished school. Though Begelman never took Goodheart up on his offer, the images had implanted themselves: the limo, the agency, the style.

During a stint in the air force, toward the end of World War II, Begelman attended a brief training program at Yale University, then took some courses at NYU. He tried his hand at insurance, but this held little interest for him. As if it were preordained, Begelman made his way into the agency business and quickly found his niche. The talents were all there: He was a shrewd negotiator, a superb judge of talent, and he was ferocious in achieving his ends.

What set him apart from his predatorlike competitors, however, was that he also had an innate sense of "class." Begelman knew how to deal with people of all strata. He understood when to be commanding, when to be obsequious, and when to reach for the check. He became a regular at "21" and the Colony and the other hangouts of the period. And somehow, along the way, the brief airforce training program at Yale became on his résumé a Yale education, then even a degree from Yale Law School. No one bothered to refute it: Begelman had the urbanity to carry it off.

The talent agency, CMA, that he built with partners Freddie Fields, Richard Shepherd, John Foreman, and others, by the late 1960's had become a powerhouse in the entertainment industry. Its clients included Paul Newman, Steve McQueen, Robert Redford, Barbra Streisand, and even Cliff Robertson. CMA was imaginative in its deal-making, aggressive in its packaging, and patrician in its style of operation. Even its stationery and trade advertisements were impeccably designed.

When Allen and Company engineered a takeover of ailing Columbia Pictures in 1973, it came as no major surprise that David Begelman would be recruited to head the studio. Begelman had the contacts and the panache for the job. Some of his colleagues, however, wondered how easily he would adjust to a corporate environment. By nature, he was a maverick, not a corporatist. His partners had to have their occasional "talks" with Begelman about expense accounts, gambling debts, and the like. These were the sorts of things he would have to keep under control as an officer of a publicly held corporation.

Begelman seemed to thrive in his new position. Though the studio had almost destroyed itself in recent years with anachronistic "groaners" like *Lost Horizon* and *Young Winston*, Columbia was suddenly identified with hot and trendy movies such as *Shampoo, Taxi Driver, Fun with Dick and Jane,* and *Close Encounters of the Third Kind*. There were flops, too, such as *The Front*, a film about the blacklist that starred Woody Allen, and *The Fortune*, with Warren Beatty and Jack Nicholson, but even these were "interesting" failures, ambitious in concept.

And when it all suddenly came crashing down around him, Begelman's explanation was poignant and to the point. "I can't stand success," he told friends. "Something within me says I don't deserve it."

Even as David Begelman was attempting to rearray his life, he was unknowingly the subject of an intense argument in Kirk Kerkorian's office in Culver City. Frank Rosenfelt, the MGM president, was arguing that a new production chief was urgently needed to replace methodical, low-key Richard Shepherd, who had occupied the job for the last four years. If the studio was to accelerate production, as Kerkorian had now agreed to do, a dynamic, high-profile executive was needed for the job—a man who could galvanize the big stars into returning to the MGM lot. And Rosenfelt knew exactly whom he wanted for the job: David Begelman.

Kerkorian listened impassively, but Greg Bautzer was apoplectic. Having long served as Kerkorian's king-maker, Bautzer was affronted by Rosenfelt's proposal. "You can't go out and hire a convicted felon," he protested, his deep voice resonating out into the corridor like rolling thunder. "This man would be in jail today if he hadn't hired himself a helluva smart lawyer." Bautzer stared over at the fourth man in the room, Frank Rothman, the prominent litigator who had defended Begelman during his Columbia ordeal. Bautzer saw Rothman and Rosenfelt exchange a lightning glance and wondered whether an understanding of some sort had been reached between them. Had Rothman surreptitiously approached Rosenfelt on his client's behalf, or was this Rosenfelt's solo caper?

As the argument continued, Rosenfelt became more tenacious. "I feel very strongly on this Begelman issue," Rosenfelt said, his high-pitched voice becoming a petulant whine. "If I don't get Begelman as my production chief, I don't think I want to remain president of MGM," he concluded.

Bautzer reiterated his objections, reminding everyone of Begelman's bizarre transgressions. Then, as was the custom, everyone turned to the man who sat, taciturn as usual, behind his big desk. "If you feel that strongly about it, Frank," Kerkorian said quietly, staring at Rosenfelt, "then I think we should go with Begelman."

The meeting ended. A still-enraged Bautzer stalked out into the hallway. Bautzer was a man accustomed to getting his way. He could not understand why Rosenfelt had taken this position or, for that matter, why Kerkorian had given in to him. It wasn't as if

Rosenfelt had shown himself a shrewd judge of manpower. No, it just didn't add up.

Unless, of course, all this was part of a much broader scenario— a strategy his canny old friend had chosen not to reveal. Bautzer knew that Kerkorian was a dedicated poker player—one who did not like to tip his hand.

On a gray, grizzly November day in 1979, Frank Rosenfelt and David Begelman sat across from each other in a small, rather seedy French restaurant in West Los Angeles. Though definitely not the sort of place industry figures would normally patronize, it was Kerkorian's choice to be the site of his rendezvous with David Begelman, his newly recruited head of production.

"Kirk is usually late for lunch," Rosenfelt warned his guest, suggesting they order. Two wilted salads were quickly placed before them. As he ate, Rosenfelt seemed elated. Kerkorian, he remarked, was intent on rebuilding MGM into a robust company, and was prepared to spend whatever was needed to achieve that end. The hotels and casinos would soon be spun off into a separate public company, leaving the film company to stand on its own. Hence, the short-term goal would be to make important pictures with important stars.

Begelman had some questions to ask. A program of this sort would require a great deal of money. Did Kerkorian understand what major studio pictures were costing these days?

Rosenfelt sidestepped the money questions. "Kirk is the original Mr. Deep Pockets," Rosenfelt said with an amiable smile. "We tell him what we need, and he writes the checks. That's the way the company runs."

Begelman looked up and saw someone enter the restaurant and head toward their table. It was Kirk Kerkorian. Begelman rose, and they shook hands. Though the two had been introduced at one or two dinner parties, Kerkorian did not show any sign of recognition.

"Good to have you aboard," Kerkorian said, as he sat down. He glanced briefly at the menu, then put it aside without ordering. An awkward silence fell over the table.

Begelman broke the silence, thanking Kerkorian for the opportunity that had been accorded him. He had learned from the past, he assured his new boss. He would work hard and toe the line.

Kerkorian smiled absently and reiterated tersely what Rosenfelt had said earlier. It was time for big movies, big stars; time to make a big splash, get the studio going again.

Begelman listened carefully to the generalities, then started to weigh in with questions, similar to those he had asked Rosenfelt.

Kerkorian responded that the studio was in strong financial shape, ready to meet its obligations. Quite suddenly, he then got to his feet. He had to fly to Chicago, he explained, matter-of-factly. As a result, there wouldn't be time for lunch.

They all shook hands once again, and Kerkorian was gone. Begelman stared at his wilted salad in confusion. Rosenfelt, however, was ebullient.

"You see? . . ." he said.

Before the Begelman era at MGM could begin, however, there was still the issue of a contract to be resolved. When David Begelman had raised the issue earlier with Rosenfelt, his response had been dismissive. "Kirk doesn't believe in contracts," Rosenfelt had declared.

Begelman countered that Columbia had been prepared to guarantee him some $500,000 a year if he'd stayed on as a producer. Given that offer, he couldn't accept the post at MGM without something in writing.

Under protest, Rosenfelt finally succumbed, agreeing to a deal calling for an annual salary of $250,000 through June 1984, climbing to $325,000 through the following year. There would also be a 5 percent profit participation in certain projects, to be selected at a later date. Beyond that, the contract also provided for a sort of "golden parachute"—a three-year production deal with a minimum of $300,000 in fees for each film, plus profit participation. This was to kick in automatically if Begelman's services as production chief were no longer required.

With Begelman in place, Kerkorian now set to work to implement his financial game plan designed to levitate his studio's ambitious new program.

Having decided to split the company into two publicly traded stocks, MGM Film Corporation and MGM Grand Hotels, Inc., Kerkorian retained 47 percent of each company. According to his strategy, he would, if necessary, build a "floor" under the stock by buying up to 1.45 million shares of the film company at five dollars a share.

As it turned out, no such "floor" was needed. The moment the shares became available, the public clamored to acquire both stocks. Indeed, the public response was so exuberant that analysts felt compelled to send up some warning flags. Kerkorian's reorganization had confused investors, said Anthony Hoffman of Bache Halsey Stuart Shields, Inc. "People feel they are getting something for nothing. In this case, they're having something taken away from them, which is the earning power of the combined companies."

Still other analysts cautioned that MGM Film Corporation, despite the Begelman appointment, was still far from a viable entity in the film industry. The only way MGM could become a "major" once again was to reacquire the distribution machine that it had so casually sold off almost eight years earlier.

This was one theory with which Kerkorian was in agreement. Indeed, he already was scanning the horizon in search of a likely candidate. His criteria were simple: He wanted a company that was reasonably healthy, that was available at a realistic price— and, most important, he wanted to be able to complete the acquisition without undergoing the sort of bloodbath he'd endured during his Columbia episode. The Columbia experience had reminded him that Hollywood still regarded him as an outsider —indeed, a somewhat menacing outsider.

The most interesting prospect seemed to be Twentieth Century-Fox. A decade earlier, Kerkorian, mindful of the internecine warfare between Darryl Zanuck and his son, Richard, had tried to make a play for the company. At the time, Fox was about to default on some $67 million in bank loans. Jim Aubrey, however, had handled the opening negotiations clumsily, and the older Zanuck had angrily called off talks.

Now, Fox represented an even more interesting target. It had diversified by acquiring a chain of foreign theaters, large resorts in Aspen and Pebble Beach, California, as well as a soft-drink business.

Just as Kerkorian was prepared to pounce, however, a new player charged into the arena—Marvin Davis, a Denver oilman. Davis was willing to pay some $720 million for the studio, paying for it in part by liquidating various assets—a plan akin to the one Kerkorian had applied to MGM.

Kerkorian was furious over Davis's unexpected intrusion. But at the same time, he was in no mood for a proxy fight.

He decided to keep looking. His next target, ironically, was United Artists, the very company that was now distributing MGM's films. Having just endured the indignity of *Heaven's Gate*, UA was a bruised and beaten company. Its corporate parent, Transamerica, had clearly become disillusioned with its entry into the entertainment business. Negotiating with Transamerica would be a lot easier than trying to make a deal with a member of "the Hollywood club." Transamerica, as Kerkorian had learned, was just interested in the bottom line. The more he thought about it, the more interesting United Artists became.

That United Artists was still around at all, after some sixty years, was in itself something of a miracle. Upon its formation in 1919, it was dismissed by the movie moguls of its era as a classic case of "lunatics taking over the asylum." The "lunatics," in this case, were an unlikely combination. There was a Canadian blonde named Gladys Smith, who, as Mary Pickford, was pulling down an amazing ten thousand dollars a week. There was Douglas Fairbanks, ultimately to become her husband, who had been a star onstage before switching to movies. There was D. W. Griffith, who, at forty-four, was the oldest of the team, and who had changed the nature of filmmaking four years earlier with *The Birth of a Nation*. And, of course, there was brilliant, enigmatic Charlie Chaplin. W. S. Hart also was part of the initial UA crew, but he pulled out when Adolph Zukor of Paramount offered him a deal calling for $200,000 a picture. Griffith, too, would soon withdraw, as a result of his mounting paranoia that his partners' films would receive more attention from the new company than his own would, since they were stars, and he was a lowly director. Zukor encouraged Griffith's exit with a $250,000 directing deal.

The initial announcement of the venture rang with idealistic dedication. The purpose of the new company, the announcement said, was "the furtherance of the artistic welfare of the moving picture industry." The notion was not only to help the filmmakers protect and nurture their own work, but also "to protect the great motion picture public from threatening combinations and trusts that would force upon them mediocre productions and machine-made entertainment."

In theory, each partner in the new company would deliver three films a year, to be produced, financed, and distributed by UA.

Though the company's initial projects were commercial successes, it quickly became evident that these stars alone could not supply a company with sufficient product. Pickford was embroiled in a messy divorce, and her budding romance with Fairbanks seemed to be more intriguing to their fans than their projected movies. Chaplin was trying to extricate himself from a $1 million contract with First National, and did not deliver his first film to the company until 1923. Instead of the comedy his partners had anticipated, Chaplin's first contribution was a melodrama called *A Woman of Paris*, in which he made only a brief cameo appearance.

By the mid-1920's, the actors had decided to hire professional management to run their company. Their recruits were two tough-minded Russian immigrants, Joseph M. Schenck and his brother, Nicholas. The Schencks had a quick remedy for UA's product problems: A merger with another young company, called Metro-Gold-wyn-Mayer. The MGM merger was agreeable to everyone except Charlie Chaplin. He believed the artists would find themselves embroiled in the same sort of "arrogant, money-grubbing enterprise" they had originally run away from.

Chaplin's dissent caused a furor among his fellow filmmakers. At a board meeting, Fairbanks called Chaplin a "kicker." A baffled Chaplin called Fairbanks a "jumper." Pickford and the Schencks couldn't figure out what either was talking about, but everyone realized the anticipated merger was a dead issue. The first effort to bind MGM and UA was doomed to failure.

While Nick Schenck ultimately became chairman of MGM, serving as Louis B. Mayer's boss, Joe Schenck remained at UA. Within the next few years, he brought into the company his wife, Norma Talmadge, his brother-in-law, Buster Keaton, and also an array of producers who would later make a considerable mark on the film business, among them, Walt Disney and Darryl F. Zanuck.

When Schenck and Zanuck ultimately departed in 1935 to take over the newly merged Twentieth Century-Fox, UA fell into the doldrums. The movie careers of Fairbanks and Pickford were history, as was their marriage. Chaplin had only made four films in his sixteen years at UA, instead of his promised three-a-year output. Pickford tried to test her mettle in running the company, but she clashed repeatedly with colleagues, losing Walt Disney over a quarrel relating to rights to his cartoons. The company endured an up-and-down record on its movies (*The Private Life of Henry VIII*, *Stagecoach*, *A Star Is Born*), but brought forth a succession of interesting filmmakers, such as David O. Selznick, Walter Wanger, and Alexander Korda.

By 1950, with Pickford and Chaplin no longer speaking, and their once-proud enterprise sinking deeper and deeper into debt, two street-smart New York lawyers, Arthur Krim and Robert Benjamin, both in their early forties, decided to step into the fray. Informing Pickford and Chaplin that their company was effectively bankrupt, Krim and Benjamin offered to take over management of the enterprise on one condition: If they succeeded in turning the company around, they would be rewarded with half-ownership.

Though the attorneys had had no experience in production, they were adept at crisis management and creative at deal-making. In an effort to attract top stars and filmmakers, they essentially reinvented the way in which distribution companies and the creative community related to one another. Under the newly evolved UA system, stars like Kirk Douglas and Burt Lancaster would become fifty-fifty partners with UA, producing as well as starring in their own films. They would have full creative control, and would own the copyright. All this represented a sharp departure from the old notion of stars as "hired hands." Top agents, such as Lew Wasserman of MCA (who later took his own company into the production and distribution business), endorsed the Krim-Benjamin formula because they saw a chance to participate in big back-end profits.

UA had other advantages to offer. It charged no studio overhead. It had no contracts with unions, so filmmakers were free to make their own deals.

Further, while the Hollywood-based studios had been hard-hit by government decrees splitting them off from their theaters, UA owned no theaters, and hence had nothing to dispose of. In short, UA's total lack of assets in itself turned out to be an asset.

Most important, UA also began to get lucky with its movies.

Producer-director Stanley Kramer, for example, had just had a turndown from Columbia on what he called a "western without action," and decided to give UA a shot at it. Indeed, he even offered the $650,000 needed to shoot the film. The project, *High Noon*, was a worldwide hit and won an Academy Award for Gary Cooper.

Another now-fabled movie, John Huston's *The African Queen*, popped up at UA almost by accident. Its producer, Sam Spiegel, was financing the project with foreign money but needed a loan to cover his dollar costs. Krim borrowed the money from Walter E. Heller, the Chicago financier, and advanced it to Spiegel in return for U.S. distribution rights.

The "new UA" was launched. Before long, the list of filmmakers doing business with the company included Otto Preminger, George Stevens, Joseph L. Mankiewicz, and such prestigious production companies as the Mirisch Company (which produced Billy Wilder's great films) and Hecht-Hill-Lancaster, Burt Lancaster's company. Movies emanating from UA were eclectic, unpredictable, and often quite successful. Among them: *Marty, The Moon Is Blue, The Apartment, The Russians Are Coming,* and *Tom Jones.*

By the mid 1950's, UA finally cut its vestigial ties to its founders. Charlie Chaplin called Krim unexpectedly in February 1955, to say he would sell his 25 percent of the company if UA would give him $1.1 million within five days. The U.S. government had been harassing Chaplin for some years now, suggesting past membership in the Communist party. Incited by these accusations, the American Legion had periodically picketed theaters at which UA films were playing. To Chaplin, now living in Vevey, Switzerland, UA represented his last link with the United States. He had surrendered his reentry permit in 1953. But now the deal was closed; Chaplin was no longer a part of the company he had helped found with such idealistic fervor.

The following year, Mary Pickford, too, decided to sell. She wanted $3 million for her share. UA borrowed $2 million and gave her debentures to cover the rest. Krim, Benjamin, and their partners now owned their company outright, and within a year sold stock to the public.

UA's fortunes, like those of other film companies, experienced wide swings over the next decade. Filmmakers who could do no wrong in the 1960's were stumbling badly in the 1970's. Billy Wilder, who gave UA *Some Like It Hot*, was now coming forth with *One, Two, Three* and *Avanti*. Tony Richardson, who'd directed *Tom Jones*, was now coming back with *The Charge of the Light Brigade*.

By 1967, Krim and Benjamin, witnessing the increased consolidation within the entertainment industry, were ready to seek a corporate "sugar daddy" to help cushion the cyclical blows. Several potential suitors seemed interested, John Kluge of Metromedia and Nate Cummings of Consolidated Foods among them. Instead, they chose a dark horse—Transamerica.

The "marriage" seemed rocky from the outset. UA's fat profits of $20 million in 1968 disintegrated into a $35 million pretax loss a year later. This sudden downswing helped exacerbate differences in the two corporate cultures. To Transamerica management, their co-equals at UA seemed profligate and overly suspicious of new business technology. The UA people, meanwhile, distrusted Transamerica's nitpicking controls.

Eric Pleskow, UA's operating chief, bridled over Transamerica's efforts to impose its procedures and wage scales on UA personnel. He also sensed that the big conglomerate, in its anxiety to assemble an energetic young management team, would imminently try to ease out his mentors, Krim and Benjamin—a prospect he found intolerable.

The tensions between the two companies exploded in the January 16, 1978, issue of *Fortune* magazine. An article quoted Arthur Krim as stating, "You will not find any top officer here who feels Transamerica had contributed anything to United Artists." Krim, Benjamin, and the rest of the top UA management turned in their resignations and formed a new company called Orion Pictures, with a financing and distribution deal at Warner Bros. HIGH NOON AT UA, *Variety* trumpeted, in announcing the extraordinary walkout. A week later, the trade paper carried a two-page ad signed by many of the top filmmakers in Hollywood, including Francis Ford Coppola, Stanley Kubrick, and Bob Fosse, in which Transamerica was chastised for letting Krim and company go. "The loss of this leadership will not only be felt by UA, but by all of us," scolded the filmmakers.

True to the style of conglomerates, Transamerica decided to show Hollywood the error of its ways by supplanting the Krim group with a new management team. It was, indeed, the standard MBA response. Andy Albeck, a Russian-born distribution man who talked in a clipped Prussian-sounding accent, was selected by Transamerica to run "a management system . . . we can understand." For the next two years, the company diligently struggled to assemble a profitable program of films. Its efforts were brought to a thunderous halt, however, by *Heaven's Gate*, the debacle that ultimately resulted in a staggering $44 million write-off.

The time was ripe for the dalliance between MGM and Transamerica to begin. The opening move was carefully choreographed by both sides. An emissary was dispatched by Kerkorian to make an offer he knew would be declined. For the grand sum of $5 million, MGM offered to buy its way out of its UA distribution deal.

James Harvey, the head of Transamerica, knew Kerkorian was a wily trader, so he decided to play along. Transamerica would be glad to consider a buyout, he said. The price, however, would be not $5 million, but $55 million.

At this point, of course, each side was intent on setting up the other. Harvey hoped that he could get Kerkorian so frustrated in his attempt to get out of the distribution deal that he would end up buying UA as a whole. Which, of course, was exactly what Kerkorian had in mind all along.

Kerkorian was in full orbit now. He flew to New York for a surreptitious meeting with his old trading partner, Arthur Krim. Though Krim, of course, had long since departed UA, he nonetheless "coached" Kerkorian through possible scenarios, supplying his estimates as to the worth of key assets.

Kerkorian assembled his key advisers in Las Vegas for a final strategy session. Reviewing the numbers tensely, Kerkorian concluded that the final price would be somewhere between $300 million and $400 million. Fred Benninger, the old aviator, was aghast. It was crazy to sink that kind of money into the entertainment industry, he protested. "Think of what that money could buy you in Vegas!" Benninger said.

Kerkorian fixed his cold gaze on his associate, and told him to shut up. "If you don't understand the deal, then don't shoot your mouth off about it," said "the boss." The room fell silent.

In May 1981, the final deal was hammered out. MGM would pay some $380 million to acquire United Artists.

News of the acquisition caused a shock wave in the entertainment industry, and also prompted a sharp debate about the terms. According to one school of thought, Kerkorian had made himself a good deal. The UA library of some nine hundred films, it was argued, combined with MGM's existing treasure trove of old movies, would create a total inventory of some forty-one hundred motion pictures that could ultimately be exploited on television and other media throughout the world. In addition, Kerkorian had picked up rights to the James Bond and *Rocky* sequels, two of the most valuable properties in the motion-picture industry.

A second school of thought argued, however, that Kerkorian had vastly overpaid for these assets. In UA, he had acquired a company with essentially no management and no product in the pipeline.

Moreover, in closing the deal, MGM had made a bizarre gaffe in the area of foreign distribution. It had been the design of MGM executives to make abundant use of the newly acquired UA foreign-distribution organization, which was one of the most respected in the world. However, the company had an existing deal whereby MGM "and its subsidiaries" would have to distribute all its product overseas through Cinema International Corporation, a company that was jointly owned with Paramount and Universal.

Mindful of the "small print" in the deal, David Begelman already had served notice to CIC that MGM intended to maintain the UA foreign operation, and that it did not consider UA to be a "subsidiary," as referred to in the CIC contract. Begelman's dictum had met with no protest. However, Kirk Kerkorian, while passing through New York, was invited to an impromptu meeting with Lew Wasserman, the head of MCA (which owned Universal) and Charles Bluhdorn, head of Gulf + Western (which owned Paramount). Ill-prepared for the meeting, and intimidated by his high-powered adversaries, Kerkorian found himself agreeing to disband

UA's foreign distribution company in favor of yet another projected joint venture, to be called UIP (United International Pictures).

"Kirk got sandbagged," one top MGM executive, who was close to the deal, observed. "Here was our guy with his grade-school education and his polyester windbreaker trying to negotiate with two of the brightest minds in the entertainment industry, and he gave away the store." MGM thus had to allocate millions of dollars to close down a superb foreign sales organization and start up yet another one, which it really didn't need.

Kerkorian's error may have been costly, but the UA acquisition had nonetheless set his company on a new course. This was quickly underscored when UA's first two films out of the chute turned out to be huge hits—*Rocky III* and the Bond film *For Your Eyes Only*.

David Begelman now had the distribution machine he had coveted. His urgent task was to consolidate managements into a streamlined new team and mobilize a program of potential hits that would carry the banner of the new MGM/UA.

CHAPTER TEN

■

THE BLACK HOLE
1984

Even as Frank Yablans's first cycle of films moved haltingly but inexorably through production and postproduction in 1984, a new array of projects was being shepherded through the development process. And they, too, were encountering unforeseen obstacles.

Of all the various cadres in the studio bureaucracy, none operated under a vaguer mandate than the development staff. While the task of business affairs was to negotiate deals, and of estimators to tote up budgets, and of marketing staff to map out new campaigns, the development staff, by contrast, carried the rather esoteric responsibility for fostering new ideas, new writers, new filmmakers—and, hopefully, nurturing some shootable scripts along the way. Their counterparts in an industrial company would be the "R&D" staff—research and development—but with one key distinction. The R&D people were held sternly accountable to produce a specified number of new products or processes or face dismissal. The development staffs at movie companies generally are not held to such rigorous standards. Artistic output could not be quantified, it was argued. A new idea for a movie might be the

184

product of several minds—a director or producer, as well as the studio personnel. It was all a question of group-think.

By the end of the first year of the Yablans regime, the warning signs had gone up that the development process was in disarray. Writers had been hired to work on some 125 new properties, but only one of the projects had begun to take shape as a movie. This was a cop story called *Running Scared*, which was limited in its aspirations, but effective in its execution.

Other projects, on the other hand, were generally foundering. Indeed, many had already been consigned to the turnaround pile. As a result, meetings of the development staff had begun to take on a disputatious edge as executives, in true bureaucratic tradition, sought to pass the buck for failures.

Tensions were further exacerbated by the recent addition to the staff of Danton Rissner, as a senior vice president. A close personal friend of Yablans, Rissner had served as a senior production executive at several studios, most recently as executive vice president at Twentieth Century-Fox. A stooped, sallow man who looked as if he'd just been released from a gulag, Rissner had a deep-seated skepticism about the development process, and enjoyed taunting the D-boys and D-girls about their labors. The task of presiding over development meetings was rotated among Rissner, David Wardlow, and me, and when Rissner was at the head of the table, the sparks would fly.

One sunny March morning in 1984, the full staff of fourteen were seated around the conference table, most looking guarded and suspicious. In addition to the development personnel, a representative of business affairs also was in attendance, alert for information that might impact on the deal-making process. And running the meeting was Rissner, ghostly pale and as acerbic as always. Before him was a long list of the scripts in development, along with the names of the executives charged with supervising each project.

"What's the situation on *Lucky Strike?*" Rissner inquired, peering at his list.

"We'll have something to read next week," replied David Wardlow.

"Isn't that what you said last week?"

"It took longer—what can I tell you?"

"How about *Nerve Endings?*"

"It's still a month away," responded another voice from across the table.

"What ever happened to the concept of delivery dates?" Rissner demanded, not looking up from his papers.

"Slow writer. Tough story. Nothing I can do about it."

"You can instruct the writer to turn in his material," Rissner shot back. "That's often how pictures get made. What's the status of the *Youngblood* rewrite?"

"I read it last night," another voice reported. "I will circulate it for weekend reading."

"Don't keep us in suspense. Is this draft an improvement?"

"Well... maybe. The girl's character has been sharpened in some ways, but there are still several areas..."

"Well, for heaven's sake, don't go out on a limb," Rissner goaded. "I mean, we would never want to pin anyone down around here. Who's looking after *Deep Cover?*"

"I am," came a halting reply. "It came in. Piece of shit."

"Put it on weekend reading."

"Why? It's terrible!"

"I like pain," said Rissner, looking as though he meant it. "Besides, I want to see what we got for our fifty thousand dollars."

Rissner squinted at the next item on the list as though it were written in Sanskrit. "If I am not mistaken, the next entry on our development list is entitled 'Grimm's Fairy Tale.' Does someone want to explain? Are we turning the studio into a day-care center?"

Ileen Maisel had an exasperated look on her face. "I'll fill you in after the meeting," she said evasively. A bright and somewhat burly young woman of twenty-six, with short, curly hair, Maisel had been Yablans's personal assistant during his producing days before following him to MGM/UA. Having just been elevated to a vice presidency, Maisel, unlike other development executives, did not need approvals from myself, Rissner, Fields, or anyone else to close a development deal. She was authorized to pursue her instincts, however expensive they might be. This being the case, she was the object of some jealousy among other staff members who were senior to her in age and experience.

On this particular morning, however, Danton Rissner was undaunted by Maisel's autonomy. "I wouldn't feel comfortable being the only person to know about your fairy tale," Rissner told her. "I think you should share this information with the entire group."

Maisel sucked in her breath. "Let's just keep this in the room, okay?" she said, with a surreptitious glance around the table. "Last week, I was tipped off to a remarkable literary discovery. A previously unknown Grimm's fairy tale was discovered in a private collection."

"I am delighted to learn that," Rissner said.

"And we have bought the movie rights!" she added triumphantly. Maisel's globose face reddened with excitement even as Rissner stared at her stonily.

"Would you care to explain why we would want to own these movie rights?"

"My God, this is a major literary discovery! . . ."

"And have you read this . . . this fairy tale?" Rissner persisted.

"Not yet, but I'm getting a copy next week."

"Ah," said Rissner, like an impatient professor. "Then we will really have something to look forward to on next weekend's reading."

Maisel looked annoyed at Rissner's obvious sarcasm. Across the room, a voice piped, "I like it, and I want to buy it." The voice was mimicking Maisel's favorite expression—one she habitually employed to describe a property that had aroused her enthusiasm. This had applied to a considerable number of projects in recent months; indeed, about a third of the development list stemmed from Maisel's personal enthusiasms—a fact that had been observed by writers and agents alike. Like wildcatters tapping a newly discovered oil field, writers by the score had been camping outside Maisel's cramped office, eager to pitch their ideas and hopefully hear those magic words, "I like it, and I want to buy it."

Maisel's peers on the development staff had hinted tactfully that she curb her appetite. But Maisel, a fitfully exuberant individual, was, by her own admission, a binge eater and a binge spender. And now, she had launched herself into her new role as a binge developer.

Danton Rissner, sensing that he had lost control of his development meeting, tapped the table impatiently. "Let's not let these literary discoveries sidetrack us," he warned. "We've got some serious business to address here."

And he returned to his lengthy list.

The scattershot development at MGM/UA had indeed become "serious business," and the problem went far beyond the freespending propensities of Ileen Maisel. Money seemed to be flying off in all directions, without logic or accountability.

One reason was that the Yablans regime had inherited a formidable number of "mandated" development deals from previous administrations. A considerable list of producers and directors, including Leonard Goldberg, Fred Silverman, and David Gerber, had guarantees or discretionary funds at their disposal. Marvin and Harold Mirisch, two venerable producers, were entitled to receive $1.5 million to supervise projects of their choosing.

Added to this was another group of actors and actresses who had been accorded pay-or-play commitments for films—George Hamilton at $500,000, Lindsay Wagner at $450,000, and Farrah Fawcett at $500,000, for example. Since they were to be paid whether or not they actually worked, an effort was made to develop projects for them.

Confronted with these obligations, Yablans and Fields proceeded to add mandates of their own. Yablans hired his live-in girl friend, Tracy Hotchner, who had scant screenwriting experience, to write a remake of *The Philadelphia Story*, the memorable Spencer Tracy/Katharine Hepburn film. Under her deal, Hotchner was paid $50,000 for her first draft and an additional $30,000 for revisions, against a final price of $150,000. Frank Davis, the studio's business-affairs chief, tried to reduce Hotchner's price until a colleague called him off with the warning, "She's a friend of the family."

Shortly after the deal was closed, Yablans summoned Leonard Goldberg to his office to inform him that the Hotchner project would be channeled through his discretionary fund—news that came as a shock to Goldberg, who'd had other plans for his development money.

Not to be outdone, Freddie Fields negotiated a deal for his ex-wife, actress Polly Bergen, to develop a property entitled *Dear Kidnapper*. He also brought in a project called *Full Moon in August*, which his present wife, Corinne, would co-produce.

Kirk Kerkorian's long-term friend, Yvette Mimieux, the one-time MGM starlet, was allocated some seventy thousand dollars to develop a musical set at a high school in Venice, California.

And two of Yablans's closest personal friends, Dino Conte and David Niven, Jr., with whom he'd shared a weekend house in Malibu the previous summer, also turned up with generous development deals.

None of these friend-of-the-family ventures survived the development gauntlet, however. The Bergen and Mimieux projects were dispatched into turnaround after their first drafts. Fields withdrew *Full Moon in August* in the teeth of withering critiques from his own development staff. And the Hotchner script was abruptly pulled off the shelves, after being read by Yablans and Maisel.

The ever-growing stream of projects into the limbo of turnaround underscored the studio's lack of any coherent policy or philosophy toward the development process. The titles of properties

on the development list themselves suggested a crazy quilt of styles
and subjects: *Clean Straw for Nothing, Arm of the Starfish, Orange
County Red, Slammer: A Brute Farce, Caged Women in Chains,* and
The Adventures of Princess Weinberg.

As if to compound the embarrassment, the development list each
week would contain a one-line summary of the particular theme
being explored in each project. Hence, the May 26, 1983, list stated:

—*Fat Thighs and Four Eyes:* A comedy about a socially inept man,
recently divorced, whose 18-year-old son shepherds him out into the
brutal world of contemporary dating.

—*Girls' School Boy:* When the first male student arrives at an all-
female prep school, all hell, and fun, breaks loose.

—*The Peeled Man:* A love story about an American artist living
on a small, isolated island near Africa amidst revolution and terror.

—*Post Office:* Neither rain nor sleet can keep these postal workers
from their appointed fun—a behind-the-scenes look at a large post
office.

Apart from the eclectic subject matter, time and again projects
would be placed in development that management would ultimately renounce. A script was financed for a remake of the classic
1958 nuclear thriller *On the Beach,* but when it reached Yablans's
desk, he decreed that nuclear thrillers were not commercial. Also
vetoed was a fine script developed by the Dutch director Paul Ver-
hoeven, which dealt with an eighteenth-century slave trader. Films
about slave traders were "not box office," it was decided.

A number of prominent artists got caught in the whipsaw. Bo
Goldman, who'd won an Academy Award as co-author of the
screenplay for *One Flew Over the Cuckoo's Nest,* delivered a brilliantly written script to the studio entitled *The Anita Factor,* which
focused on the relationship between a prep school student and his
troubled father. Goldman had written the script for a mere $60,000
against an ultimate payment of $400,000 because the studio pro-
fessed a willingness to let him direct the movie—his first directing
stint. The door was slammed on these hopes, however, when Goldman was abruptly notified that the studio didn't care for the subject
matter.

Producers holding multipicture deals at the studio didn't fare
much better. One case in point was Linda Gottlieb, a vivacious
and fiercely energetic New Yorker who was guaranteed $150,000
a year against her producer fees to develop projects for the studio.
Having been duly assigned to a lavish corner office at MGM/UA's
New York headquarters, Gottlieb had her first run-in with studio

bureaucracy when she asked the office manager to remove a painting from her wall. The office manager was stunned. "This used to
be David Begelman's office," she informed Gottlieb, "and that used
to be Mr. Begelman's favorite painting. It is a very expensive work.
He commissioned it from his son-in-law."

"I appreciate its illustrious history," Gottlieb replied, "but I'd
still like it removed."

The first project submitted by Gottlieb was a ten-page treatment
entitled *Double Sunrise*, which she wanted to develop into a full
screenplay. Written by Richard Maxwell, *Double Sunrise* was a love
story involving two young scientists who fell in love at Los Alamos
in the early 1940's, even as the basic elements of the atomic bomb
were coming together. The story was based in fact—his parents
had met at Los Alamos. David Wardlow and I both liked the story,
but, in the process of closing the deal, made the mistake of mentioning it at a production meeting. His curiosity piqued, Yablans
asked to read it, and several days later buzzed me on the intercom.
"That Los Alamos piece," he said, "it's a nothing. Forget it."

"Hold it, Frank," I countered. "I think it's worthy of development. Besides, it's Linda Gottlieb's first project. I don't want to
start things off by shooting her down."

"It's a nothing," was Yablans's retort, as he clicked off.

Gottlieb received the news philosophically. "I'll just have to
come back with something better," she sighed.

And she did. Over the next few weeks, several writers were hired
to work on her various stories. One was an offbeat summer romance
set at a Catskills-type summer resort. It was called *Dirty Dancing*.

Several weeks after rejecting *Double Sunrise*, Frank Yablans
found himself meeting with Roger Donaldson, the Australian-born
director who had recently finished a Mel Gibson film, *The Bounty*.
In the course of exchanging ideas, Donaldson expressed his keen
interest in the period when nuclear energy was first harnessed.
"There's got to be an important film to be made about Los Alamos,"
he declared.

Yablans got a flash. "By the end of the day, you'll get a treatment,"
he announced. "It's exactly what you're looking for."

That afternoon, Donaldson received a copy of *Double Sunrise*,
the material that Yablans had earlier rejected. Within two weeks,
Donaldson and a writer were at work on the screenplay.

Gottlieb was visiting the studio later that month when she spot-
ted a new project entitled *Double Sunrise* on the newly issued development report.

Encountering Yablans at the commissary, she decided to thank him for changing his mind about the idea. Yablans seemed distracted. "Oh, the nuclear thing...sure..."

"I hear Roger Donaldson is also involved," Gottlieb said. "I look forward to working with him."

Yablans eyed her warily. "You're not part of the deal," he advised.

"Not part of the deal..." Gottlieb repeated numbly.

"In this business, you win some and you lose some." Before she could reply, he gave her a patronizing pat on the behind and hurried off.

Over the course of the succeeding months, Gottlieb put eight projects into development. None were made by the studio. *Dirty Dancing* ultimately went into turnaround, was acquired by Vestron, and became a hit. *Double Sunrise*, however, never came to fruition.

If Linda Gottlieb was struggling, Roddy McDowall, who had a similar producing deal, also found himself baffled by the development maze. McDowall, to be sure, was more than an ordinary producer. He'd been a child actor of considerable renown who'd essentially grown up on the MGM lot, attending the studio school alongside the likes of Linda Darnell and Elizabeth Taylor. In the course of this incubatorlike upbringing, McDowall had become a living, breathing encyclopedia of film lore, and I, among others, had often utilized this resource. When I found myself weighing a project that sounded vaguely familiar, for example, I would tap into McDowall's data bank to determine its true origins.

Now well into his fifties, McDowall had long since lost his apple-cheeked, child-star demeanor and had turned into a slender, rather wan man of considerable graciousness. Whenever he visited MGM, his presence would evoke an extraordinary stir. Studio old-timers, whether they were guards, grips, or cleaning women, would greet him as though he were family. In a sense, he was.

Given his abilities and insights, it was my notion to bring McDowall onto the lot in a capacity where he could put his knowledge to work for us. Besides looking for new projects, he could address himself to another important task—identifying those films from the MGM past that would lend themselves to remakes.

McDowall and I shared a somewhat heretical approach to remakes. "Everyone is always looking to remake the fabulously successful movies," he observed, "but I think it's a better idea to look to the flops rather than the hits."

He had a point. The big hits of Hollywood's golden years often resulted from some magical fluke of casting—a Hepburn-Tracy picture, for example, or a Bogart-Bacall vehicle. It would be ludicrous to try to recapture that magic, especially since the stories often didn't hold up as well as the cast.

On the other hand, there was also that occasional film that, despite a strong premise, nonetheless flopped because of disastrous casting or some other factor relating to studio politics. Roddy McDowall could summon up a substantial list of once-promising films that had fallen victim to sexual intrigue—the casting of a studio chief's girlfriend, for example.

Installed at his offices on the lot, McDowall set about reviving an old Robert Montgomery vehicle called *The Earl of Chicago*, which had been a box-office failure in 1938. Its central character was a Chicago gangster who, upon release from prison, was informed that he was the sole heir to an earldom, replete with English manor house and servants. He must only return to his ancestral home to claim his prize. All this came as a complete surprise to the gangster, who, upon settling into his new house, found himself sliding into the manner and style of "a proper gentleman."

The original Robert Montgomery movie started out as a lark, but by the third act had plunged into dark melodrama, culminating in the hanging of the central character. It was McDowall's notion to spin it off in a more comedic direction.

Upon developing his script, McDowall was informed by the studio that his project indeed held promise—provided that Eddie Murphy could be signed to play the earl. McDowall pointed out that Murphy, while a superb comedian, was under exclusive contract to Paramount. MGM was unmoved. *The Earl of Chicago* was left to die on the vine. McDowall subsequently developed other subjects, one of which became *Overboard*, which finally came to fruition two regimes later as a Goldie Hawn vehicle.

Shortly after Roddy McDowall moved onto the MGM lot, his friend Joan Rivers also signed a deal with the studio. At the time, Rivers was at a high point in her career. As the "permanent guest host" of the Johnny Carson show, she commanded TV ratings equal to if not greater than those of the durable Carson. Movie and TV deals were being tossed her way with regularity. Hyperkinetic and abrasive, Rivers was indisputably "hot."

There was cold logic in her decision to sign with MGM, however. Tracy Hotchner, Yablans's companion, was a close friend. Rivers and her husband, Edgar Rosenberg, had logged many dinners with Yablans and Tracy. And Yablans had promised to help Rivers advance her film career, long a source of frustration to her. Rivers had written and directed one low-budget film, *Rabbit Test*, which had not been well received.

During the couples' dinners together, ideas would ricochet back and forth across the table for projects that Rivers could adapt and perhaps even star in, but no one could identify an initial vehicle to trigger the process. The problem was exacerbated by Rivers's habit of wildly overbooking herself on Las Vegas engagements, TV guest shots, and one-night performances around the country. Convinced that "being hot" was a fleeting phenomenon—a sage prediction, in her case—Rivers saw to it that every waking hour was devoted to the cause of maximizing her income and notoriety.

Since I, too, had known Rivers and her husband for many years, the assignment fell to me to sort through the blizzard of one-liners and zero in on a property. This was no easy objective, given that Rivers preferred to hold her meetings as she moved from one gig to the next. The sheer act of being in transit, rather than wasting time sitting in a room, seemed to get her juices flowing.

These on-the-run meetings were further complicated by the intense security that followed her every movement. Given her appetite for controversy, Rivers received periodic death threats from TV viewers, and she took them so seriously that her comings and goings resembled those of a head of state.

We were in the midst of a story discussion as we arrived at the NBC studios one night and headed toward her dressing room. As we walked, I noticed the security men taking up positions around us, chattering into their walkie-talkies in their usual gibberish of code names.

"Spitfire heading for bunker," one security man muttered into his walkie-talkie. "They are now passing waterfall." The "bunker," I assumed, was the dressing room; "waterfall" was the security guard we were just passing, and "Spitfire," no doubt, was an apt name for Rivers, who took no notice of any of this, holding forth all the while on some arcane story points as though she were strolling in Central Park.

"I don't have a fix on the love interest yet," she explained in her usual nervous rasp. "I have the structure down pat, I have the gags, but I don't have the romance."

We had reached the dressing room now, and Rivers, in midsentence, turned the knob to find it was locked. Behind us, the murmurs continued. "Spitfire is at bunker," the ubiquitous security man mumbled into his walkie-talkie, taking no notice of the fact that Rivers was locked out. Caught up in her own thoughts,

Rivers kept describing details of the script, suggesting possible cast, etc. Minutes were rolling by as we continued our corridor conversation.

Finally, Rivers peered quickly at her watch. Realizing she was minutes from broadcast time, she wheeled on a security man, screaming, "Spitfire is locked out of her fucking bunker, you idiot, and is going to miss her fucking show!" The guards dropped their walkie-talkies and all but knocked the door off its hinges.

After weeks of negotiation, a deal was finally agreed to whereby Rivers would write a screenplay for a story entitled *Mental Case*. Its central character, to be played by Rivers, was a somewhat crazed psychic who, while solving murder cases, managed to muddle them up, pointing the finger at the district attorney or some other unlikely suspect.

Rivers had offered to write the script for scale—that is, the minimum fee allowed by the Writers Guild. The one proviso was that if the studio opted not to proceed with the project, Rivers would be paid a "kill fee" of $150,000.

Content with this arrangement, Rivers started work on her screenplay. When the deal memo came through, however, the "kill fee" was mysteriously absent. Rivers informed business affairs that she and Yablans had shaken hands over the "kill fee," and that he would confirm it. Yablans, however, was now professing a memory lapse, and couldn't recall the agreement.

In response, the volatile Rivers announced she was walking away from the deal. "I have to be a friend of Frank Yablans to get shafted like this," she declared. "Imagine what would happen if I were his enemy."

In an effort to mollify the tempestuous comedienne, Yablans proposed that *Mental Case* be set aside and another project be substituted to initiate the Rivers-MGM relationship. After several submissions and countersubmissions, a property entitled *The Big Kiss* by John Guare was confirmed as the new project.

Rivers seemed pleased. She admired Guare's writing, and promptly launched into a round of meetings with potential directors to get the project off the ground.

Rivers had just completed one such interview when she received a call from her manager. The redoubtable MGM business-affairs department had phoned to report a technical problem, he declared. It seems the studio, upon further investigation, had discovered it did not in fact hold the rights to the Guare project after all, and therefore was not entitled to assign it to Rivers.

For Joan Rivers, that was the last straw. Like many others before her, she had come to the conclusion that MGM/UA was not the place where her film career would flourish.

The Rivers imbroglio only reinforced in Frank Yablans's mind a determination to develop projects in concert with prominent Hollywood personalities. There were too many obscure writers working on too many obscure scripts, Yablans lectured his staff. It was time for the studio to develop links to the superstars. And he knew the perfect person to serve as the "point man" for this campaign. Namely, Robert Towne.

Like many writers, Bob Towne had fought frequent battles with that syndrome known as "writer's block." When the work was going well, Towne had turned out such brilliant scripts as *Chinatown* and *Personal Best* (which he also directed). When things were going badly, however, the slender, saturnine Towne would become twitchy and start looking for other diversions.

Frank Yablans, long a friend of Towne's, decided he had an excellent solution to Towne's dilemma. MGM/UA would pay Towne some $250,000 a year, and Towne would not have to write a word. Instead, he would serve as a sort of ambassador plenipotentiary to the community of superstars, hopefully guiding them toward an association with MGM/UA. Through his screenplays, Towne supposedly had gained the confidence of Barbra Streisand, Jane Fonda, Goldie Hawn, and others. Now was the time to put these relationships to work for him.

To Towne, this was a writer's dream. He felt like a coal miner who had suddenly been instructed not to dig anymore, but to advise others how to dig. Even as he cashed his first check, Towne commenced discussions with Streisand and Fonda about possibly teaming on a turn-of-the-century story dealing with sweatshops.

Meanwhile, the industrious Towne had also sold Yablans on yet another hot notion. Towne proposed to set up a company that would encompass the industry's top cinematographers—men such as Gordon Willis, Haskell Wexler, and the like. These cameramen would become exclusive to MGM/UA. And since the world's top directors by and large wanted to work with these craftsmen, then they, too, could be lured more easily to the studio.

Yablans thought this was a terrific idea, and he encouraged Towne to begin his round of meetings with the studio's blessing.

As the months wore on, however, it became abundantly clear that none of Towne's ambitious schemes were taking hold. Streisand, Fonda, and Towne had several felicitous talks about sweatshops, but could not get around to agreeing on a writer, much less hammering out a narrative. The cinematographers' company, meanwhile, developed one small hiccup: None of the cameramen in question saw any reason to start a company such as Towne envisioned, since such an entity might complicate their lives rather than simplify them.

Bob Towne continued to pick up his $250,000 annual fee, but he decided to drag himself back to his computer to start writing once again.

Slumped behind his desk, Freddie Fields looked disconsolate. Two executives from business affairs had just left his office after going over a list of a dozen or so projects that had just been put into turnaround. Fields, as president of MGM, had done the appropriate acquiescing and initialing, but the experience had left him drained. He stared across the room at Wardlow, Rissner, and me, and gave a helpless shrug. "Where did all this stuff come from?" he asked. "I mean, we're putting projects into turnaround I never even heard of."

"Beats me," said Wardlow.

"There's this project, *The Adventures of Princess Weinberg*. Did anyone really want to develop a script called *The Adventures of Princess Weinberg?*"

"I think it came from one of the discretionary funds," Rissner offered.

"They're gonna start laughing at us out there," Fields said, as though talking to himself. "They're gonna think we're a fucking joke." He looked up for a reaction, but everyone was avoiding his gaze. "Did anyone see the cake in Ileen's office today? I never saw anything like that in my life." Fields shook his head in bewilderment. "I mean, if that doesn't mean they're laughing at us ..."

Fields was referring to a birthday cake delivered earlier that day to Ileen Maisel from Creative Artists Agency. It was a normal cake, except for one detail. Sculpted in icing atop the cake was a rather large penis—an allusion, perhaps, to Maisel's scatological sense of humor. Given the fact that the cake emanated from the customarily cautious and conservative folk from CAA, the cake generated ripples of surprise. Maisel herself seemed undaunted, however. Indeed, she'd cheerfully started slicing her cake for distribution along the corridor until one of her female colleagues almost fainted as she recognized the object into which the knife was penetrating. As others helped the colleague to a chair, Maisel hurriedly banished the cake to the inner recesses of her closet.

"We've got to start acting like grown-ups," Dan Rissner was

intoning, as Fields nodded his agreement. "We've got to stop these bullshit deals."

Wardlow and Fields were each chipping in their own analyses now, but I was only half-listening to the dialogue. Instead, I found myself scrutinizing my colleagues as though for the first time. Here they were—Wardlow, Fields, Rissner, and the others—they were hardly stupid people. Indeed, they were highly intelligent, and represented a remarkable breadth of life experience. And yet, within the confines of their present environment, they'd become essentially dysfunctional. It was as though some form of group paralysis had swept through the corridors. Men and women who'd distinguished themselves in previous careers were, within these walls, mired in inertia.

Freddie Fields had been one of the most innovative agents of his era. Wardlow had been a pillar of integrity in the agency business. Rissner had been a tactful and highly effective studio executive. Even the various D-girls and D-boys along the halls were an imposing lot if one talked to them one-on-one. They were smart, well-meaning people.

Yet collectively, all of us, here and now, were caught in some sort of intellectual gridlock. There was no sense of innovation, no lively exchange of ideas. There were no wonderful surprises leaping from the pages of projects in development or from those before the cameras. There was no energy, no dynamic. Instead, there was only a pervasive suspicion, a sense that something had gone wrong, and that a time of reckoning was at hand.

Nor had I been a scintillating exception to the rule. Though highly effective in three previous executive stints, at MGM/UA I had found my own projects going sour. I had chased what I thought were promising properties and packages, only to have them elude my grasp. Either they foundered in negotiation, or their principals decided to back away from MGM/UA at the last minute. It was as though MGM/UA had become the black hole of the entertainment industry. People and projects that ventured through its portals would never be heard from again.

It wasn't simply a Frank Yablans problem or a Frank Rothman problem or even a Kirk Kerkorian problem. It was rather the cumulative impact of all those men and others, too. It was the pervasive cynicism that gripped the studio, the omnipresent scent of betrayal. And it was dragging everyone down.

The day after the meeting in Freddie Fields's office, Hal Ashby came by for lunch, and we sat in the commissary, reminiscing about the filming of *Harold and Maude* and the sixties in general.

Ashby had survived bouts of ill-health and personal bankruptcy and other setbacks, but there was still a twinkle in his eye and a determination to laugh at the world. In the middle of our lunch, a heated discussion among MGM/UA financial executives broke out at a nearby table. Strident phrases like "interest shortfall" and "cost overruns" resonated through the executive dining room.

Noticing Ashby's wan smile, I said, "Can you imagine what it would have been like, trying to make *Harold and Maude* here?"

Ashby shuddered. "Maude [the Ruth Gordon character] would have looked around and said, 'Bad karma, man. Real bad karma.' "

And she would have had a point.

CHAPTER ELEVEN

■

RENAISSANCE
1981

ONE day after Kirk Kerkorian completed his acquisition of United Artists in 1981, a harried-looking Frank Rosenfelt burst out of Kerkorian's office clutching two ragged scraps of paper. As it turned out, they would come to represent very expensive scraps. On them had been scrawled a series of boxes, arrayed in the shape of two pyramids, representing the proposed management structures of the new MGM/UA.

Kerkorian's conception of his new company contained some big surprises. Instead of one consolidated, cost-efficient entity, as everyone had expected, Kerkorian was now presenting a blueprint for two separate and distinct companies, each with its own president, chief financial officer, business-affairs department, production executives, etc. His scrawled management charts had instantly added millions of dollars to the company's overhead.

Rosenfelt and his associates stared at the sheets of paper with all their empty boxes in stunned silence. "What does this mean?" someone finally asked.

"It means we've got to fill these boxes!" Rosenfelt shouted, his hand moving from box to box. "We need new names in all these boxes, and we need them now!"

Even as Rosenfelt's aides wandered back to their offices, they were still trying to digest the implications of Kerkorian's dictum. Everyone had assumed that Begelman would become production head of both MGM and UA, but now it seemed he would take over only one of those entities, and it was still unclear which one. And the key question remained: Why had the ever-mysterious Kerkorian chosen this course of action?

It made no sense—unless, of course, Kerkorian intended to turn right around and sell off one of his two companies. Perhaps the old Armenian had yet another secret scenario that no one was as yet privy to.

For the moment, the priority was to "fill the boxes." The lines formed outside of Rosenfelt's and Begelman's offices as they interviewed possible candidates. Joseph A. Fischer, who, as Columbia's chief financial officer, had been a strong advocate of Begelman's dismissal during the check-forging scandals, was now chosen to be executive vice president of MGM. Shortly, he'd be moved over to UA as president with Donald Sipes, a TV executive at Universal, installed as president of MGM.

Meanwhile, Raphael Etkes, another longtime Universal executive, who had been appointed senior vice-president of UA the week before the company was sold to MGM, was told by Rosenfelt that he would now report to Begelman. Begelman quickly corrected that impression: Etkes, Begelman advised, would report to no one—he would be fired and his one-year deal paid off.

On the production side, the moves were equally confusing. Richard Shepherd, once Begelman's old partner at CMA, had lingered on as the head of production for MGM. The first he'd heard of Begelman's appointment was from a guard at the MGM gate. Shepherd had just returned from Europe when, as he arrived at the studio, the guard greeted him by saying: "You must be happy that your old friend is working here!" Shepherd, who knew nothing about Begelman's appointment, asked, "What friend?" "David Begelman," came the reply.

When Shepherd marched into Frank Rosenfelt's office, Rosenfelt apologized profusely, saying he'd been too busy to notify Shepherd of the management changes. "Don't worry, you and David have always worked well together," he said reassuringly.

Before long, Begelman summoned Shepherd to inform him to the contrary. "You'll be happier with a producing deal," Begelman told his former colleague. "Besides, you'll make more money."

Shepherd could not know that the man who would ultimately succeed him as production chief at MGM would be none other than Freddie Fields, their other former partner at the CMA agency. Paula Weinstein, meanwhile, took over as head of production at UA. Fields and Weinstein were a study in contrasts: Weinstein was a feisty feminist and crusader for liberal causes, while Fields was coolly calculating and steadfastly nonideological.

There was still one key player whose role had not as yet been revealed—namely, David Begelman. The "box" that Kerkorian had reserved for Begelman was that of chairman of the newly acquired UA.

To be sure, the underlying reality was that it was David Begelman, whatever his title, who controlled the destiny of the new MGM/UA. Indeed, even as all the high-priced executives at MGM and UA were checking into their new offices, their fate had already been sealed by decisions made by Begelman during his first eighteen months in office. He had already closed the big deals and signed the big checks. All that remained was for his schemes to run their course.

On paper, at least, the projects that Begelman had managed to assemble prior to the UA acquisition represented an imposing mix of talent. He had decided, for example, to resurrect the career of the seventy-five-year-old impresario Billy Wilder with a vehicle entitled *Buddy Buddy*. Based on a French farce, the movie showcased Wilder's two favorite actors, Jack Lemmon and Walter Matthau.

Begelman had also signed Richard Dreyfuss to star in a well-received play entitled *Whose Life Is It, Anyway?* The protagonist was an accident victim, paralyzed from the waist down, who was fighting for his right to determine the moment and means of his death. John Badham, who had scored a spectacular success with *Saturday Night Fever*, signed on as the director.

Begelman also enlisted the services of two vivacious actresses, Candice Bergen and Jacqueline Bisset, to team as disputatious friends and rivals in *Rich and Famous*. Robert Mulligan had originally been signed to direct, but he withdrew during a strike-induced delay, to be replaced by another distinguished septuagenarian, George Cukor. On quite a different tack, Begelman closed a deal with Robert Aldrich, another filmmaking veteran, to make a raucous comedy about female wrestlers entitled *All the Marbles*. And he gave the green light to Franklin Schaffner, the director of *Patton*, to make *Yes, Giorgio*, a rather mannered film about opera that would mark the movie debut of Luciano Pavarotti.

At the other end of the artistic spectrum, Tobe Hooper, the brash young filmmaker who had made the cult classic *Texas Chainsaw Massacre*, was entrusted with a "special effects" thriller called *Poltergeist*, produced by Steven Spielberg's company. And another promising young director, thirty-year old Martin Brest, was set to direct a techno-thriller entitled *WarGames*.

By far the riskiest of Begelman's films was *Pennies from Heaven*, a piece written by the idiosyncratic British author Dennis Potter. Shifted from England to Chicago in the Depression years, the film version starred Steve Martin with Herb Ross directing.

Potter's conceit was to intercut lip-synched songs and dances into the format of realistic drama. In the midst of somber dramatic exchanges, Martin and Bernadette Peters would suddenly start miming period tunes. Steve Martin even danced to Bing Crosby's rendition of "Did You Ever See a Dream Walking?"

Produced on a modest budget for British television, *Pennies from Heaven* was lauded in London, but re-created now as a $20 million studio extravaganza, it was a dicey proposition. Indeed, studio veterans winced at the notion of this surreal musical—almost a parody of the traditional MGM musical—being shot on the very stages where *Singing in the Rain* and *Meet Me in St. Louis* had once been created. Was this a brainstorm—or a travesty?

Though Begelman was already taking heat for his more adventuresome forays, even his worst critics agreed that, in a brief span of time, he had infused energy and excitement into the old studio. Legendary filmmakers were checking into long-deserted offices. Shabby corridors were being repainted and offices refurbished. There were recognizable faces in the commissary for the first time in years. The whole place was buzzing.

To the amazement of the film community, the studio had actually contrived to reinvent itself. Its patchwork management was presenting a united front to the industry. Deals were being closed, bills being paid. To add to the momentum, *Rocky III* was turning out to be the surprise bonus of the UA acquisition, earning some $65.7 million in domestic theatrical rentals.

Given the basic volatility of the company, skeptics wondered how long the honeymoon could last. Behind closed doors, to be sure, the cracks were already beginning to show.

One major source of tension: the soaring costs of levitating the whole operation. With two fully staffed studios, MGM and UA, now in operation, millions of dollars were rolling out each month in overhead expenditures and commitments to new projects.

At the same time, the cost of Begelman's initial slate of films was running higher than projected. While budgets under Melnick and Shepherd rarely exceeded $5 million, Begelman's appetite was far more voracious. (In addition, the costs of filmmaking had spiraled in the interim.)

In any case, the hard data sent chills through Kerkorian's conservative executive committee. *Yes, Giorgio* would end up costing $14.9 million, *Cannery Row* would end up at $13 million, and *Whose Life Is It Anyway?* at $12.5 million (including interest, overhead, and overages). The most alarming news, however, emanated from the set of *Pennies from Heaven*, where shooting had fallen some twenty-two days behind schedule. When production finally came to an end, costs had soared to $27 million, some $7 million over budget.

While the executive committee totted up the costs, the "old pros" in the commissary were fretting over the issue of commerciality. Over lunch each day, there were dark forebodings that Begelman's projects were too upscale—indeed, too arty. The Begelman pictures, it was agreed, were in deep trouble.

With portents of crisis looming all around him, Kirk Kerkorian remained, as always, an isolated figure, sitting alone in his office, staring at columns of figures. Despite the burgeoning activity on his lot, Kerkorian had chosen not to mingle with the newcomers. Indeed, he barely knew even his most trusted senior studio executives—veterans like Roger Mayer, who ran the studio plant, or Frank Davis, who presided over business affairs. Kerkorian rarely greeted employees whom he passed in the corridors and usually climbed the two flights of stairs to his office every morning rather than take the elevator. Ostensibly, he liked the exercise of climbing stairs, but to studio employees it was yet another manifestation of his isolation.

Having distanced himself so effectively, Kerkorian now turned for advice not to a studio executive or even an industry figure but rather to an attorney—Frank Rothman. As a partner in the high-profile law firm of Wyman, Bautzer, Rothman & Kuchel, Rothman had often represented MGM's interests over the years. Indeed, it occasionally seemed as though he represented everyone connected with the studio as well. He'd served, of course, as Begelman's attorney during his battles at Columbia. He'd represented Frank Rosenfelt from time to time and was even now representing Richard Shepherd in his divorce proceedings.

Rothman was indeed the "ultimate insider" and so, in their own way, were his partners. Eugene Wyman had been a long-term leader of the state Democratic party. Thomas Kuchel had been a

U.S. senator for twelve years. And Bautzer had long functioned as friend and adviser to "The Boss," although Kerkorian had been showing signs of backing away from the relationship. Bautzer, a man of considerable bombast, had long boasted that he was the "real" decision maker at MGM—a claim that increasingly rankled Kerkorian.

Suddenly Rothman seemed to be turning up wherever Kerkorian was and appearing at key meetings. To experienced Kerkorian-watchers, the message was clear. The Boss had found himself a new consigliere.

In April 1982, barely five months after the "boxes" had been filled at MGM and UA in accordance with Kerkorian's mandate, yet another new box was now placed atop the pyramid. Frank Rothman was formally declared chairman and chief executive officer of MGM/UA, a position that Kerkorian had earlier declared would not even exist.

On the surface, Rothman's quiet ascension seemed to spell good news to the embattled David Begelman. The two had become friends during the Columbia ordeal. But during that period, Rothman had functioned as Begelman's "hired gun." And now he was Kerkorian's.

In his new role, Rothman almost immediately began to take a dim view of his old client's performance—reflecting, no doubt, the opinions of his patron. To Rothman's logical, lawyerly mind, the cost overruns on Begelman's films seemed unthinkable. So, too, was the atmosphere of administrative disarray. Notes about deals were scrawled haphazardly on the backs of envelopes, and occasionally one hand did not seem to know what the other was doing.

Begelman's critics within the studio claimed, too, that he was so caught up in stitching together his superstar packages that he wasn't paying sufficient attention to the underlying material. Begelman's *modus operandi*, it was said, was to impulsively acquire projects based on their "elements"—their actors and directors—and not on analyzing the commerciality of the screenplays themselves.

What frightened Rothman was that the studio's managerial clumsiness was now becoming common knowledge throughout the filmmaking community. The widely publicized firing of Raquel Welch had seen to that.

The fact that Welch had now filed suit against MGM was in itself an embarrassment. Welch, after all, had long been an MGM stalwart. She had been on hand with Cary Grant for the groundbreaking of the MGM Grand. Yet now she was publicly charging that she had been made the scapegoat for cost overruns on *Cannery Row*.

The movie, one of the first to be green-lighted by Begelman, had been troubled from the start. David Ward, the young writer-director (he had previously written *The Sting*) was making his directing debut on the film, and he and Welch had not seen eye to eye from the first day of shooting. Welch, he claimed, had demonstrated a "difficult attitude"; for example, she'd been requiring three hours for makeup every morning. An argument had now erupted over the actress's proposal to apply her makeup at home. Even as all this was being negotiated, Welch was abruptly fired from the film. Her response was to file suit against the studio, charging, among other things, that MGM executives had been secretly negotiating for Debra Winger to replace her even as she was attempting to work out her differences with the studio. (Welch ultimately carried the day, winning a $10 million award from a jury.)

While the Raquel Welch case had exacerbated Rothman's impatience with David Begelman, the UA chairman, a proud and rather imperious man, found himself equally appalled by Rothman's utter lack of show business "savvy." Begelman found he could almost always count on the fact that, if he liked the work of a particular filmmaker, Rothman would find some reason to disdain it. Even when they traveled together, it seemed like a bad marriage. One aide recalls Begelman's indignation after a joint visit to the *Yentl* set in London. Begelman was an exuberant fan of Barbra Streisand, admiring both her personality and her talent. But Rothman, after meeting her, made an offhand remark about how much less attractive Streisand seemed in person than on the screen. "I thought Begelman would bash him," the aide recalls.

Whatever Begelman's frustrations, there was one reality he could not ignore: It was Rothman who clearly held the corporate reins. To drive home this point, Rothman decided to apply the brakes to his UA chairman. The company was in a cash crunch, he announced. As a result, all new projects were on hold. Everything would have to be examined from a new set of criteria.

Suddenly, several favored projects that Begelman had lined up were in jeopardy. *WarGames* could not move forward because it exceeded a newly mandated $7.5 million lid on budgets, imposed by the banks. Begelman was about to lose another project he loved—a touching drama called *Terms of Endearment*. He had closed a deal on the property, but now was about to forfeit his option because of the "crunch." (The film would shortly go into turnaround, ending up at Paramount.)

Exasperated, Begelman tried to determine whether these new restrictions were real or imagined. On several occasions since joining the company, Begelman had questioned Rothman and Rosenfelt alike about the limits of his production budget, pointing out that a specific budget had been assigned to him at Columbia. "Don't worry," he'd been assured. "We don't need budgets here. Kirk has all the money we need."

But if Kerkorian indeed had the money, he was showing a sudden disinclination to spend it. Greg Bautzer, for one, was not surprised. "Kirk thought MGM and UA combined would be an instant 'money machine,' like Vegas," he observed. "Suddenly, he was getting a whiff that things weren't going right, that the first films out of the pipeline weren't going to be *Star Wars*."

One insight as to Kerkorian's mood was revealed at an executive committee meeting early in 1982. Arriving late, Kerkorian interrupted the flow of discussion with a seemingly irrelevant question. "This Dino De Laurentiis guy—where does he get his money?" Kerkorian wanted to know. Aides explained the basic concept of foreign pre-sales, which De Laurentiis had pioneered, but added that no one really knew where De Laurentiis managed to find his seemingly inexhaustible supply of production financing. They then used the question as a wedge to return to a related issue—that MGM/UA needed to find its own fresh sources of funding.

The UA acquisition had been financed mainly with bank debt. Now, with interest payments soaring, the company's top financial advisers had been advocating new instruments, such as long-term subordinated debt. The company, they contended, had grown too vast to be financed like a corner grocery store. Walter Sharp, a longtime member of the executive committee and himself a former bank executive, still talked of the bank as "Mother Hen," and would drop lines like, "Mother Hen is a bit impatient with us this month." The time had come, aides now argued, to forget about "Mother Hen" and start looking for new avenues, especially since the first Begelman films were opening to disappointing business.

Alarmed about the box-office results, Kerkorian made one of his rare phone calls to a top marketing man in the company. "What happened to the numbers?" Kerkorian asked, as he ticked off a list of limp grosses. Though the adman tried to avoid being pinned down, Kerkorian persisted. Finally, in anguish, he said, "Dammit, Kirk, our pictures are too 'uptown.'"

"Uptown?..." Kerkorian repeated, puzzled.

"You know—uptown, upscale..."

"They're not commercial?..."

"Yeah, that's one way of putting it."

"I see," said Kerkorian, clicking off the line.

Not only were such Begelman films as *Rich and Famous, Pennies from Heaven*, and *Buddy Buddy* opening to weak business, but so were the pictures inherited from UA. Again, they were "uptown" projects such as *The French Lieutenant's Woman, True Confessions*, and *Cutter's Way*.

To Kirk Kerkorian, the fortunes of MGM/UA had reached a crossroads. Something drastic would have to be done.

The job of dismissing David Begelman was assigned to Frank Rothman, as the chief executive officer of MGM/UA. This was a rather awkward role for him in view of the fact that Rothman had, of course, been Begelman's attorney and prime defender. Indeed, the Begelman-Rothman relationship had just been held up to public scrutiny yet again in a long piece that ran in the January 7, 1982, *Los Angeles Times*. Based on an "advance peek" at the forthcoming book *Indecent Exposure*, by David McClintick, the article reviewed the Begelman forgeries and Rothman's successful efforts to keep his client out of prison. Although these lurid events had taken place five years earlier, the *Times* report somehow seemed to blur the time barrier and create a sense of immediacy.

The *Times* story sent shockwaves through the MGM/UA hierarchy. It was almost as though the forgeries had just occurred that week—even though everyone had been well aware of the incidents at the time Begelman had been hired.

When Begelman arrived in his office at 8:45, Friday morning, July 7, 1982, Rothman was waiting for him. "This is very uncomfortable for me," Rothman declared, "but we are going to have to let you out of your agreement." Devastated, Begelman demanded to know what that meant. Begelman was accustomed to Rothman's penchant for "legalese." Was Rothman now saying he was fired, or was he also saying "the contract has been invalidated"?

Rothman replied curtly he could not discuss the issue any further at the present time. An announcement would be released at noon that would disclose Begelman's dismissal as chairman of United Artists, Rothman said. Then he added, "You don't have any friends on the board, you know. No friends at all." And with that, Rothman left Begelman's office.

Begelman tried to gather himself. He'd realized his situation had become troubled, but he couldn't believe they'd pull the rug out from under him after only eight months at United Artists, and barely two and a half years with the company. He'd made some mistakes, to be sure; he'd rushed into some situations that he should have assessed more carefully. But that was only because Kerkorian wanted to see quick results.

Begelman was gripped by a sudden sense of betrayal. In a short span of time, he had presided over one of the biggest acquisitions in motion-picture history, helped recruit the managements of two companies, and assembled a formidable program of films. And now, even before most of his movies had been given a chance to prove themselves in the marketplace, Rothman was putting him out to pasture. His supposed defender! His attorney!

It was a few minutes after nine o'clock in the morning now, and Begelman noticed that all of his lines were already clogged with incoming calls. His secretary had a look of desperation on her face. He quickly realized what was happening: Rothman had told him he was releasing the announcement at noon, but he'd misled him. He'd released it at noon, New York time, which meant 9:00 A.M. in Los Angeles. He could hear his secretary already explaining to callers, in a panicked tone of voice, that she had no knowledge that her boss had been fired, that Mr. Begelman would return the call later in the day.

Begelman cursed in frustration. Rothman hadn't even given him the courtesy of breaking the news to friends and associates. They would have to learn about it on radio or television.

Later that day, he was to receive even more ominous news. MGM had no intention of honoring the remaining three years of his contract. Studio attorneys informed him that in view of his "past difficulties at Columbia," it would be unwise for Begelman to try to seek legal remedy, because that, in turn, would compel MGM/UA management to bring "certain things" to light about Begelman's performance at the company.

Begelman was furious. He had nothing to hide about his work at MGM/UA, he protested. Furthermore, he resented what he felt were the efforts of his own former attorney to intimidate him.

Yet he sensed that MGM/UA, for whatever reason, would not back down. And, whatever the cost, he resolved that he would not back down, either. He'd been through tough times before. He'd endured the taunts and embarrassments of public disclosure.

He had nothing to lose now.

*   *   *

The sudden departure of David Begelman in mid-1982 created an immense power vacuum at MGM/UA. The company found itself with a sprawling, redundant management structure and with two production chiefs—Freddie Fields at MGM and Paula Weinstein at UA—who did not hold the confidence of top management. Frank Rothman, as chief executive officer of the company, was now bent on collapsing all the "boxes" that Frank Rosenfelt, only two years earlier, had so diligently tried to fill. Suddenly, everyone in the company seemed to be stepping on everyone else's toes. The obsessive topic of conversation at the commissary was who was going to get fired, and when.

Kirk Kerkorian, meanwhile, was going through his own typically introverted reassessment. Kerkorian was stung. He had allowed himself to be persuaded by his advisers that the time had been ripe to build a movie company, and he had spent half a billion dollars to buy United Artists, hire an assemblage of high-powered executives, and put a slate of expensive movies before the cameras.

And what had he got out of it? A gigantic bank debt, for one. A lineup of money-losing negatives, for another. Wherever he looked, all he saw was feuding executives, angry stockholders, hostile bankers ... and leering critics.

Kerkorian knew who he was: He was a trader. He had made hundreds of millions of dollars buying low and selling high. And now he'd allowed himself to be talked into an entirely different and unfamiliar role—a creator of companies, a builder of dynasties.

"Bullshit!" thundered Kerkorian, to his tight circle of intimates. Never again would he allow himself to be hustled!

He was going back to what he understood. It was time to start trading again.

CHAPTER TWELVE

■

UNDERTOW
1984

T HE arrival of spring in 1984 brought mounting signs that Frank Yablans was in trouble at MGM/UA, and he knew it. "I feel like I'm caught in an undertow," he confided to a friend, "and I'll be damned if I know what to do about it."

Clashes with Fred Benninger and Walter Sharp, Kerkorian's two long-term representatives on the executive committee, were becoming more frequent. Yablans wanted the committee's approval for some overall deals for top stars, including Sylvester Stallone, but was turned down. When Yablans closed a major deal with the ubiquitous Dino De Laurentiis, Sharp and Benninger protested that they hadn't been kept apprised of the negotiations. Resenting their implication that he'd had some "private agenda" in making the De Laurentiis deal, Yablans defended the arrangement, arguing that the studio was at risk for only 60 percent of the negative cost of the films, and still owned all video rights. His opposition on the executive committee countered that De Laurentiis's record had been dismally weak in the U.S. market.

The projects involved were indeed a bit dicey. One was an epic called *Red Sonja*, starring Brigitte Nielsen (and Arnold Schwarzenegger in a cameo) and yet another was *Year of the Dragon*, directed by none other than Michael Cimino (his first job in the five years since *Heaven's Gate*).

Adding to the tension was the unrelenting storm of criticism about budget overruns, especially on *Red Dawn* and *2010*. Though they didn't know it, the executive committee did not see the same data as the production staff, but received instead specially prepared yellow pages that contained a "pad" of 6 percent on each picture. Even these contingencies were now being invaded, however.

Yablans protested that he was applying strict controls to the films. He reminded his recalcitrant executive committee that despite the increased activity on the lot, he had still managed to reduce overhead by some 10 percent since taking office.

What was really behind the criticism, Yablans concluded, had nothing to do with budget overages or Stallone deals. The real issue was Kirk Kerkorian.

To Kerkorian, Yablans realized, MGM/UA was still a privately owned company (Kerkorian controlled 51 percent of the stock, and the rest was in the hands of the public). Hence, any sharp increase in the price of the stock, or any newly declared dividend, would have a dramatic impact on Kerkorian's personal fortunes.

And this represented the real "trap" of Yablans's job. Kerkorian wanted strong earnings. But there was no way to produce earnings of this magnitude and still cover the high interest payments coming due on the junk bonds sold by Michael Milken. Not unless the company wanted to return to the policy of stripping assets, as in the Jim Aubrey era.

Yablans understood the basic risks of these deals. The music company that Kerkorian had sold for $62 million a year earlier already had been resold for twice the price (it would be sold yet again in two years for five times the 1982 price).

In a modified way, Yablans already had resorted to this sort of tactic to pump up first-quarter earnings. He'd negotiated a controversial deal to pre-sell MGM/UA pictures to German television in return for some $60 million. As a by-product of the negotiation, however, MGM's own video company had to pay back millions on earlier video deals, since the video values had been directly affected.

Even as Yablans was struggling to reassess his priorities, he sensed that more and more, he and Frank Rothman were working at cross-purposes. At a time when Yablans was trying to persuade Barbra Streisand to take a more vigorous role in promoting *Yentl*, for example, he learned that Rothman was simultaneously seeking to penalize her for budget overruns on the film. While Yablans was trying to elicit greater cooperation from the powerful Creative Artists Agency, which controlled many top stars, Rothman was triggering a lawsuit with Sean Connery, a top CAA client, over monies due him on old James Bond movies. Rothman also opposed Yablans's $15 million Stallone deal on *Rocky IV*. (The $15 million was for acting, writing, and directing.) Yablans defended the deal on the grounds that, among other things, Stallone had promised to keep actual production costs to about $12.5 million.

Whenever Yablans left town on business, Rothman was increasingly insinuating himself into delicate studio situations. During one of Yablans's absences, for example, Rothman summoned Lin Parsons and David Wardlow to his office, waving the production report of *Teachers* at them. "They're one and a half days behind!" he exclaimed, face reddening. "You tell them that if they don't make up that day and a half, I'm going to fire the director. That'll show the town that I mean business."

Parsons and Wardlow left the room in a daze. *Teachers* was one of the few projects that was still on budget—why pick on it? When Yablans learned of the confrontation, he hopped the next plane back to Los Angeles.

The already troubled Yablans-Rothman relationship took another bizarre twist as a result of a "Frank Rothman Roast" that was staged to raise money for the Los Angeles Free Clinic. Several hundred tuxedo-clad guests attended the dinner, including Kirk Kerkorian. After the usual band of comics that play the "roast circuit," including Norm Crosby and Phil Foster, quickly exhausted their inventory of lawyer jokes, Crosby demanded to know what they were all doing there. "Does anyone here really know this Rothman character?" Crosby asked. "Can anyone tell a single joke about him?"

There was a rumble of discomfited laughter in the ballroom. Couples were exchanging "how-soon-can-we-get-out-of-here?" glances.

And now, Frank Yablans rose to speak. Not one to shrink from a challenge, Yablans was clearly determined to salvage the evening. It is true, he said, that Frank Rothman was a very private man—indeed, he had never even given a newspaper interview. But now, Rothman had finally decided to break his code of silence; an interview would soon be published in the *Los Angeles Herald-Examiner* in which "Rothman tells all."

The interview was apocryphal, of course. It was a joke to lead into Yablans's comedy turn. But the audience was not quite sure of this, as Frank Yablans started to read from the so-called newspaper article.

In his make-believe interview, Rothman admitted that though he had long resisted "going show biz," he was finally succumbing. Louis B. Mayer's boarded-over private elevator had been secretly restored to operation for the purpose of ushering starlets directly to the executive suite. This revelation was met not with laughs, but with stunned silence.

As Yablans doggedly pushed ahead with his speech, the silence became, in fact, deafening. Phil Foster jumped from his seat and yelled at Yablans, "Don't give up your day job."

"Sit down," came a call from the audience, and Greg Bautzer, sitting next to Kerkorian, applauded the heckler.

Incredibly, Yablans still pushed on, shortening his speech as he went. When he finally sat down, the room cleared so quickly, a waiter was heard to ask, "What happened—food poisoning?" Neither Rothman nor Kerkorian said good night to Frank Yablans on the way out.

"This has been the most awful night of my life," Yablans remarked to Tracy Hotchner as they left the ballroom.

There were no public repercussions of the Rothman roast, but senior executives detected a palpable tension in the upper reaches of the Thalberg Building. Though Rothman and Yablans had adjacent offices, their visitations became less frequent. "If Rothman told you to do something, you could count on the fact that Yablans didn't know about it, and vice versa," observed one senior studio executive who saw both every day.

Amid these intrigues, Kirk Kerkorian expressed his restlessness in a characteristic fashion—by announcing a Byzantine financial maneuver. At a quickly assembled meeting one morning, Yablans breathlessly announced that Kerkorian had decided to buy back all shares of MGM/UA stock that were now held by the public, thus "taking the company private." Neither Yablans nor anyone else could explain precisely why he had decided upon this action, but Yablans was clearly ebullient. "It'll be great for all of us," he enthused. Without the scrutiny of outside stockholders and regulatory agencies, he explained, the company could finally write off its unsuccessful pictures. It could also design more exotic deals with stars, and even provide more compelling incentive programs for its executives. The most pleasing incentive for Yablans, however, was not having to worry about the price of the shares anymore.

Less than a month later, all these expectations were deflated.

Kerkorian, it seemed, had changed his mind. As usual Kerkorian wasn't talking, nor were his aides. According to one theory, his nine-dollars-a-share offer to stockholders was deemed so dangerously low as to invite stockholders to file suits rather than buy shares. Wall Street's valuation of movie stocks had begun to rise as a result of rumors that Rupert Murdoch was shopping around for a studio. And Kerkorian's buy-back was considered too miserly.

Frank Rothman, ever the stoic parent figure, remarked, "It's all for the best." Yablans, on the other hand, was so angry he wouldn't talk to anyone. Instead, he embarked on one of his frequent trips to Europe.

For Yablans, his European forays increasingly had come to represent a necessary escape from the tensions of the studio. When he was traveling, he was the "king" of MGM—the man who held court to the world's filmmakers at the finest hotels and restaurants. There was no executive committee to hold him back, no Frank Rothman, no Kirk Kerkorian.

As a by-product of his European travels, Yablans was becoming increasingly involved in the quest for "pickups"—independently made movies that the studio could acquire for distribution. Here was one sector of the studio's affairs in which Yablans could function unilaterally, the way he liked to work. He could wheel and deal with producers and financiers, concocting complex deals involving tens of millions of dollars. In the United States, MGM/UA still hovered near the bottom of the list of companies with which important filmmakers would want to do business. In Europe, however, the company still had a magic name, and the prospect of an MGM/UA distribution deal symbolized prestige and financial gain.

In theory, pickups held certain attractions for a movie company. MGM/UA could acquire distribution rights to a project at a set price, often after the film had finished shooting. Hence, there were no concerns about budgets, development costs, etc. The price paid could either be a set figure or a cut of the gross, or both. In the deal between MGM/UA and Cannon Films (the film company run by two bombastic Israeli cousins, Yoram Globus and Menahem Golan) Cannon received a 30 percent share of the gross, climbing to 65 percent. The Cannon deal resulted in one surprise success called *Breakin'*, but also in several embarrassments, including *Bolero*, starring Bo Derek.

Another MGM/UA pickup that turned out to be a surprise hit was *Hot Dog*, described by Richard Graf, the studio's distribution chief, as a "tits-and-ass ski movie." Frank Rothman had opposed picking up the film on grounds that it was "too risqué," but Yablans and Graf had overruled him this time, and the film opened in January 1984 to a strong $4.5 million weekend.

Successes like *Hot Dog* were the exception to the rule, however. Most filmmakers with viable projects choose to make them through conventional channels. Hence, the pool of independently made product usually consisted of recycled genre movies—karate movies and the like.

The arena of foreign-made pickups also remained the murkiest sector of major studio activity. Occasionally, rumors of payoffs and bribes would resonate throughout a company after a controversial project had been picked up for distribution. Jim Aubrey, whose regime was distinguished by such dubious pickups as *The Green Slime, In the Black Belly of the Tarantula,* and *Night of the Lepus* (which dealt with man-sized carnivorous rabbits), had threatened to file charges against one of his senior executives as a result of an alleged bribe on a pickup.

Despite these inherent risks, Yablans followed the consummation of his Dino De Laurentiis deal with a stepped-up program of pickups. He pursued a curious Moroccan-made "weepy" called *Misunderstood*, which dealt with the struggle of a boy to come to terms with the sudden death of his mother. Despite a fine performance by Gene Hackman, the film died a quick death at the box office.

Yablans also tried to acquire *Pirates*, the ill-starred $30 million comedy directed by Roman Polanski. The project originally was to star Jack Nicholson as a roisterous, bumbling pirate, but ended up with an obviously miscast Walter Matthau in the lead. The film ended up with another distributor. It flopped.

But the quest continued. Somewhere, somehow, a pickup would come along that would be the answer to all the studio's problems. Or so Yablans seemed to believe.

By chance, one of Frank Yablans's frequent visits to London happened to coincide with one of my infrequent ones. My mission was twofold: The studio had financed two films that were now being edited in London, and it was my job to view the cuts and confer with the filmmakers about further work to be done. I also intended to see some agents in search of new properties. I did not know what had brought Yablans to town, but I would shortly find out.

The London sojourn had come along at a propitious time. I, too, had wearied of studio intrigues. At Yablans's suggestion, I had taken along my wife, Leslie, to share the amenities of Claridge's. And though my wife, like many others of the Irish persuasion, professed to be a vehement Anglophobe, she, too, enjoyed the shopping, the theater, the lively crowds—even the afternoon tea.

But while London proved a constant source of surprise and delight, the two projects assigned to me did not. The task of viewing "first cuts" often poses a stern test of patience and tact. The early versions are almost invariably much too long—perhaps thirty to forty-five minutes over their final running time. Since there's no music or special effects, one has to make the appropriate allowances.

Given these deficiencies, it is easy to misjudge a first cut, even for an experienced observer. I sat next to a major distribution executive watching an early cut of *Jonathan Livingston Seagull*, and heard him predict a $75 million gross. The film was a notorious turkey. On the other hand, Paramount's foreign-sales chief warned me, after seeing the first cut of *The Godfather*, that the film would fail miserably because it was "too talky." The film, of course, was a huge hit.

Mindful of these hazards, I tried to frame my words tactfully as the lights came on following the screening of *Martin's Day*, a thriller starring Richard Harris, which MGM/UA had financed. The version I had seen was clearly too long, perhaps by twenty minutes, and it was not difficult to pinpoint those areas where the action lagged. Those were clearly the points to focus on. What would remain unsaid was the deeper flaw: This was one of those thrillers that was uniquely unthrilling. The story didn't build. There was no point in puncturing the filmmakers' morale at this juncture. Besides, there was always the chance that I was wrong, that the film, when honed and polished, would magically rise like a soufflé. I had seen that happen, too.

The second film on my list, *Electric Dreams*, held greater potential. It represented the combined effort of two enfants terribles of the London scene. Its director was Steve Barron, a hot young video director. Co-financing the film was Richard Branson, the innovative founder of Virgin Records and Virgin Airlines. The plot of their film focused on an unexpected romantic triangle involving boy, girl, and computer—the computer, enlisted by the boy in wooing the girl, developed its own emotional attachment for her. The narrative was to be embellished with music, cartoons, and all manner of special effects. An inexpensive project, *Electric Dreams* seemed to have the elements of a delicious surprise, an oddball pastiche.

Midway through the screening, I began to realize that this particular recipe wasn't cooking. Despite the fecund imaginations involved in the project, the result was curiously bland—indeed, lifeless. The moments that should have been bold seemed lamely derivative; and what could have been cute was instead cloying. I was devastated.

After the screening, I congratulated everyone, told them to keep up the good work, made a few suggestions, and exited as quickly as possible. These were all people I liked, and yet, despite the good intentions, we'd all let one another down. The best thing to do was get out of there and take a long walk.

In the street, I noticed that Rusty Lemorande, the American line producer of the film, was on my heels. "You were being polite," he called after me.

"What can I say?"

"I appreciate good manners, mind you," Lemorande continued. "No one in this business has good manners anymore."

"Thank you, Rusty."

"When you see the opticals, when you hear the music . . ."

"I'm sure you're right," I replied.

"And the special effects—you won't believe the special effects."

I nodded. He peered at me balefully. "You don't think it has any juice, do you?"

"I'm rooting for it like crazy. . . ."

"Do you know what Steve will do if this picture flops?" Lemorande said, referring to the director. "This is his first picture. His mother, Zelda, is directing her first feature, too. Can you imagine—competing against your own *mom?* If her film is a hit, and his goes into the toilet . . ."

Unable to finish his sentence, Lemorande just stood there shaking his head.

"Oedipal filmmaking is something new to me," I responded, softly. "I hope both pictures are hits." We shook hands, and I started on my walk.

Having seen these two films back-to-back, I found myself wondering whether or not some sort of jinx had indeed settled over MGM/UA. I knew that the opposite could be true—it was possible for a studio to acquire a sort of subliminal momentum. In the days when Yablans and I were at Paramount, I recalled working on films like *The Longest Yard*, which, though undistinguished in execution, seemed to levitate themselves to surprising success. "Sleepers" like *Paper Moon* kept appearing with regularity. It seemed as though everything we touched for three or four years acquired a life of its own.

At MGM/UA, by contrast, projects seemed to get sucked into cinematic quicksand. During the short-lived Begelman era, perfectly intelligent, well-made films such as *Fame* and *Whose Life Is It Anyway?* seemed to drop from sight. Even *WarGames*, after an outstanding start, trailed off much sooner than anyone expected.

Peter Guber, the chief of Columbia Pictures, who doubles as a UCLA professor, often talked about a "movie god" who presided, by whim, over the fate of movie projects. If there was indeed a "movie god," he was not now looking kindly upon Culver City.

When I reached my hotel, my wife informed me that Yablans had called. When I returned his call, he announced that he would be screening a movie in an hour and wanted us to be there. "Are you sure you want me?" I asked. "I'm not doing too great this week. I'm beginning to feel like the Typhoid Mary of screenings."

Yablans snickered. "This will change your luck," he said.

My wife and I trekked dutifully to Elstree Studios, arriving just as Yablans and Tracy Hotchner entered the screening room. Frank was beaming with anticipation.

The lights dimmed, and I got my first glimpse of a film that was ultimately to occupy a small but significant niche of MGM history.

The film was called *Oxford Blues*, and it was reminiscent of an old MGM property entitled *A Yank at Oxford*. The film related the story of a young American hustler, played by Rob Lowe, who, at the start of the movie, parks cars for a hotel in Las Vegas. Lowe becomes infatuated with Lady Victoria, a lissome young member of British royalty whose photo regularly decorates the tabloids. The Lowe character wins some money in Vegas and uses it to travel to Oxford University, where he enrolls, falsifying his past academic record. His intent, of course, is to encounter his "dream girl."

As luck would have it, our protagonist is not only good-looking and ambitious, but also has the potential to be a champion rower, a skill he masters at Oxford.

Before the film is over, Rob Lowe is not only winning races, he is also triumphing before the debating society. In the end, he beds down his English dream girl, only to end up in the arms of Ally Sheedy, the unpretentious American coed who'd pursued him from the outset.

Even as the film was drawing to a close, I tried to organize my thoughts. Yablans, I could sense, loved the film. He would turn to me any minute now and say, "This is a helluva winner, isn't it?" thereby placing me in the no-win position of being the professional naysayer.

As the house lights came on, however, I was saved for the moment by the entry of Elliott Kastner, the gregarious American producer who had funded the film independently. Kastner, himself a minor legend in the industry, was all over Yablans and Hotchner—there were hugs and kisses and an exchange of congratulations. It was clear that a deal had already been made on this picture, or at least an understanding had been reached—an understanding that had made both Kastner and Yablans very, very happy.

As my wife and I headed for our car, we agreed to meet Yablans later for dinner. "We'll talk about the movie," Yablans said, as he strolled off with Kastner.

There was silence in the car as we rode back to the hotel. "Say something," Leslie finally said.

"What do you want me to say?"

"I saw a terrible movie," she said. "A bad movie, a dumb movie. I didn't believe a moment of it. And he just bought it, didn't he?"

"That's the conclusion I drew."

"Who's going to see it? I mean, *what is it?*"

My wife, indeed, had a point. *Oxford Blues* was a cinematic oddity. Not funny enough to be a comedy, not affecting enough for a love story, too "creaky" to pass itself off as an American "coming-of-age" film, this was clearly a film with an identity crisis.

Robert Boris, the clever young American writer-director, had done a creditable job in mounting his film, especially since this was his first directing stint, but he'd clearly had a lot of problems to overcome. First, the film had been shot on the proverbial shoestring. The uneven performances suggested a lack of coverage. Crowd scenes had a familiar shot-on-the-run quality. Some of the material, at least in this cut of the film, simply didn't match. Moreover, the Las Vegas section of the story was sketchy in the extreme. There was no time to flesh out the Rob Lowe character or suggest his backstory.

Elliott Kastner, the producer of *Oxford Blues*, was a maverick filmmaker with a history of ventures of this sort. A stooped, rumpled, wizened little man, Kastner had a reputation in the industry for coming up with deals that were far more intriguing than his movies. Though over the years he'd produced a couple of high-profile films such as *Missouri Breaks*, the Brando film directed by Arthur Penn, he'd also proven remarkably adept at funding obscure films that failed to find audiences.

"Let's try to steer the conversation to some other topic," my wife suggested, as we pulled up to Langan's Brasserie, the popular London hangout for the entertainment industry where we were to meet Yablans.

Even as we entered the restaurant, we could tell that the evening was not getting off to a propitious start. There was a solid clot of trendy-looking types awaiting their tables, but Yablans and Hotchner were at the front. I saw Yablans slip a large bill into the maître d's hand. The maître d' then signaled the captain, who started to lead them up the stairs toward the mezzanine.

No sooner had they taken a few steps then we saw Hotchner's hand clamp down on the captain's shoulder.

"Where do you think you're taking us?" she demanded.

"To a table, *madame*," came the officious reply.

"No," corrected Hotchner, "to the balcony."

"A table on the mezzanine, *madame*."

"You are taking the president of Metro-Goldwyn-Mayer to the fucking balcony," Hotchner advised, articulating her words carefully, "and that won't do."

The captain stared at her, clearly unprepared for this direct onslaught. Yablans himself stood at the bottom of the stairs, scrutinizing the main floor for a table, as though not listening.

"Allow me a moment, *madame*," the captain said, retreating to the refuge of the maître d's desk. He burst out of the huddle a few seconds later, giving Hotchner a quick signal to follow him to the one empty table on the main floor—a table, perhaps, that had been reserved for another party who would now languish in the Siberia of the mezzanine.

The moment we were seated, the look of annoyance disappeared from their faces. In their minds, the incident had been forgotten, the maître d' had been another minor obstacle to be dispensed with. Indeed, the conversation at dinner was downright jovial. Yablans's rapier wit was directed at a variety of topics, ranging from studio politics to the British aristocracy. Hotchner, too, was funny and insightful.

Inevitably, however, the conversation drifted back to *Oxford Blues*. Our disagreements were candidly stated. Yablans and Hotchner both thought the film delightful. Leslie and I both found it lacking. The assessments couldn't have been more divergent.

The only touch of rancor occurred on the issue of cost. Yablans vehemently disputed my suggestion that it looked like a "cheapie." "They couldn't have spent more than two million, Frank," I guessed.

Yablans disagreed. In his view, it was a well-crafted film—"a rich-looking film," he said.

I cited specific scenes that looked to me like "cheats." Yablans felt my analysis was hypercritical.

Eager to change the subject, Leslie lifted her glass and drank a quick toast to "all those Rob Lowe fans who will make it a hit." Everyone seconded the motion.

The following day, my curiosity piqued, I placed a few calls in an effort to find out how much *Oxford Blues* really cost. The information, I felt, would be useful in framing an appropriate deal.

The network of production managers in London is a tight one, and, within hours, I had in my hotel room what was described to me as the top sheet of the budget. The totals confirmed my suspicions. The film had cost slightly over one million pounds below the line—that is, the actual cost of shooting the film. This translated to about $1.5 million at the 1983 exchange rate. The above-the-line, which included such items as cast and director, came to the equivalent of $250,000, but this did not include fees for the producer and the financing. Hence, according to the production manager, the film cost slightly under $1.8 million.

By the time I'd received the budget, Yablans had already flown on to New York, which was also scheduled to be my next destination. Ileen Maisel, Yablans's assistant, was also in New York at the time, and in reviewing a variety of subjects, I mentioned to her in passing to remind Yablans that I had come up with the *Oxford Blues* budget. Within an hour, an ominous message awaited me at the hotel. Frank Yablans wanted to see me urgently and immediately.

Yablans made no effort to mask his anger when I arrived at his suite at the Carlyle. It was a military-style interrogation.

"How long have you been in possession of this budget?"

"I received it the last day in London."

"And why did you not bring it to my immediate attention?"

"Because I knew I was going to see you in New York."

"Why did you decide to search for the budget?"

"*Search?* Hey, we're not talking Scotland Yard here! I made a couple of phone calls...."

"And then you found it, but decided to conceal it from me?"

"Why are you making a federal case ...?"

"Because we're talking about loyalty here...."

I looked at Yablans, aghast. I took the top sheet and placed it atop his coffee table.

"Here it is," I said. "Do with it as you see fit."

"That will be all," he said.

"We have an agenda of urgent business to discuss."

"That will be all," he repeated.

I left his suite angry and perplexed. Clearly, I had touched a raw nerve with *Oxford Blues,* but the nuances of the situation still eluded me. I found it hard to believe that this whole issue rested on a matter of pride—that Yablans was incensed because he'd overestimated the cost of the film. What difference did it make? If he still wanted to acquire the picture for distribution, he could adjust the price accordingly. We'd get a cheaper deal.

Returning to California, I managed to put *Oxford Blues* out of my mind. Four days later, however, while sifting through mail that had accumulated during my travels, I found wedged in among the deal memos an inter-office memorandum to Karla Davidson, the studio's chief attorney, from Dean Stolber, the company's astute executive vice-president. I glanced at the memo, started to put it aside, and then began reading carefully.

Its contents were, to say the least, surprising. According to the deal memo, MGM had acquired domestic distribution rights to *Oxford Blues* for a cash price of $6 million. The producer, Elliott Kastner, would also receive 60 percent of all net profits from the film.

Another page was stapled to the initial deal memo. It was dated the following day, but was intended as an addendum. It stated that an additional $1 million would be paid to Kastner "as a deferred pick-up price, which sum shall be payable at a time and in a manner to be determined in the sole discretion of Frank Yablans."

This was an extraordinary provision for a deal such as this— indeed, for any deal. Kastner had not only made a windfall in the sale of his picture, but one day later had been awarded a $1 million deferment—and only Frank Yablans could determine when and how it could be paid.

It's very rare for a producer to get all his money back prior to release, and from a single source. Kastner himself had been offering *Oxford Blues* to other companies for less money—Richard Berger at Disney had been offered the project for $4 million. Even *Crocodile Dundee,* the most successful pickup of all time, was acquired for a modest advance that by no means covered its cost of production.

The entire transaction was also unique in terms of the apparent alacrity with which it had been implemented. Given the leisurely ways of the business-affairs functionaries, deals of this sort often meander through the layers of bureaucracy for weeks, if not months. *Oxford Blues* had been stamped for quick attention.

So quick, in fact, that the business-affairs executives had never even seen a budget of the film. Elliott Kastner had notified the deal-makers that the film had cost $6 million dollars to make, exclusive of his fee. When asked for documentation, he declined. When presented with a memo certifying the cost, he replied that he never signed memos of this sort.

Another person who had never seen a budget was the director, Robert Boris. In the case of most films, a director helps prepare a budget and then is asked to sign it. In the case of Boris, however, no such request had ever been made. Indeed, numbers were mentioned to him only once, and that was during his initial meeting with his producer. At that time, Kastner had told him that he had between $2 million and $3 million at his disposal in England to finance a movie. "Do you have anything I can make at that price?" Kastner had asked him. Boris had thought about it, then suggested the *Oxford Blues* story line. Kastner had reacted positively to the idea and paid Boris to develop it.

When the script was completed, Kastner read it and approved it. The project, he felt, could be delivered for his target price. From that time on, Boris never saw a budget or discussed cost.

On several occasions during the thirty-day shoot, Kastner had asked Boris to cut a few scenes together that he could show to potential investors—backers who could "take him out."

Boris, during this period, had kept pressuring his producer for additional shooting time. He especially wanted more scenes in Las Vegas, which would serve to amplify the Rob Lowe character, but Kastner had turned him down. Though potential backers had liked bits and pieces of the film, he'd replied, no one had been willing to write "the big check."

No one, that is, until Frank Yablans came along. By that time, of course, the movie was long since finished, and Boris had delivered his cut.

Now that "the big check" had been written and cashed, the MGM/UA establishment seemed anxious to get the incident behind them. The day after seeing the deal memo, I encountered Frank Davis, chief of business affairs, emerging from the commissary.

"Frank," I started, "about *Oxford Blues*..."

Before I could say anything more, an enigmatic half-smile creased his face. It was a smile that had become well known at the studio over a period of twenty years; it was known as the "hear-no-evil, speak-no-evil" smile.

"You've seen the deal memo, I take it," I said.

Davis nodded and said nothing.

"You've been here a long time," I continued. "Have you ever seen one like it?"

Davis peered at me gravely. "Life at MGM," he proclaimed, "is a process of continuous education." And with that, he strolled off, smiling once again.

Though *Oxford Blues* officially disappeared from the agenda of issues to discuss at MGM/UA, the subject continued to intrude itself from time to time in subsequent months and years. As Frank Yablans's critics on the executive committee intensified their pressure, the *Oxford Blues* transaction was reviewed once again, and the matter was turned over to Kerkorian's friend Greg Bautzer for scrutiny. Upon studying the details of the transaction, Bautzer's recommendation was that the entire question be turned over to the District Attorney's Office for investigation.

Bautzer also proposed that the D.A. probe charges that had been made concerning the Dino De Laurentiis deal—charges that *The Wall Street Journal* was also investigating as part of a planned story on Yablans and MGM/UA. The *Journal* had hired an investigator to look up the property records to the house in Tuscany occupied by Yablans and Hotchner, but had found that while records of other houses in the region were readily available, this particular house appeared to be uniquely anonymous. While emphasizing that they were not drawing any conclusions or inferring culpability, the *Journal*'s reporters had asked Bautzer for comment.

The irascible Bautzer, who'd once been a supporter of Yablans, made it quite clear that he'd disapproved of Yablans's performance. While declining to speak "on the record," he confirmed to the reporters that if he had his way, the district attorney would soon be looking into all these matters.

Indeed, Bautzer soon got his way. Even Kirk Kerkorian, while dreading the glare of publicity that could result from actions of this sort, supported the notion that the issue would have to be brought to the attention of the proper authorities.

The District Attorney's Office was not quite so obliging, however. Those officials charged with looking into "white-collar crimes" stated that they were so backed up with cases involving far greater sums of money that they could not deal with the MGM/UA case at this time. Not unless MGM/UA wanted to press charges, that is.

The company mulled its options, then decided not to push the matter further—a decision that sat well with Frank Yablans. The only reason he'd made the *Oxford Blues* deal to begin with, he insisted, was in response to his company's desperate need for product. "We needed the damn picture," Yablans told friends, acknowledging nonetheless that the deal represented "the biggest embarrassment of my career." It was a mistake—an innocent mistake, he insisted.

The box-office returns did not ease his embarrassment. The film opened on August 24, 1984, to bad reviews and weak business, bringing in only $2.4 million during its initial week of release in 1,075 theaters.

In subsequent years, Elliott Kastner continued to contact MGM/UA to request the final million dollars mentioned in the addendum to his deal. The million dollars was supposedly intended for him, he reminded everyone, but what had happened to it? No one could answer him.

Though the *Oxford Blues* incident had been officially buried at MGM/UA, it nonetheless helped resolve an important question in my mind. I had to get out. And the sooner, the better.

When I confided this intention to three or four friends and advisers, the uniformity of their response surprised me. "What took you so long?" was the oft-repeated question. I had clearly fallen out of favor with the regime, and the regime had fallen out of favor with the community. It seemed to be unanimous all the way around.

In the movie business, there are three ways to engineer one's departure. One can unfurl one's "golden parachute," and depart with salary and benefits intact. Unfortunately, my contract contained no such parachute. Second, one can simply walk away clean, which provides both emotional satisfaction and financial impoverishment.

I decided on the third course, which is to orchestrate an "exit picture." The idea was to have my contract assigned to a specific film, attaching myself as co-producer. I thus fulfill my contract, but in a different capacity.

The next film scheduled to start production was *Youngblood*, starring Patrick Swayze and, ironically, Rob Lowe. In this case, Lowe would play not a Las Vegas hustler, but rather a talented young hockey star getting his start on the junior hockey circuit. This was still, to be sure, a "reach" for Lowe, but at least he wouldn't have to win any debates at Oxford. The director of *Youngblood* was a bright young documentary filmmaker named Peter Markle, who would, I felt, be a delight to work with.

With this scenario in place, I informed Yablans's office that I wanted a meeting. Usually, this results in a summons to his office, but in this case he soon appeared in mine. He looked tired and dispirited.

"What's up?"

"Frank, I feel a bit out of synch with the way things are going around here, as I think you know...."

"Like what?..."

I drew a breath. "I had a teacher who used to tell me, 'Don't give me the facts, give me the truth.'"

"What's that supposed to mean?"

"It means I don't want to debate the facts with you. I just want to tell you the truth, which is that I want out."

"I think you need a shrink...."

"I don't think that's a suitable response....I have a year to go on my contract. I would like to co-produce *Youngblood*..."

"That's it? Just like *that?*"

"Look, Frank, we've logged a few miles together. I'd hoped all this would turn out better—"

"I'll have business affairs work it out," he cut in. "How much time?"

"That's up to you, of course. My experience has always been the sooner, the better."

"Business affairs will work it out," he said.

He was poised at the door now.

"We should have done better, Frank. Both of us. We should've been able to turn things around."

"Not here," Yablans said softly. "Not this fucking place..."

He wheeled suddenly and was out the door, slamming it behind him. My odyssey at MGM/UA had come to an end.

CHAPTER THIRTEEN

■

DEMOLITION DERBY
1984

IT would all come down to the numbers. Frank Yablans had understood that from the start. The pictures would have to stand on their own. After all the pontificating in the boardroom, all the posturing at Morton's, all the negotiating and position taking at CAA and ICM, the final verdict would be cast by the kids in the suburban shopping malls.

By Christmas of 1984, the verdict on MGM/UA had begun to look discouraging. Films like *The Pope of Greenwich Village, The Aviator, Until September, Garbo Talks, Electric Dreams,* and *Martin's Day* had already been written off as box-office failures. *Teachers* had registered a respectable but unexciting $15 million in domestic rentals. Marketing tests on two films, *O.C. & Stiggs* and *Movers and Shakers* had been so disappointing that their release had been indefinitely postponed. Even more shocking, *Mrs. Soffel* had also been added to the list of projects that were "on the shelf."

The much-heralded *Red Dawn* had miraculously been completed in time for its August 10 release date and had opened in a huge number of theaters—some 1,822. The strategy was to pull in as wide an audience as possible before the reviews came out, and it proved successful. The film grossed an excellent $8.2 million on its opening weekend. But the combination of damning reviews and unenthusiastic word of mouth quickly plunged the numbers into a tailspin and, by Labor Day, projections had been downgraded to about $18 million in domestic rentals (the film had finally come in at a cost of $19 million).

Yablans and General Haig had dreamed of catching a right-wing wave and riding it blissfully to shore, but the wave never came, either in the United States or Europe. Indeed, Europeans seemed more frightened than entertained by images of a Russian-occupied United States, and critics were thoroughly alienated by the entire exercise.

The failure of *Red Dawn* to live up to its lofty expectations stepped up the pressure on *2010*, which had been assigned the prized Christmas release date. Unless *2010* could establish itself as a certified hit, the box-office totals achieved by Yablans would not even match the levels of the Begelman years.

Given the importance of *2010*, Yablans had appropriated a grandiose war chest of $16 million to open the picture, and he personally presided over most marketing meetings, grilling the executives in charge of each phase of the campaign. "I've never seen anything like this," a perspiring Irv Ivers confessed to colleagues after one marathon session. "It's like Hitler in his bunker." Ivers, who'd been personally recruited by Yablans as president of worldwide marketing, began to look like a man suffering from a terminal illness. When Rothman asked how he was feeling, the normally mild-mannered Ivers turned on him and snapped, "Once we open this picture, I'm never going to work for Frank Yablans again as long as I live."

Though the echelons of advertising and publicity men were performing yeoman service, a pervasive sense of doom hung over the department. "It's such a cold goddamn picture," blurted one of the senior advertising men after the first screening. "It's my picture, and even I couldn't get involved in it." Nonetheless, the official "party line" was that the film was nothing short of immortal, worthy of the massive ad campaign and the posh London opening, replete with royalty, etc.

On December 7, 1984, the studio took on the trappings of a campaign headquarters the night of the presidential election. Teams of technicians stood by to analyze incoming data and review the results of exit polls. The reception accorded *2010*, everyone realized, would determine whether the present regime would remain in office, or would be swept to oblivion.

The initial weekend was heartening. Opening wide in 1,126 theaters, the film took in $7.4 million for an average of $6,500 per screen—not a sensational opening by industry standards, but vigorous nonetheless. By the end of the first week, the total had risen to $12.1 million, and the second week brought a decline of only 16 percent.

Back in the bunker, these portents prompted conflicting interpretations. Frank Yablans was now confidently projecting a huge hit; subordinates analyzing the exit polls were bearish. Audiences respected the movie, but didn't find it particularly entertaining, they reported ruefully.

Kirk Kerkorian's reaction to the opening was, as usual, down-to-earth. He had already started interviewing Frank Yablans's potential replacements.

"What do you think *2010* will end up doing?" Kerkorian asked one candidate for the job several days after the opening.

"I figure about twenty million domestic," was the response.

"I don't get it," Kerkorian replied. "This morning, Yablans told me it would hit a hundred million dollars in the United States."

"He must be seeing some numbers the rest of us don't see," came the discreet reply.

Within three weeks, however, even Yablans was ready to concede that *2010* would do only slightly better than *Red Dawn*. Indeed, the company's "numbers crunchers" were already at work calculating the devastating impact of this news. Projections for the next quarter, ending February 28, 1985, would show a 24 percent decline in revenues from the previous year, resulting in an alarming $82.2 million loss.

MGM/UA was hemorrhaging once again. Indeed, Kerkorian's advisers were now urging him to take a series of stern actions that he had till now fiercely resisted—firing Yablans (who had drawn down $981,000 in pay that year), taking massive write-offs on Yablans's losing films, and publicly disclosing that the Yablans regime had cost the company some $250 million in losses.

Kerkorian balked. Reluctant, as always, to pin the blame on any individual, Kerkorian didn't want to make Yablans his "fall guy." "He'd done his best," Kerkorian told his advisers.

Kerkorian recalled, too, that Yablans himself had advocated taking write-offs on the Begelman films only two years earlier, but Kerkorian had vetoed the move, arguing that it would limit the company's borrowing ability.

While halfheartedly defending his production chief, Kerkorian nonetheless harbored a festering resentment over the grand promises Yablans had given him—a repeat of the "cons" perpetuated by previous production chiefs. Kerkorian was observing the soaring results achieved by competitive entertainment companies such as Paramount and Warner Bros. And now, yet another budding success had appeared on the horizon—the Walt Disney Company, under its new regime headed by Michael Eisner, Frank Wells, and Jeff Katzenberg, was already bursting with activity. Yet Kerkorian, who owned two of the proudest logos in the industry, MGM and UA, was still dead in the water.

Kerkorian's interest in the Disney turnaround was far from academic. In the early 1980's, Disney had fallen into a corporate torpor under the management of Walt Disney's son-in-law, Ronald W. Miller. In mid-1984, however, Kerkorian had decided to throw his weight behind a raid on Disney. Saul J. Steinberg, the porcine chief of Reliance Insurance Company, had made a tender offer at $72.50 a share (within three years, shares would be selling at over $370). Kerkorian had quietly struck a bargain with Steinberg under which, if the raid succeeded, Kerkorian would buy the Disney film production business for $447.5 million. (Steinberg's tender offer for 49 percent of Disney stock aggregated out at some $325 million.)

As it turned out, the Steinberg raid quickly atrophied, but Steinberg realized a handsome gain. Disney directors voted to pay him some $59 million to go away—an award that was promptly called "greenmail" by stockholders. The stockholders filed a class-action suit against Steinberg, against the ubiquitous Drexel Burnham Lambert, which functioned as his adviser, and against the entire Disney board of directors.

Stung and confused by these various setbacks, Kerkorian responded with his customary whirlwind of financial maneuvers. He announced yet again that MGM/UA would be transformed into a privately owned entity. Then he changed his mind. He increased his stake in MGM Grand Hotels from 50 percent to 70 percent, and proposed that MGM/UA buy back the 15 percent interest held by public shareholders in MGM/UA Home Entertainment. The latter move prompted a lawsuit from Sumner Redstone, a major power player in the entertainment industry, who charged that Kerkorian had deliberately concealed an earlier offer that was considerably higher than the announced price.

Kerkorian chose this time of chaotic maneuvering to come forward with his newest recruit to take over the production reins of his company—forty-eight-year-old Alan Ladd, Jr. There were two things Kerkorian found especially appealing about Ladd. First, after two masters of self-promotion—Begelman and Yablans—

Ladd's understated, self-effacing style seemed a therapeutic relief. Second, Ladd's was one of the few Hollywood names that carried weight in the investment-banking community.

"Laddie," as he was known to the trade, was the man who had given a green light to *Star Wars* when he headed Twentieth Century-Fox. Later, running the Ladd Company, which distributed through Warner Bros., he had fostered *The Right Stuff* and *Police Academy*.

Though his father had been a celebrated star in Hollywood's golden era (he had appeared in MGM's *The Badlanders* as late as 1958), Laddie did not fit the stereotype of the "movie brat." He was, for one thing, scrupulously polite. He regularly uttered curious phrases like "thank you" and "please," rarely heard in Hollywood's executive suites. In contrast to Yablans's bombast, Ladd spoke so softly visitors had to lean toward him, straining to pick up his phrases. His succinctness gave birth to myriad anecdotes. One aggressive producer-director realized after a meeting that he had "pitched" his project for a full hour, during which Ladd had uttered only a single but conclusive word: "No."

Yablans was in New York when he learned of the Ladd appointment and rushed back to Culver City to try to salvage his job. He was greeted by a surprise, however. According to Rothman's assurances, Yablans would not be replaced by Ladd, after all. Instead, he and Ladd would serve as co-equals, Yablans at MGM and Ladd at UA, both reporting to Rothman. Indeed, Yablans was even promised an extension of his contract and a $250,000 annual raise if he would stay on under the new arrangement.

From the outset, the new structure exhibited stresses and strains. Irrespective of the cheery announcements, producers and agents assumed Ladd was the new power in Culver City, and channeled their attention accordingly. Several key Yablans executives surreptitiously arranged meetings with Ladd, soliciting jobs at UA. Ladd, meanwhile, was hiring the nucleus of his own team, consisting of Jay Kanter, Richard Berger, and John Goldwyn.

Only six weeks after the new structure was announced, Rothman suddenly declared that he didn't think it was working. On March 14, 1985, Frank Yablans announced his departure, thanking colleagues for their support, pointing with pride to the company's achievements and saying all the polite things to disguise his underlying bitterness. A day later, Alan Ladd, Jr., was confirmed as president and chief operating officer at MGM/UA. Serving under Ladd, Kanter would nominally head MGM and Berger UA, but the implication now was that the company would once again be unified.

Ladd had won the day, but he had no illusions about the problems facing him. Though two sequels, *Rocky IV* and *Poltergeist II*, were in preproduction, he was appalled by the quality of the other Yablans projects in development.

Indeed, one hundred properties were quickly put in turnaround, representing an investment in the millions. (They may have been too hasty about one of them: *Dirty Dancing*, developed by Linda Gottlieb at MGM/UA, as mentioned earlier, would become the biggest hit in Vestron's history.)

Ladd and his associates, concerned with the task of maintaining a continuum of product, had assumed that the flow of submissions would start to rise once again, but, contrary to their expectations, the phones at the studio had grown oddly still.

The reason: Rumors were rampant on Wall Street that MGM/UA once again was "in play." According to the insiders, Kerkorian had started active conversations with several potential buyers for MGM, UA or both. The buyers encompassed a wide range of people and institutions—an Arab, a Dutch conglomerate, etc.

For Ladd, the For Sale sign represented a major obstacle. The top talent he was courting would have no interest in making a film for a company that was about to be sold. Too many filmmakers had gone through the nightmare of starting a film under one management, only to find another, unsympathetic regime charged with the responsibility for marketing it.

To add to Ladd's woes, word was leaking out that Kerkorian, always the tough Vegas game-player, was determined to get "his price," even if it took years. For Kerkorian, this represented a once-in-a-lifetime deal. Though sick and tired of staring at red ink, Kerkorian was nonetheless convinced that the asset value represented by the combined MGM and UA libraries had reached cosmic levels and that someone would step up and pay the price. "Kirk became obsessed with the notion that there was a sucker out there," recalled one aide. "He knew it in his gut."

Faced with Kerkorian's hard bargaining, however, the prospective buyers one by one faded away—the Arabs, the Dutch, even a few interested Japanese. The landscape, which had once looked so promising, suddenly seemed bleak.

And then along came Ted Turner.

Ted Turner never liked being thought of as a conventional man of commerce. "I am an adventurer, not a businessman," he will casually tell a visitor, adding that he did not set out to be "a Donald

Trump." Sir Francis Drake and Magellan were his role models. "I am happiest when I am on the edge," confides Turner, a twinkle in his eye.

Over the years, skeptics have dismissed this kind of talk as hyperbole. Ted Turner, old friends concede, has a need to dramatize himself, to make himself larger than life. In point of fact, Turner was a rich man's son; family money and family contacts provided the cornerstones of his success.

Perhaps to confound these doubters, Turner in 1985 abandoned the conventions of prudent business behavior and, in effect, blasted off into outer space. For a year, he was like an out-of-control comet, careening between constellations of money and power.

No one knows precisely what triggered this blast-off. Some attribute it to psychological aberration; some relate it to the incipient stagnation that was afflicting many of his favorite enterprises. His cherished baseball team, the Atlanta Braves, were mired in mediocrity. His Atlanta superstation, whose programs are relayed via satellite, was suffering a profits squeeze; advertising revenues were not keeping pace with fast-rising movie fees. Indeed, some movie distributors, such as MGM, were refusing to sell films to Turner at any price.

Whatever the cause, Ted Turner concluded early in 1985 that the major networks and distributors were trying to put the squeeze on him, and he started to wonder, What would Magellan or Sir Francis Drake have done in such a situation?

One answer, Turner felt, was to launch an assault on that sanctum sanctorum of media power, CBS. By any standard, it was an astonishing foray—a classic business scenario of the minnow trying to swallow the whale. But even as Turner was announcing his offer and marshaling his allies, William Paley, the baronial figure who founded CBS and still presided over its affairs in times of emergency, snuffed out the uprising as a feudal lord would quell the rebellious serfs.

Less than a week after the CBS debacle, the dauntless buccaneer was circling around a less awe-inspiring but still formidable target—MGM/UA. Kirk Kerkorian, like Turner, had not been having much success operating his company lately, and, like Turner, he was a dealing man. Most important, MGM/UA had a treasure trove of movies, some thirty-five hundred of them, embracing not only the studio's own product but old RKO films and pre-1950 Warner Bros. films as well. And it also had *Gone With the Wind*, Ted Turner's favorite. To Turner, a southern boy, he was not just buying another company—he was buying Tara.

And he wanted it with a passion. The fact that there were certain obvious obstacles did not alarm him. For one thing, the assets of Turner's broadcasting and sports empire aggregated a mere $354 million, and Kerkorian would surely ask over $1 billion. MGM/UA might not be CBS, but it was still a Goliath to Turner's David. Moreover, advisers warned him of the dismal lineup of films the studio was about to release. It was not a list that would assure a strong cash flow once Turner had taken control.

These arguments may have had weight, but would Magellan have turned back in uncharted waters? No! Turner was determined to hold firm to his course.

From his very first meeting with Kerkorian, Turner knew that, as he put it, he had gone "sailboat racing in a hurricane." Kerkorian's price was a staggering $1.5 billion, and he didn't intend to spend the whole summer talking about it. What it all boiled down to was Turner's willingness to pay twenty-eight dollars a share for MGM stock that was actually selling at nine dollars—a considerable leap of faith.

Wherever he turned, friends and advisers told him not to make this deal. "Kerkorian is trying to give you the biggest screwing in the history of American business," a top associate warned. Industry seers recruited in Hollywood, such as attorney Ken Ziffren, also judged the price too high. Their objections focused on simple mathematics. Combined earnings of Turner and MGM/UA would optimistically total about $200 million a year, yet the aggregate payments to service the debt would come to three times that amount.

Turner, as Kerkorian would soon learn, had evolved his own scenario for bridging this gap. Two weeks after negotiations had commenced, the forty-seven-year-old Georgian found himself seated at his desk, signing the six hundred documents that constituted the purchase agreement. What looked like a sale, however, was in fact a short-term lease. No sooner had Turner signed the documents than he was on the phone to ask Kerkorian for a small favor. The negotiations had taken place so quickly, he said, that his people had not really had time to review the books. Could he send a "a couple of men" to study the numbers? Kerkorian said yes, and Turner promptly dispatched a forty-man team of accountants and attorneys to complete his "due diligence."

What they found was not encouraging. For one thing, even as the negotiations were in progress, the management of MGM/UA had committed a bizarre faux pas that had compromised the value of the library. Stealing a page from Mel Brooks's comedy *The Pro-*

ducers, what the company had effectively done was to sell its pay-TV rights twice. Moreover, the deal with the second buyer, a program distributor called Rainbow Service Company, prohibited MGM/UA films from being shown on many cable TV stations— among them Ted Turner's WTBS! Kerkorian was hard put to explain these contractual errors, since his chief executive, Frank Rothman, was himself a lawyer. Indeed, MGM/UA's legal fees to Rothman's old law firm totaled $1.5 million a year. The studio would now have to foot $35 million of the $50 million settlement needed to extricate itself from the Rainbow deal.

While the Turner and the MGM/UA attorneys were fencing over these glitches, Turner himself was coming to terms with a more urgent issue. Drexel Burnham Lambert informed Turner that it was having trouble finding buyers for the junk bonds Turner hoped would finance the MGM acquisition. The investment-banking firm had pulled the rabbit out of the hat for MGM/UA once before when it sold some $400 million in junk bonds, but apparently it couldn't do it again. Its efforts were being undermined by the release of one bomb after another—*Marie, 9½ Weeks, Dream Lover,* and *Fever* were the latest disasters. (*Fever* was directed by Richard Brooks and produced by Freddie Fields, the team that had misfired on *Road Show.*) With a $26 million loss forecast by MGM/UA for the next quarter, the investment-banking firm was fighting too strong a tide.

Ted Turner was starting to sink beneath the waves, and the person who had the biggest stake in keeping him afloat was Kirk Kerkorian. The old trader knew he had made a good deal—too good a deal, in fact. Now it was time to hammer out some adjustments—perhaps a small change in the scenario could bring about the same happy ending. With this objective in mind, the following was put on the table: Turner would buy MGM/UA for $1.5 billion, plus assume certain MGM debt, Kerkorian would in turn buy back UA for some $480 million. This would greatly relieve Turner's burden, and he would be free to cushion the deal still further by selling off other assets. Kerkorian, meanwhile, was already laying plans to take UA public as a separate company.

Now the deal was starting to make sense both to Kerkorian and to Turner. To Alan Ladd, Jr., however, who had been watching from the sidelines, it was becoming a fiasco. He had learned that Turner was already in negotiation with Viacom and with the two Israeli cousins, Menahem Golan and Yoram Globus, to sell them half of MGM's production and video operations for $225 million. To Ladd, the message was clear. This was no longer a corporate acquisition; this was a demolition derby. He petitioned both

Turner and Kerkorian to sit down one more time and try to evolve a deal that would keep the production company intact.

Responding to these pleas, Turner and Kerkorian now arrived at yet another permutation. Kerkorian would buy back UA, and would also pay another $300 million for the MGM logo. Hence, months after the negotiation had started, the MGM and UA names would once again be united.

As far as Ted Turner was concerned, he was now left with the library of films—his main target to begin with—plus the historic forty-four-acre studio in Culver City. Turner quickly found a buyer for the studio—its prime tenant, Lorimar-Telepictures, which paid some $190 million for the facility.

Turner had thus managed to ride out the hurricane in his stalwart sailboat—but barely. He had realized his dream of owning MGM, but had managed to hold on to it for a mere seventy-four days. In that brief period, he hadn't had time to green-light a single film, but he'd come close. He had put his okay on a pickup of an Australian picture called *Crocodile Dundee*, which had been offered to the studio for distribution. Turner and Ladd had both liked the film. The Australian producers, however, were worried about MGM's financial instability. They decided to reject MGM's offer and instead take a lesser offer from Paramount.

Had Ted Turner succeeded in closing that one deal, the proceeds from *Crocodile Dundee* alone would have turned his company around.

Turner had to swallow another bitter pill, as well. As a result of the added debt assumed by Turner Broadcasting, he would no longer wield sole operating control over the company. There would instead be rule by committee.

Kerkorian, too, was tallying up his gains and losses. By paying back $780 million to Ted Turner, he'd been able to keep UA and MGM, but both companies had effectively become corporate shells. It would take hundreds of millions of dollars to levitate them once again.

Kerkorian clearly had the capital, if he wanted to spend it. Not only had he reaped hundreds of millions of dollars from the Turner deal, but he'd also, along the way, sold off the lion's share of his hotel and casino holdings for some $286 million—a sum that, according to aides, was less than he'd hoped for, but still a considerable amount of money.

In addition, Kerkorian personally had realized an astonishing paper profit of over $150 million during the first two days of trading of his newly listed UA stock. The public demand for the stock was a source of private amusement to Kerkorian's aides, who had worked feverishly over the previous weeks to dream up a balance sheet, assign assets, and basically invent a new company. Indeed, the arbitrariness of their actions helped trigger a class-action law-suit alleging that Kerkorian had schemed against the interests of his public shareholders to end up with more than 80 percent of the new UA for himself. According to the suit, Kerkorian had understated the true value of UA to discourage his old shareholders from buying their fair share of the deal. Adding to the furor was a story in *Fortune* magazine, which estimated that Kerkorian had emerged from the maze of transactions with a fortune of well over $600 million, much of it liquid.

If Kerkorian's wealth was soaring, his credibility in the community had plummeted to an all-time low. Kerkorian had always been thought of as the "nice guy" who received bad advice. Now, suddenly, Kerkorian found himself portrayed as the "bad guy," and he wasn't happy about it. His aim from the start had been to sell MGM/UA as a whole, not break it up. That was done to accommodate Turner, and now Kerkorian was getting the blame. Second, Kerkorian had never wanted to end up with 80 percent of the new company—a company which he would have to keep afloat with his own money.

Having effectively hid from the press for many years, Kerkorian now began to wonder whether he shouldn't start presenting his case to the public. He even did what would have been unthinkable a few years earlier: He sought out the advice of a Hollywood publicist, Jim Mahoney, to discuss his concerns.

Though Kerkorian was now taking more than his fair share of criticism, the facts nonetheless spoke for themselves. The two once-great companies that had been under his stewardship had become mere logos.

MGM no longer had a studio, a library or any of the other components comprising a viable entertainment company. The new owners of the lot were already dismantling the immense, three-ton MGM sign atop the studio water tower and supplanting it with a new banner proclaiming Lorimar-Telepictures. (Since the studio was quickly sold yet again to Warner Bros., this sign, too, became an instant anachronism.)

There were other telltale reminders of MGM's now-lowly status. At a studio screening, the audience erupted in boos and hisses when they discovered that a new MGM logo had secretly been substituted for the old roar of Leo the Lion. The Latin motto, *Ars Gratia Artis*, also disappeared after sixty-one years. The motto, which translates as "Art for Art's Sake," had always been a curious conceit, but its disappearance at this particular moment in history seemed ominous.

The *Los Angeles Times* canvassed some of the MGM stars of the past to elicit their reaction to these sudden changes. "I feel like a part of me is gone," June Allyson confessed. "It makes me very sad."

"It's like they were tearing down the Statue of Liberty and putting up condos," commented Jackie Cooper.

Only Mickey Rooney took a more hardheaded view. He'd cried a decade before when Kerkorian had sold off half the back lot, he admitted, "but it's a little late to get sloppy and slobbery now."

Ted Turner seemed to agree. When a reporter asked him if he regretted participating in the dismemberment of the studio, he replied, "MGM died long before I came along."

As if to underscore this view, rows of dumpsters appeared one day behind the Thalberg Building, and they were quickly filled with files and papers. A film buff started sifting through the material and, to his amazement, found correspondence between Louis B. Mayer and many top stars of the thirties, along with other material of historic interest.

When asked why they hadn't contributed the material to the Academy of Motion Picture Arts and Sciences, or to other archivists, the Lorimar-Telepictures executives declined to reply. The past, they seemed to be saying, belonged in a dumpster.

Once Ted Turner had packed his bags and led his squad of lawyers and accountants back to Atlanta, show-business analysts sat down at their computers to figure out if he'd made such a bad deal after all.

Hollywood had dismissed him as a yokel and a megalomaniac—epithets he seemed to relish—but now some people had begun to wonder whether there had been an intriguing method to his madness. Turner was about to launch yet another important cable venture called TNT—Turner Network Television—for which the newly acquired films would be a pivotal asset. Given his usual gift for understatement, Turner estimated the actual value of films he'd acquired to be in excess of $1 billion, claiming they constituted "thirty-five percent of all the great movies ever made." This percentage was subject to interpretation, but Turner had, in fact, acquired some thirty-five hundred properties in all—"Turner's treasures," as he liked to call them, including, among other things, "every Ronnie Reagan movie ever made." Before making the deal, Turner confessed, he had never seen a Garbo film, but now he had watched them all. Moreover, he planned to rerelease movies like *Anna Karenina* and *Ninotchka* under a new process whereby the black-and-white films would be "colorized"—a prospect that affronted the lingering sensibilities of Hollywood artists.

Ownership of the films, Turner noted, would put him in an even stronger position because he would be able to distribute the films himself, rather than relying on middlemen. Though everyone had focused on his debts, Turner said, the time would come when they would instead start ogling his profits.

Turner's optimism was buttressed by the nation's top cable operators, who, realizing Turner's intrinsic importance to their industry, helped bail him out with some $568 million in new equity. Given this infusion, Turner's prognosis by mid-1989 seemed to be growing brighter. The company, which had been announcing losses quarter after quarter, suddenly was at break-even with revenues rising some 27 percent. And a key to the upbeat reports was the synergy between the new TNT and the MGM library.

Perhaps Ted Turner had landed his Tara after all.

Finding himself in control of UA once again, like someone discovering an unexpected present under his Christmas tree, Kerkorian decided that the company needed a dynamic new presence. It had been almost a decade since UA last had its own distinct identity. Clearly something dramatic had to be done to refurbish its image.

Kirk Kerkorian, it turned out, felt he had found just the man for the job, but, in his usual furtive manner, had not seen fit to tell anyone about him. One of the first to learn his identity was, coincidentally, Alan Ladd, Jr. He'd been watching a football game at the home of his old friend Guy McElwaine, the onetime ICM agent who had gone on to become head of production at Columbia Pictures after the Begelman scandals. About an hour into the game, the doorbell rang and in walked Jerry Weintraub.

A big, ebullient man with an overbearing presence, Weintraub was especially high-spirited this afternoon. The reason, he explained to his startled companions, was that he had just become Kirk Kerkorian's "partner" at United Artists.

Ladd and McElwaine exchanged a blank stare. "Partner," they

knew, was not a word in Kerkorian's vocabulary, but Weintraub was already busily explaining the new arrangement. Weintraub would invest some $30 million of his own money in the company. In return, UA would become his fiefdom. He would make all decisions—there would be no second-guessing from the executive committee or even from Kerkorian. "My partner," Weintraub reiterated, "has given me a free hand."

As word of the Weintraub appointment spread quickly through the industry over the next forty-eight hours, a variety of skeptical questions were raised. Would Weintraub's $30 million investment really qualify him as a "partner" in Kerkorian's eyes? Kerkorian's investment in the company, after all, would total in the hundreds of millions. Indeed, would Kerkorian ever grant anyone the sort of autonomy Weintraub now claimed—even a man who had put up his own money?

There was another question being asked, as well. Though everyone knew that Jerry Weintraub had made a lot of money in the entertainment business, did he really have $30 million in loose change to toss into a caper like this?

For his part, Kerkorian was, as usual, maintaining his invisibility, so no one could put these questions directly to him. As for the burly, hard-driving Weintraub, his responses were unswerving. "UA is mine," he explained succinctly, warning observers to buckle up for a thrill-packed ride.

Though many men might be wary about the ambiguities surrounding his new position, Jerry Charles Weintraub, age forty-nine, seemed to rejoice in them. Weintraub was, after all, a genuine Hollywood character. A son of the Bronx, and a graduate of the ubiquitous William Morris mail room, Weintraub looked upon the Hollywood power game as an existential exercise.

In the "real world" of business, he understood, power was obtained through money and privilege. In Hollywood, however, the key weapons were bluff and illusion. And Weintraub had become a master at wielding these weapons.

His mannerisms and life-style seemed to spill from the pages of *The Great Gatsby*. The vast parties at his Malibu estate, called Blue Heaven (San Simeon South, others dubbed it) were Gatsby-like in their opulence. Clad proudly in his two-thousand-dollar custom-made Brioni suits, a valet always at his elbow, poised to light his Havana, Weintraub presided over the swarms of strangers—some of them important strangers—who always seemed to overflow his grounds. And while not everyone would necessarily get to shake hands with the host, all would, at the very least, confront the life-sized portraits of Weintraub and his wife in stained glass that adorned the house. (In Weintraub's portrait, he is talking on the phone.)

As with Gatsby, there was something dangerous and mysterious about the details of his personal life. There were murmurs about his womanizing, his occasional outbursts of violence with colleagues and even with women. But the Jerry Weintraub who was on display at Blue Heaven was always controlled and convivial.

While Gatsby, however, was content to watch from the periphery, Weintraub compulsively had to be at the center of things—the center of wealth and power, the man who made and broke careers. There would be incessant references to his "close friend" George Bush, who occupied a neighboring summer house at Kennebunkport, Maine. Unlike Gatsby, Weintraub courted publicity, and his need for self-promotion often got out of hand. A story in the *Los Angeles Times*, for example, quoted him as reflecting: "When I try to sit back and look at what I've accomplished and what I've done, it's pretty awesome, you know? Pretty awesome."

In another interview he boasted: "I'm one of the richest people in the world." (Not according to *Forbes* magazine, however, which declines to list him among the four hundred wealthiest people in America.)

The son of a jewelry salesman, Weintraub fell in love with movies working as an usher at the Loew's Paradise, which was his neighborhood theater in the Bronx. After taking a stab at acting lessons, Weintraub launched himself into the gauntlet of show-biz entry-level jobs. He was successively an NBC page, then a flunky in the William Morris mail room, finally emerging as an apprentice agent at giant MCA, the monolith headed by Lew Wasserman.

An avidly impatient man, Weintraub quickly found ways to accelerate his climb. He married his first important client, singer Jane Morgan (whose family, old Maine residents, ultimately introduced him to Bush). Then he shifted into the more entrepreneurial and lucrative field of personal management. He was a proficient "signer," linking his fortunes to the soaring careers of Neil Diamond, John Denver, and the Beach Boys.

Weintraub's entry into film producing occurred through a fortuitous meeting with the iconoclastic director Robert Altman, after a John Denver concert in Carnegie Hall. Weintraub ended up co-producing *Nashville*, which Altman directed. From there, he went on to involve himself in an eclectic array of movies, such as *Oh,*

God!, Cruising, Diner, and, of course, *The Karate Kid,* the oddball hit that mixed the *Rocky* and Ninja formulas with a bit of New Age philosophizing.

The success of *Karate Kid* lent Weintraub the cachet to mingle with Hollywood's proprietary class; indeed, it fueled his ambition to become a member. Having briefly worked for Lew Wasserman, Weintraub now yearned to *become* Lew Wasserman. In his mind, he already had the key accoutrements: He had the contacts, he had his estate, he had his Rolls. Wherever he went, there was a coterie of butlers, D-girls, and other aides to smooth his way.

And now Kirk Kerkorian had come along to provide Gatsby his sultanate.

While Alan Ladd, Jr., was cautiously trying to regroup his forces in Culver City, Jerry Weintraub hurled himself into a frenzy of activity. "Jerry was determined to create an 'instant major,'" observed one aide. "He was going to do it overnight." It was as though his whole life had been a prelude to this moment.

At UA's handsome new offices in Beverly Hills, Weintraub assumed the role of a modern Medici, dispensing largess to his favored artistes. One filmmaker after another was ushered into Weintraub's lavish suite of offices, where wine and cheese were served by the omnipresent butler while Weintraub held court and listened to the pitches and entreaties. It was a sort of never-ending party—a Weintraub celebration.

And at the end of many meetings, Weintraub would smile grandly and say, "You've got yourself a deal." An aide from business affairs was then summoned to codify the proceedings, and everyone went away happy.

Recalls an executive at UA at that time: "As with many great salesmen, enthusiasm came naturally to Jerry. But unfortunately, Jerry had no idea how to run a company. He'd never run *anything* before. Only in the movie industry can a guy get himself appointed to manage a company who had never even run a grocery store."

Weintraub's operating style constituted a startling contrast to that of Alan Ladd, Jr., who remained in semi-exile in Culver City. While the taciturn Ladd disdained hyperbole, Weintraub had developed it to a high art. Ladd could trigger a $20 million picture in the same dull monotone others reserved for the weather report. By contrast, Weintraub could make someone being hired for a humble rewrite feel as though he'd just won a Pulitzer Prize.

While Ladd had customarily avoided announcements, Weintraub issued fusillades of press releases, and also peppered the trade papers with full-page ads bearing his name. "When people think of UA, I want them to think of Jerry Weintraub," he admonished his chief of advertising. "I *am* UA!"

On the charisma index, Weintraub was clearly leaving everyone in his dust. The buzz at Morton's was about UA and its "action." The big packages were being taken to Weintraub, and his dealings were ranging far and wide. One moment he would be closing a deal for Frank Sinatra to star in an American version of *La Cage aux Folles*. The next, he would be co-funding a concert film in Russia with Ted Turner.

Though some questioned his taste in projects, no one could refute the fact that Weintraub was signing up some formidable talent. He closed a mammoth Stallone deal, much broader than the one Frank Yablans had tried unsuccessfully to fight past his executive committee. He even managed to persuade the illustrious Billy Wilder to emerge from retirement yet again and become a sort of "elder statesman" at UA.

The seventy-nine-year-old Wilder, who had made some of his greatest films for UA, would now be afforded the opportunity not only to develop his own material, but also to guide young filmmakers through the difficult shoals of preproduction. Wilder was given a large office and, naturally, a press conference, with Jerry Weintraub presiding.

Soon Wilder was greeting stars and directors at Weintraub's side, spinning his colorful anecdotes and dispensing wisdom.

It was a disaster from the start. Wilder was appalled at the quality of the material Weintraub was acquiring. And when Weintraub would screen completed films with Wilder, the elegant but blunt-spoken old filmmaker would simply throw up his hands and advise that they were beyond redemption.

A case in point was a film called *Wise Guys*, which had been green-lighted in the waning days of the Yablans administration. Its director, Brian De Palma, had made some powerful thrillers in his time, but he was less sure-handed when it came to comedy.

After Weintraub and Wilder screened the film together, Weintraub turned to his newly anointed elder statesman for his suggestions. *"Suggestions?"* Wilder snorted. "What sort of suggestions?"

"Ideas to tighten the picture," Weintraub offered.

"This picture is a big pile of shit," Wilder shot back. "Perhaps I could tell you how to make it into a smaller pile of shit, but it would still be shit!"

Weintraub smiled a pained smile. He informed the old director that he thought he could prove him wrong.

Within weeks, the film opened to generally mediocre reviews and empty theaters.

Though his judgments were often skewed, Weintraub succeeded in conveying to filmmakers a sense of enthusiasm and supportiveness. Indeed, he occasionally admitted that he wished he could be at their side, participating more closely in the creative process. "If I hadn't decided to become Kirk's partner," he told one visitor, "I would have become a film director myself."

While filmmakers enjoyed these words of support, they winced at suggestions of intrusion. And word was starting to seep out about Weintraub's impulsive and unannounced expeditions to the editing room.

Coincidentally, the target of one of his earliest forays was the film called *Youngblood*, on which I had been working after my exit from the Yablans regime. I had spent eleven weeks in Toronto during the shoot, and had been pleased with the results. It was not the sort of film that would win awards at film festivals or that critics would compare to *Jules and Jim*. But it was a solid, well-crafted piece of filmmaking that had run up outstanding scores at audience previews.

Youngblood had been an "underdog" project from the start. At a time when studios were focusing their resources on $20 million or $30 million projects that could play the key summer dates, *Youngblood* was one of the few modestly budgeted films to squeeze through the system. It had two "comers" playing its leads, Rob Lowe and Patrick Swayze (who was shortly to make his big splash in *Dirty Dancing*). It had scope and action, yet its budget was still under $6 million—a bargain by current standards.

In genre, *Youngblood* was a "rite-of-passage" story. Its protagonist was a talented but poverty-bound young hockey player, who, desperate to make the ranks of the professionals, becomes embroiled in the brutal, atavistic world of Canadian junior hockey. To him, hockey was still a game; to those competing with him, however, the prospect of a pro career represented their lone opportunity to escape poverty and anonymity. They would claw and maim and do whatever else was necessary to climb to the top.

Peter Markle, the director, had himself survived the hockey wars, but had opted for Yale University rather than a career as a pro. He had wanted to shape his film as a gritty, realistic account of teenage blood lust—a sort of *Battle of Algiers* on ice. To reinforce the aura of realism, he had even hoped to cast a real hockey player in the lead.

Frank Yablans had other ideas. He would green-light the film on the proviso that Rob Lowe play the young hockey star. Both Markle and I swallowed hard over this notion. Though an obliging young actor, Lowe's talents clearly lay in light comedy rather than gritty action. He was, irrevocably, a "pretty boy."

Yablans steadfastly resisted Markle's pleas that he reconsider. Lowe, meanwhile, promised to practice his skating and to attend every hockey game in town. He even proposed to wear an artificial scar during the shoot to lend him a "tougher look." (The "scar," of course, failed to make him look tough; it just made him look like a pretty-boy-with-a-scar.)

Faced with the choice of making his film with Rob Lowe or not making it at all, Markle resigned himself to Lowe. He also set about to alter his screenplay to accommodate his young leading man, adding some lighter moments, heightening the romantic interludes, etc. He understood the risks: He was "softening" his picture, rubbing away the edges. He was waking up in the middle of the night, arguing with himself about the changes. But at least he was getting his picture made. That was a triumph by itself.

Having drastically altered the tone of the film, Yablans, of course, was not around to see the finished product. It was Alan Ladd, Jr., who attended the successful previews in Chicago and Dallas. When audiences turned in their preview cards, it was discovered that between 90 percent and 92 percent had rated the film either "very good" or "excellent." Ladd was elated, and so was Peter Markle. Strong previews usually motivate studios to spend more money on their advertising campaigns, and this, too, augured well for the picture.

There were, to be sure, some editing changes that Ladd felt would help the picture. He outlined the various cuts and trims to us after the second preview. We both agreed that they were thoughtful and constructive, and set the editor to work to implement the changes. Ladd was already discussing plans for the film's release. MGM/UA, as usual, did not have an abundance of product, and *Youngblood*, he felt, was "a sleeper."

An unexpected memo from the business-affairs department brought these plans to an abrupt halt, however. It seemed that no one had noticed that *Youngblood* had arbitrarily been designated a United Artists picture when Frank Yablans had approved it for production. At the time, this designation carried no significance whatsoever, since UA existed in name only.

With the appointment of Jerry Weintraub to head UA, however, all this carried ominous import. If *Youngblood* was going to carry "his" banner, Weintraub intoned, it would also have to bear his stamp.

To achieve this end, yet another screening was scheduled for Weintraub and his entourage. The group included several surprise guests, such as John Avildsen, who had directed *The Karate Kid*, and Bud Smith, who had edited that film. Also in attendance was Tony Thomopoulos, whom Weintraub had just recruited as president of his TV and movie operations. A former president of ABC Television, Thomopoulos, with his dark blue suit, his mane of white hair, and his zipped-up expression, still seemed more a network functionary than a movie executive.

The screening took on a festive atmosphere with the arrival of Weintraub's butler, who brought with him a variety of alcoholic beverages, including a huge pitcher of screwdrivers. As the screening progressed, Weintraub's manner grew increasingly boisterous, thanks to the refreshments. He and his coterie were exchanging a steady stream of banter. It was becoming less a screening than a party.

After final credits, Weintraub remained in his seat, discussing the film with his guests. Finally, he dispatched an aide to inform the director and producer that he would have no comment until the following morning at eleven.

The next day, Weintraub wasted no time with amenities. "I can make it better," he announced. "I know where it drags and I know where it moves." The job of "fixing" the picture would take a week, he advised. Bud Smith, the *Karate Kid* editor, had been hired to carry out the job. Weintraub planned to join Smith in the editing room and personally preside over the reediting.

Though Weintraub related all this as though he were doing both the picture and the filmmakers an enormous favor, Peter Markle looked anything but pleased. Indeed, he was sputtering indignant protests.

"You're going to *change the whole picture*?..." Markle demanded.

"I'm going to make it better," Weintraub said.

"It doesn't need to be better," Markle replied. "It needs to be left alone."

I reminded Weintraub that the film had been previewed twice to excellent results and that Ladd had made his suggestions before approving this version for release. Weintraub would thus be the third studio chief to have his input. Weintraub was not swayed. The picture needed work, he reiterated. Once his changes had been completed, he would hold yet another preview. If the results did not equal or surpass those of the earlier previews, he would, if we so desired, return the film to its original form and release it that way. Having delivered his ultimatum, he rose and exited the office.

For seven days, Weintraub and his editor worked on their new cut. Word leaked out of drastic changes being made, but Weintraub himself had nothing to say.

True to his promise, a preview was then scheduled to which Markle and I were duly invited. It was not a full-fledged preview in a regular movie theater, as before. Instead, a research company had been hired to invite a supposedly representative sample of young moviegoers to the MGM Studio Theater. After the screening, questionnaires were distributed and the results evaluated.

Weintraub was on hand to view his handiwork, flanked by Bud Smith and Thomopoulos. Peter Markle stood next to me behind the last row and, as the film progressed, grew increasingly manic. The reedited film was some fourteen minutes shorter than the earlier version, but, due to the curious alchemy of filmmaking, it seemed considerably longer.

In an effort to "speed it up," key reaction shots had been trimmed, transition scenes truncated, bits of color and nuance eliminated. "It's just...television," was all Markle could say at the end—the ultimate condemnation from a director of theatrical features.

The next morning, Markle and I found ourselves seated once again in the UA reception area, awaiting our next scheduled audience with Weintraub. A tense-looking secretary soon appeared. She would show us into Thomopoulos's office, she said.

That office was empty, but moments later a door burst open and in strode Weintraub and Thomopoulos, both of them in dark blue suits now and looking grave. Thomopoulos started to sit down, then noticed that Weintraub intended to remain standing, so he, too, stood.

"I made a deal with you," Weintraub told us. "I stick to my deals."

The results of the previous night's screening, he explained, had showed a dip in the number of "very goods" and "excellents" from 90 percent to 67 percent. This disparity, he said, stemmed mainly from an error in the survey techniques, not from the editing changes, but, nonetheless, those were the numbers, and he would abide by them. "Do you want the picture released your way or my way?" he asked.

"Our way," Markle and I chorused.

"You got it," Weintraub said, already wheeling. Thomopoulos had started to shake hands, then hesitated when he saw his boss abruptly withdraw, but his network manners took the upper hand. He grasped my hand and said, "Good luck," then hurried after his boss into the hallway.

I looked over at a perspiring Markle, who stood motionless, as though in shock. "Well, we survived that one," I said, in a lame effort to comfort him.

Markle was not assuaged. "We're gonna spend the rest of our lives previewing this picture," he murmured. "Just wait—after Weintraub, there'll be another..."

Jerry Weintraub's draconian appetite for deals was rapidly leading United Artists into a form of administrative gridlock. Aides were constantly scrambling to catch up with all the projects to which Weintraub had committed, only to find that in some cases Weintraub had either forgotten about the deals or had changed his mind. "I'd go to Jerry and say, 'I've got the deal in place now,' and he'd look at me and say, 'I never told you to make that deal,' " a top aide said.

To add to the confusion, Weintraub would sometimes ask two different executives to negotiate the same deal. One aide even heard Weintraub instructing his butler to check out the rights on a property.

Meanwhile, Weintraub continued to regale the press with his ambitious production plans. In some interviews, he would refer to his "partner," Kirk Kerkorian, and to their shared enthusiasm for the upcoming slate of films.

But if Kerkorian did, in fact, share Weintraub's enthusiasm, he was not giving evidence of it. Indeed, while the financier was maintaining a low profile, his key aides were starting to make their presence felt—always a sign of impending trouble. Fred Benninger and Walter Sharp, known through the company as "Kirk's hit men," were not routinely "copied" on Weintraub's inter-office deal memos, but they nonetheless suddenly seemed armed with all of them, and were peppering senior UA executives with questions. Their chief concern: that Weintraub was building up a huge overhead at a time when there were no immediate films in the pipeline. Too many of his deals were geared to projects and relationships that could not bear fruit for one or two years, if ever. The only cash flow in the interim, therefore, would stem from Kerkorian's checkbook.

Old Kerkorian-watchers had seen this pattern before. First would come the period of heightened observation and analysis—the calm before the storm. Then, inevitably, an incident would occur to provide the flash point.

For his part, Weintraub seemed oblivious to the warning signs. If anything, his flamboyance became more extreme. At his insistence, the company made an offer to purchase the expensive Beverly Hills office building at which United Artists now had its offices. A man given to grand entrances (he showed up at the most recent Cannes Film Festival aboard a 176-foot leased yacht), Weintraub's arrival at industry functions now took on the pomp of a head of state. He posed for a magazine-cover photo seated atop a prize white stallion, attired in the regalia of a country squire. At Christmas, a veritable army of messengers fanned out across town to deliver Dom Pérignon from UA's new benefactor.

Even Kirk Kerkorian found his way onto Weintraub's gift list—a fact that surprised "the boss," in view of the widely observed fact that Weintraub had apparently been forgetting his name of late. In speaking before groups of bankers and securities analysts, Weintraub had picked up the habit of referring to "my UA"—an idiosyncrasy duly reported to Kerkorian.

The long-predicted crisis was triggered by an innocuous-looking deal memo circulated to senior executives that disclosed terms of yet another "overhead deal." This time, the beneficiary was Guy McElwaine, the man who, as production chief at Columbia, had nurtured Weintraub's producing career. McElwaine had given him the "go" on *Karate Kid* and had funded his staff of D-girls, who'd been developing myriad new projects at Columbia. With McElwaine now jobless, Weintraub was in a position to return the favor. McElwaine's producing deal at UA called for a $1 million a year guarantee—a hefty sum for any producer, especially one who had never produced a picture. Moreover, UA's executive committee had not been forewarned of this generous arrangement.

The morning after the McElwaine deal memo was circulated, an eerie stillness settled over the UA corridors. Executives avoided eye contact as they passed each other in the hall, as though not wanting to acknowledge their incipient panic. Weintraub himself was locked behind closed doors, fielding phone calls from Kerkorian's designated crisis manager, Stephen Silbert. By late morning, the doors to Weintraub's suite were suddenly flung open and Weintraub marched out of the building, trailed by his secretaries, aides, and butler.

Within moments, the news had circulated through the building.

Jerry Weintraub had been summarily dismissed by his erstwhile "partner," Kirk Kerkorian. There would be no press conferences, no statements of regret, nothing. Weintraub was history; it was as simple as that.

The financial settlement was arrived at with surgical precision, in sharp contrast to the messy Begelman separation. Though Weintraub had never actually written out a check for $30 million, as he had claimed, he had in fact borrowed some $12 million from a bank to buy shares of unregistered MGM/UA stock in the hope that they would sharply appreciate in value. MGM/UA agreed to buy back these shares, thus allowing Weintraub to pay off his loan at the bank. This settlement was promptly "leaked" to outsiders in slightly distorted form. Weintraub, it was said (and subsequently published) had received a $12 million contract settlement from Kerkorian—news that came as a considerable surprise to "the boss," who was shocked that anyone would think Jerry Weintraub would receive a $12 million payoff for five months of work. As was his custom, however, Kerkorian decided to remain silent rather than to publicly refute the error.

Jerry Weintraub was devastated. He had dreamed all his life of heading a studio, and now he'd been sent on his way without having signaled one green light, without having seen one day of dailies, without having presided over a single world premiere. With all of his bravado and press conferences and trade ads, he had not done any better than Ted Turner; but at least Turner had his library.

Weintraub was in no mood to face the town. Rather than return to Blue Heaven in Malibu, Weintraub decided to take refuge at his summer home in Kennebunkport, Maine, where his next-door neighbor, George Bush, understood the evanescence of power. There, at Kennebunkport, Weintraub would nurse his wounds and dream of starting his next venture—a company where he alone would hold the reins, and where there would be no phantom partner who could, on impulse, sweep him away as though he were an errant schoolboy. Next time, Jerry Weintraub told himself, *he* would be "the boss"!

CHAPTER FOURTEEN

■

THE BLOCKBUSTER
1986

W ITH the departure of Jerry Weintraub, Kirk Kerkorian was
faced with yet another power vacuum. From Spago to the Hard
Rock, the town's power players and hangers-on alike were all speculating about his next moves. Indeed, watching the swings and
contortions within MGM/UA had by now become a favorite Hollywood pastime.

A subtle change in terminology had taken place, however. People
now gossiped about "Kirk's next victim," instead of his next studio
chief. Prospective buyers of MGM or UA were now referred to as
"Kirk's next suckers."

Increasingly, when Kerkorian's representatives inquired about
the availability of a given executive, they were greeted with instant
rejection. Indeed, one of the quickest turndowns came from a grizzled, combat-hardened sixty-eight-year-old onetime advertising
man named Lee Rich. Rich, together with his partner and financial
backer, Merv Adelson, had spent twenty years building Lorimar
into a television powerhouse on the strength of such shows as
Dallas, Knots Landing, Falconcrest, and *The Waltons,* among others.
During that time, Rich had acquired a reputation as a superb

251

salesman, and, too, as an astute student of the "bottom line." In a universe of hustlers and promoters, Rich was single-mindedly practical. "If Lee Rich were any more down-to-earth, you'd have to plant him," went a typical industry epithet.

These traits had come to Kerkorian's attention through his designated spies and seers. Indeed, even before the Turner deal, Kerkorian had sent Stephen Silbert to sound Rich out about a possible position, but Rich had indicated that he had no intention of becoming another pawn on Kerkorian's chessboard. Besides, at the time, Rich was enmeshed in his own corporate caper. He was trying to foster a merger between Lorimar and a big syndication operation called Telepictures. Through this marriage, Rich would not only realize a considerable financial gain, but he would also achieve another urgent objective—distancing himself from his partner. Though the Rich-Adelson partnership had been long and lucrative, the two men had never been particularly compatible. And in recent years, their flare-ups had grown more volatile.

With the departure of Jerry Weintraub, Silbert once again decided to get in touch with Lee Rich. Though the Lorimar merger had now been effectuated, Rich was still skeptical. This time, at least, he expressed a willingness to meet Kerkorian and hear what he had to say.

Kerkorian's pitch was as persuasive as it was self-effacing. "I have made a lot of money from this business," he explained, "but I have never been successful at it. I want to be successful this time. I want to build a company."

Lee Rich's job, Kerkorian explained, would be to take overall command of MGM/UA. The Boss said he understood that Rich was a corporate manager, not just another attorney like his previous chiefs. As such, Rich would select his heads of production at MGM and UA and would himself retain final say over which films got the green light for production. If he accepted the job, Rich would be given the opportunity to benefit from his own success in that he would be offered the chance to buy one million shares of restricted (i.e., unregistered) MGM/UA corporate stock. This purchase would mean that Rich would have to borrow some $11.8 million, but, if the company's stock rose from its depressed levels, the acquisition could represent a potential windfall.

Much to Rich's own surprise, he was now seriously considering a job that he had rejected out-of-hand a year earlier—a job that had been a graveyard for many careers. Why should he believe he could succeed where so many others have failed? he asked himself.

He marshaled the counterarguments. Perhaps as a result of the

Weintraub incident, Kerkorian had finally learned his lesson. Perhaps he would really give Rich a chance to succeed or fail on his own merits. Rich, after all, had demonstrated at Lorimar his ability to build a business. Surely Kerkorian understood that.

And then there were the other considerations—the intangibles. Lee Rich was beyond retirement age for most companies. How many men at this stage of their lives are given the chance to step into the job that once belonged to Louis B. Mayer?

For four weeks, Lee Rich stewed over these issues, then told Kerkorian that he had decided to accept. If Kerkorian would live up to his end of the bargain, Lee Rich would live up to his end: He would turn the company around.

Kirk Kerkorian had bought himself yet another chief executive, but this one, as he would soon learn, was markedly different from his predecessors. Lee Rich was no Frank Rosenfelt. He was older, tougher, wealthier, and vastly more cantankerous. Indeed, he was a man who, as he freely informed his friends, had "no intention whatsoever of putting up with any shit from Kirk Kerkorian."

I received an early education on the foibles of Lee Rich when I was a young columnist on *The New York Times*, reporting on news of Madison Avenue and the media. Rich, at the time, was a fast-rising media expert at the Benton & Bowles advertising agency who could always be counted on for a pithy quote. While other young admen were guarded in their public utterances, Lee Rich would always say exactly what was on his mind. A rather homely and uncoordinated man who walked like someone perpetually trudging through a field of mud, Rich was nonetheless able to dominate a room with his high-energy wit and booming exuberance.

More than a decade later, when we next connected, both of us had started second careers on the West Coast. I was vice president for production at Paramount. Rich had helped found a new company, which was getting off to a rocky start. Its first movie, *The Sporting Club*, was a clinker. Even the name of the new company, Lorimar, turned out to be a faux pas: It was an acronym of the first names of the two women whom Rich and his new partner, Merv Adelson, were about to divorce.

From the outset, Rich and Adelson seemed to be scurrying toward opposite destinations. Taut and self-contained, Adelson was fascinated by the movie world. As a young man, he had delivered food to the homes of movie stars while working for his father's grocery business. Now, he wanted to be invited to those homes as an honored guest. He felt he'd earned the right; he'd made a fortune in Las Vegas real estate, then channeled his Vegas money into the La Costa resort near San Diego. One of his investors was Moe Dalitz, the onetime Cleveland operator with whom Kerkorian had had dealings.

Rich, by contrast, was suspicious of movies and felt the future of Lorimar lay in television. While Adelson was acutely discomfited by the process of "pitching" ideas to the networks, Rich waded uninhibited into the fray. Before long, while Adelson was still trying to put together movie deals, Rich was shoehorning show after show onto the network schedule.

By 1978, with six shows on the air and their arguments about movies growing more intense, the two partners decided to bring an executive into the company charged with heading a new movie division. The job of "picking" movies would thus, theoretically, be transferred from Adelson's control to that of the new recruit. That new recruit turned out to be me.

Initially, I was as wary of the Lorimar job as Lee Rich was of Kerkorian. Having departed Paramount in 1976, I had learned to relish life devoid of corporate intrigue. I'd produced two movies, *Fun with Dick and Jane*, with Jane Fonda and George Segal, and *Islands in the Stream*, which reteamed actor George C. Scott with director Franklin Schaffner (they had recently won all manner of awards for *Patton*). I'd also started writing books once again, and this, too, nurtured a much-needed change in biorhythms.

Paradoxically, it was one of my books that led to my acceptance of the Lorimar job. Having offered me a substantial salary to become president of Lorimar's new motion-picture division, Adelson and Rich also casually let it be known that they were paying $250,000 to acquire the movie rights to a new novel entitled *Destinies*, thus outbidding UA and other studios. Since I was the co-author of *Destinies*, Lorimar's decision to acquire the book impressed me considerably. Indeed, in a deft bit of self-delusion, I rationalized that Lorimar's good taste in books might also spill over into movies. That was enough: I decided to accept the job.

My decision was not an inspired one. Adelson, it became clear, had no intention of relinquishing the reins. In my two years at Lorimar, I managed to shepherd a few successful films through the decision-making maze, including *Being There*, Hal Ashby's mordant comedy starring Peter Sellers, and a remake of *The Postman Always Rings Twice*, the steamy thriller with Jack Nicholson and Jessica Lange. But the dauntless Adelson also committed the company to such curious entries as *The Fish That Saved Pittsburgh*, a basketball comedy that couldn't find an audience, and *The Avalanche Express*, a Cold War thriller that needed massive surgery before it could be released.

And Lee Rich was unrelenting in his hectoring. "Merv just doesn't understand the movie business," he would confide, to which Adelson would reply, "Lee is really a creature of television."

Rich's prognosis was nothing if not candid. "Merv and I are like one of those bad marriages where one mate is always waiting for the other to file for divorce," he observed.

Having survived two years of Lorimar with only minor whiplash, I was hardly surprised when I learned that Rich had finally terminated his partnership to test the waters at MGM/UA. Certainly Rich had proved his staying power and his ability to build a business. Now was his chance to replicate his success on a far grander scale.

Establishing himself at the Beverly Hills suite of offices that formerly housed Weintraub's princely entourage, Rich set about the task of yet again restructuring the ragtag enterprise called MGM/UA. Tony Thomopoulos, having weathered the vicissitudes of the Weintraub regime, deserved a shot at running UA, Rich decided. As for MGM, who was better qualified than Alan Ladd, Jr.?

During the twelve months of the Turner negotiations, Ladd had become a sort of Wandering Jew of executives, which was ironic since he was one of the few non-Jews ever to become a head of production. Having been originally hired to head UA, then moved over to MGM/UA, then over to Turner Broadcasting, Ladd by now had difficulty figuring out which office to go to in the morning. Indeed, the only encouragement he had encountered during the past year emanated from Ted Turner, who, unlike Kerkorian, loved arguing about movies, but readily confessed that he had no money to finance any.

During his final months in limbo, Ladd and his associates found themselves headquartered in an ungainly Aztec pyramid across the street from the old Thalberg Building but off the MGM lot. Though barely completed, the structure already had become an industry in-joke. The pyramid, it was said, looked like a place where human sacrifices would be taken, not movies made. Ladd tried to smile at the joke, but he understood that the town anticipated that he might be among the first of the sacrifices.

The town was wrong for a change. Ladd now emerged as chairman of MGM with instructions to mount a new program of pictures as quickly as possible. The *modus operandi* from Lee Rich was straightforward: Ladd and Thomopoulos were empowered to develop whatever projects they chose. At such point as they had assembled a script, budget, director, and a list of possible casting, then Rich would issue his "yes" or "no." Rich reminded associates that he was a voracious reader. "Bring as much as you can to me," he urged. "It's time for action."

In addition to assembling his production team, Lee Rich also made another key appointment—one he would live to regret. As his president, he selected Stephen D. Silbert, a forty-four-year-old attorney from the Wyman Bautzer firm, who had been a key officer at Tracinda, Kerkorian's holding company. Slim and severe-looking, with cold blue eyes, Silbert exhibited an understanding of the business side of the corporation and also clearly held the confidence of The Boss. Though Frank Rothman was still a member of the executive committee, there was growing indication that he had quietly been dropped from "the loop."

"Why don't I ever find out about anything until after it happens," Rothman had complained to one top aide during the Turner negotiations. The aide had been tempted to reply, "Figure it out for yourself," but had managed to restrain himself. But just as Rothman had been deftly slipped into the top echelons of power replacing Frank Rosenfelt, so now Silbert seemed to be nudging out Rothman.

With the key appointments in place, executives at MGM/UA suddenly were talking to one another about topics other than office politics and contract settlements. Waiting rooms began to fill up once more with visitors other than attorneys pressing claims about broken deals. There were stirrings of life at MGM/UA yet again.

Having piloted several "start-up" operations, Alan Ladd, Jr., knew that the quickest way to find new "product" was to focus first on the pool of screenplays that had been cast into "turnaround"—i.e., scripts that companies had given up on and turned back to their writers or producers.

On a trip to Canada, Ladd and his lanky, keenly intelligent aide John Goldwyn (grandson of Samuel) had read a script called *Moonglow* that had just been added to the turnaround stockpile. An amusing but anomalous script by John Patrick Shanley, *Moonglow* had had a troubled past. Sally Field had admired the piece and had optioned it under her Columbia deal, but no one except Field believed she was right for the leading role. The moment her option lapsed, Norman Jewison, the director to whom she'd once offered it, pounced on the project and, since he, too, had a deal at Columbia, dispatched it to the newly enshrined president of the studio, David Puttnam. No one knows whether Puttnam ever read the script—the pontifical Englishman vastly preferred speechmaking to script reading—but word soon got back to Jewison that Columbia had no interest in *Moonglow*.

Hence, it was MGM's turn at the table. Goldwyn enthusiastically supported the project and, though other colleagues dissented, Ladd seconded Goldwyn's analysis. The project was rechristened *Moonstruck*, and Cher was signed for the role once coveted by Sally Field. MGM had secured its first future hit.

A second one was about to crystallize, as well. When John Cleese, the marvelously daft and erudite veteran of the Monty Python movies, told Ladd and Goldwyn an original story, Ladd was sufficiently confident of its potential that he offered Cleese $1 million if he would take the project off the market. This was an especially "macho" gesture in view of the fact that the script was not yet complete, nor had the property yet been dubbed with its ultimate title—*A Fish Called Wanda*. Ladd's enthusiasm was punctured, however, by a call from Michael Shamberg, Cleese's producer, rejecting the offer. Contractually, Shamberg reported, Universal had the first shot at *Wanda*. Several weeks later, to Ladd's surprise, Universal read the script and plunked it in turnaround, and Ladd promptly plunged in.

Ladd had also been waiting for the propitious time to make another phone call. That was to George Lucas, whose *Star Wars* had launched them both on a ride into movie fantasyland. Ladd's timing was adroit. Lucas had just received a script called *Willow* he was eager to talk about.

The film, to be directed by Ron Howard, who'd scored with *Cocoon* and *Splash*, was to cost an estimated $35 million, but MGM would put up only $20 million of that total, along with prints and advertising costs.

While the MGM ship was definitely afloat again, the transition was proving more arduous at UA. Indeed, the surviving UA staff felt like denizens of a banana republic. Their leader, Jerry Weintraub, had been abruptly swept aside in a "coup" so unexpected that they were ill-prepared for the problems of succession. Adding to the strain was the fact that Tony Thomopoulos was a network person by background, not a "features" person. And his production chief, Robert Lawrence, thirty-two, had never before held a position of such lofty responsibility. Thomopoulos, gray-faced, silver-haired, swathed always in dark blue, was known as the Suit around the office; Lawrence, who was boyishly good-looking, unstintingly trendy, and a habitué of the late-night club circuit, was known as the Kid. And it was no secret that the Suit and the Kid had no enduring fondness for one another.

Indeed, the only thing they had in common was the fact that both had managed to survive Jerry Weintraub. Unfortunately, a few of Weintraub's projects had survived, as well. One was *Bright Lights, Big City*, a numbingly dull screenplay based on the best seller by Jay McInerney.

Even under the most skillful guidance, *Bright Lights, Big City* was a difficult property to translate to the big screen. The novel was essentially an interior monologue; its plot was as thin as its narcotics were abundant. Weintraub had been drawn to the project because it was a "hot" book and, even more important, because Michael J. Fox had committed to play the lead. Inside UA, however, the movie had few, if any, fans: One senior financial executive took pity on a Japanese investors' group that was about to help finance the film, urging them to shift their money to *A Fish Called Wanda*. The Japanese rejected the suggestion as vaguely racist, however. If they wanted to invest in fish, they declared, they would open a sushi bar.

With Lee Rich constantly prodding his UA team that their MGM counterparts were far outperforming them, Thomopoulos and Lawrence pushed *Bright Lights, Big City* into production with disastrous results. The initial director, a newcomer named Joyce Chopra, was soon replaced by a veteran named James Bridges, who had directed *Urban Cowboy*. Bridges shut the picture down and rewrote the entire script. Even as they watched dailies on Bridges's revisionist version, however, UA executives knew they had a loser on their hands.

In another calculated gamble, UA also gave a "go" to a $13 million Jim Belushi picture called *Real Men*, which marked the debut of a neophyte director named Dennis Feldman. A nerdy, inarticulate young man, Feldman had become a hot item through his screenplay for the Eddie Murphy vehicle *The Golden Child*. After only a couple of weeks of shooting, however, it became clear that whatever Feldman's literary gifts, they did not seem to be translating to the screen. (After unsuccessful test-marketing, *Real Men* was never accorded a full-fledged national release.)

Given the fierce pressure to feed the distribution machine, both MGM and UA now were plunging ahead with some high-risk ventures: *Road House* at $20 million, *Union Street* at $21 million, *Last Rites* at $13.2 million, *Overboard* at $27 million, *Spaceballs* at $20 million, *Fatal Beauty* at $19 million, *Walk Like a Man* at $11 million, and *Baby Boom* at $17 million. Though some of the projects had commercial elements (Patrick Swayze, Diane Keaton, Jane Fonda) there was mounting apprehension that the company might be repeating past mistakes. Projects were being pushed into production before they were ready and before their screenplays could be fully honed. "We were trying to accomplish in weeks what should actually require years," said a senior production aide. "We were running a 'shoot now, pray later' operation." And the prayers were not being answered.

While UA was struggling with its slate, even MGM seemed to be reaching too feverishly for "high concept" projects. *Fatal Beauty*, in which Whoopi Goldberg starred as a female Dirty Harry, was a classic example of a concept-in-search-of-a-movie. *Overboard*, directed by the usually dependable Garry Marshall, seemed to labor tediously in the service of its formula plot. Indeed, though *Moonstruck*, *A Fish Called Wanda*, and, to a lesser degree, *Willow* were clearly headed for excellent results, there was a growing disquiet about the ominous "downdraft" being created by the weaker entries.

Every echelon of both MGM and UA now seemed caught up in an epidemic of second-guessing. The frenzy of activity had given way to a sudden outbreak of self-doubt. Lee Rich was battling with his distribution chief, Richard Graf, over sales strategy. The mild-mannered Ladd was furious with his superiors because, despite his pleas, *A Fish Called Wanda* was allowed to be released as a CBS-Fox video rather than through MGM/UA's own video company. To Ladd, this decision reflected a lack of respect for his business judgment. Tony Thomopoulos had grown sufficiently impatient with Robert Lawrence, his young production chief, that he had started shopping for a replacement. There was rampant infighting among the staff over development deals, production overages, ad campaigns, even expense accounts.

The most senior executives, far from being a calming influence, seemed consumed with their own battles. Lee Rich argued forcefully that Kerkorian should drastically reduce his personal holdings in MGM/UA—a position opposed by Sidney Sapsowitz, the company's chief financial officer, among others. By selling more shares to the public, Rich contended, the company could raise more working capital and achieve greater stability. His opponents, reflecting the position of The Boss, warned against a loss of control and a dilution of stock.

On this and similar issues, Rich found himself clashing as well with Stephen Silbert, the man he'd chosen to serve as president. More and more, Rich charged, vital information was reaching Kerkorian's office before it reached Rich's. Confronting Silbert on this issue at a staff meeting, Rich accused his appointee of disloyalty. "You're not working for me, you're working for Kirk," he warned.

To attorneys and agents doing business with MGM/UA, the company seemed to be plunging into disarray, its self-confidence shattered. What the company desperately needed was a shot in the arm—not just a hit picture, but a "monster" hit of the sort that had eluded the company in the twenty years of Kerkorian's ownership. If lightning didn't strike soon, it was predicted, MGM/UA would plunge into the same chaos that characterized the final days of the Begelman and Yablans regimes.

What no one knew was that the seeds of the long-awaited blockbuster had already been planted. The movie that would alter the future of the company was not exactly a high-profile project. Indeed, it was, if anything, the subject of derision and disdain, even as it was struggling through the bureaucratic thicket of development.

The project was called *Rain Man*, and it was to become the company's biggest hit since *Gone With the Wind*. Indeed, *Rain Man* was ultimately to fulfill every dream and expectation that Lee Rich could ever have conjured up.

But it would come too late to save him.

It all began with a "pitch," that humblest and most demeaning form of movie salesmanship. Barry Morrow, a thirty-seven-year-old television writer, dropped by the office of an acquaintance named Stan Brooks to pitch a story about an idiot savant.

Like most Hollywood meetings, this one, in the spring of 1986, was basically a waste of time, and both participants sensed it. Morrow conceived of his idea as a feature project, but had no experience writing features. Brooks was a TV executive at the Guber-Peters Company, an independent production company housed at Warner Bros. Hence, a TV writer was pitching to a TV executive an idea he was determined *not* to write for TV.

Incredibly, however, this exercise in futility was to trigger a chain reaction that was ultimately to enmesh four illustrious directors (including Steven Spielberg), six writers, eight producers— and Dustin Hoffman and Tom Cruise. Before events ran their course, *Rain Man* would alter many careers, spew forth eight Academy Award nominations and four Oscars, and ignite one of the biggest financial bonanzas in the history of the motion-picture industry for its stars, its director, and also for the talent agency, CAA, that represented all of them.

One of the enduring ironies of the movie industry is that its "blockbusters" almost always have inauspicious beginnings, while historic flops were eagerly embraced from the outset. *ET* endured years in turnaround, while *Heaven's Gate* was treated like a gift from God.

Rain Man was no exception to the rule. Though important figures in the movie industry later laid claim to having fostered the project, *Rain Man* in fact was nudged along by obscure individuals who never get their names in the trade press, and who had to overcome the persistent skepticism of their celebrated employers.

Barry Morrow, who not long before had been selling ladies' shoes, came upon the notion for *Rain Man* while researching an earlier TV project called *Bill*, which starred Mickey Rooney as its mentally retarded protagonist. Morrow had become fascinated with an idiot savant named Kim, who, though technically retarded, could memorize entire phone books. In *Rain Man*, Morrow decided to use such a character as the focus of a family fight over money. Charlie Babbitt returns to his hometown to discover that the family fortune has been bequeathed to his autistic brother, whom he never even knew existed. He therefore "kidnaps" his brother, and the two begin their now-famous trek across country.

Upon hearing Morrow's story idea, several issues worried Brooks. Apart from Morrow's inexperience as a feature writer, the subject of *Rain Man* could be construed as depressing. He knew that the two men who owned his company, Peter Guber and Jon Peters, leaned more toward high-energy, high-tech projects (they subsequently produced *Batman*). Nonetheless, he decided to pass Morrow along to Roger Birnbaum, a bright and aggressive young man who had just joined the company as his co-equal on the feature side.

Once he heard the story, Birnbaum had no reservations whatsoever. Without informing his superiors, he shepherded Morrow over to Lisa Henson, a Warner Bros. production executive, in the hope that the studio would finance development of the script. Henson, to Birnbaum's surprise, did not share his enthusiasm. Moreover, she pointed out that Warner Bros., as part of its massive development program, also had a project that dealt with autism and that one property on that topic was quite sufficient.

Stung, Birnbaum headed across town to UA, where his friend Robert Lawrence was production chief. Lawrence's reception was more enthusiastic. In fact, he informed Birnbaum and Morrow that they were not to leave the UA Building until a deal had been closed.

Morrow was astonished. After the Warner Bros. meeting, he'd steeled himself for ignominious rejection, and here he was, a prisoner at the UA Building!

If either Lawrence or Birnbaum had expected any praise or encouragement for having made their deal, they were to be sadly disappointed. When the project was first discussed at the UA development meeting, there were dour looks around the conference table. Tony Thomopoulos said it sounded to him like a TV movie— one of those "affliction-of-the-week" stories. Birnbaum, meanwhile, was accorded an equally glum response. "Movies don't happen this way," lectured Guber, the sort of person who even whispers at the top of his lungs. "Movies happen when you buy a best-seller like *Witches of Eastwick*. They don't happen when you develop pitches from TV writers."

Morrow was shielded from this negativism. Delighted with his eighty-thousand-dollar deal, he busily set about to get *Rain Man* on paper.

As events turned out, this wall of negativism would serve as useful preparation for the obstacles that would present themselves once the screenplay had been turned in. Far from changing anyone's mind, the draft of *Rain Man* still evoked no enthusiasm from the top levels. Lawrence and Birnbaum knew that they would need to enlist a major "element" to advance their cause. Since the subject matter was more cerebral than flashy, they decided to pursue a "name" director rather than a star.

And they got nowhere. Neither Sidney Pollack nor Martin Brest nor Larry Kasdan nor Paul Brickman nor Barry Levinson would agree to come aboard. As in most such situations, no one was quite sure of the reason for the rejections, or, indeed, whether the directors themselves had ever read the material or rather had it "covered" by their readers. In Hollywood, rejections customarily come in the form of a one-sentence phone call from an agent. "Marty Brest has passed," is usually the full content of the conversation.

While dining at Morton's, Lawrence expressed his distress to a friend, David O'Connor, an alert young CAA agent who had only recently graduated from being an assistant to Mike Ovitz, CAA's reigning czar. O'Connor's response was typically more upbeat. To begin with, he reminded Lawrence, Marty Brest had even turned down *Beverly Hills Cop* five times before finally committing to the project. Even more important, the UA strategy of pursuing directors for *Rain Man* was a mistake. Since the film had two colorful male roles, the script should go to stars like Bill Murray and Dustin Hoffman.

CAA's strategy for *Rain Man*, which was quickly cleared with Ovitz, took the following shape: Murray would play the role of the idiot savant (which ultimately went to Hoffman), and Hoffman could play his brother (the part that ultimately went to Cruise). If Hoffman were offered the idiot savant, it was reasoned, he might feel it was too close to the sort of Ratso Rizzo type he portrayed in *Midnight Cowboy*.

Though CAA's "grand designs" often met with great success, this one was sent spinning by two developments: First, Bill Murray said he didn't want anything to do with *Rain Man*. Second, Dustin Hoffman announced that he wanted to play the idiot savant. Apart from the fact that he liked the script, he also happened to have seen a *60 Minutes* segment on idiots savants, and had found it very moving.

For four hours at a Malibu restaurant, the scrupulously thorough if not obsessive Hoffman questioned Barry Morrow about the background of his story and about the real character upon which it was based. Morrow emerged from the meeting exhilarated. As a neophyte writer, he had been warned that once the heavy hitters get involved, the writer usually becomes the forgotten man. But here he was, consulting with Dustin Hoffman!

But not for long. Indeed, Barry Morrow's Malibu meeting would mark his last contribution to *Rain Man*. With Hoffman now in tow, an entire new cast of characters was about to descend on his once-disparaged project. The procrastinating Marty Brest suddenly had a renewed interest in *Rain Man*. Tony Thomopoulos, having dismissed the project as a TV movie, now started representing UA at meetings instead of a frustrated Lawrence. Peter Guber was suddenly highly visible, instead of Roger Birnbaum. Barry Morrow, meanwhile, had been dropped from the loop.

With the "first team" in place, discussions now began over the last key issue—namely, who should play Dustin Hoffman's brother? The part was not as challenging as Hoffman's. Indeed, Charlie, as written, was something of a cad—loud, self-centered, materialistic. The role did have one unique asset, however: the opportunity to play opposite Dustin Hoffman.

Even as the UA staff was drawing up its list of actors in Hoffman's age group, CAA announced that it had a better idea. The young ticket buyers in the shopping malls had already demonstrated their reluctance to see two fifty-year-olds playing opposite one another—a fact underscored most recently by the failure of *Ishtar*, which co-starred Hoffman and Warren Beatty. After that fiasco, CAA had decreed that Hoffman, in his next film, should be teamed with one of its hot young stars—someone like Tom Cruise, for example. Indeed, Cruise had been slipped the script to *Rain Man* and had loved it.

The notion of a Hoffman-Cruise movie sent UA into paroxysms of excitement—quickly followed by total confusion. The age gap between the two stars was twenty-eight years! How could they be believable as brothers? *Rain Man* was supposed to be a story about an idiot savant, not about a biological accident. The casting of Tom Cruise, UA officials fretted, would require a massive restructuring, a rewrite....

Not at all, argued the seers from CAA. Though Hollywood might be cognizant of the age gap, the great unwashed wouldn't even notice. The charisma of the actors would carry the day.

As events would soon prove, CAA turned out to be right on two counts. First, the much-feared age gap did not become an issue. But even more important, the emotional bond that quickly developed between the two actors would prove crucial to the survival of *Rain Man*. Dustin Hoffman and Tom Cruise not only liked their roles, they also liked each other. And both levels of devotion would be put to a stern test by the succession of false starts and erratic decision making that dogged the film's progress.

It would be reasonable to assume that any project that starred Dustin Hoffman and Tom Cruise, and that had the avid support of such institutions as CAA and UA, would glide smoothly and unobtrusively through preproduction. But nothing came easily to *Rain Man*.

The initial crises concerned rewrites. Though everyone had said they'd liked Barry Morrow's screenplay, everyone was now eager to improve upon it. Martin Brest had his own checklist of creative nips and tucks. So had the actors. And each participant also had his favorite rewrite man.

Within months, the screenplay of *Rain Man* would turn into a literary smorgasbord, as one "script doctor" after another paraded past the table. Ron Bass, a lawyer-turned-scenarist, took the first pass at the rewrite, then departed for a vacation. Martin Brest had admired Bass's previous screenplays, but when he read the new *Rain Man* draft, he was troubled. With a possible directors' strike looming, Brest opted to bring in another writer, Richard Price, who'd written *The Color of Money*. But now, reading Price's first pages, Brest was even more troubled—and Dustin Hoffman was troubled by the fact that Brest always seemed troubled. Soon Brest was off the picture due to what Hollywood likes to call "creative differences." Another writer, named Michael Bortman, was brought in to do some work, but there was no director to lend guidance to the project, which was clearly drifting now.

Discouragement turned to instant rapture as Steven Spielberg suddenly entered the mix. Spielberg found the project enticing, but he wanted Ron Bass to try another tack. Both he and Dustin Hoffman felt the Raymond character was too cuddly and affectionate. They wanted him more cantankerous, hard-to-reach, realistically autistic, and that is what Bass now set out to create. By the time he'd finished, however, Spielberg was consumed by problems of his own. He'd promised his good friend George Lucas that he would be available to start preparation of the vaunted *"Indy III"*—*Indiana Jones and the Last Crusade*. There was no way, Spielberg realized, that he could do *Rain Man* without a major delay on his other enormous project.

Now, the dogged Hoffman turned to his old friend Sydney Pollack, with whom he had worked (and warred) on *Tootsie*. Pollack had already turned down *Rain Man*, but Hoffman was persistent, and Pollack agreed to give it another try. The director, of course, had his own choices in rewrite men—David Rayfiel and Kurt Luedtke. Tackling the script yet again, Pollack and his writers were intent on making *Rain Man* less picaresque and more of a love story. After several weeks, however, they reported ruefully that they were not making progress. They couldn't seem to get a handle on the story.

Morrow's narrative had by now gone through all sorts of permutations and contortions. Charlie Babbitt, who originally ran a sleazy phone-solicitation company, now was a salesman of imported cars. His girlfriend, once an attorney, had become his secretary. His brother, Raymond, the autistic savant, who in Morrow's script had moments of lucidity, had become zipped up and feisty. The boy-gets-girl aspect of the story had now become boy loses girl and boy loses brother, as well. A story about skewed relationships had become more of a "road picture."

Amid all the pontificating and rewriting, the project had clearly lost its way. A superstar "go" picture had become one of the world's most expensive development deals.

And the frustration was tearing up UA. Management had looked hungrily to *Rain Man* to help dramatize its comeback, but all it had got for its time and money was a stack of abandoned scripts.

Tempers were wearing thin. Robert Lawrence, who'd first made the deal for *Rain Man*, felt he could have guided the project to fruition, but, instead, he'd been excluded from meetings. The free-spirited Lawrence made little effort to conceal his impatience with the cool, highly political Thomopoulos. "The thing Tony really cares about most is whether he gets a good table at Morton's," Lawrence would tell associates.

Mindful of Lawrence's frustration, Thomopoulos decided to take him out of his agony. Summoning Lawrence to his office, Thomopoulos told him he was no longer the production chief of UA. Indeed, his successor had already been hired. He was Roger Birnbaum, who, as an employee of Guber-Peters, had first brought *Rain Man* to Lawrence. The project had come full circle.

Determined to resolve *Rain Man*'s problems, Thomopoulos set up a breakfast with Hoffman, but twenty minutes into the meeting, he found himself more disheartened than ever. Hoping to find a committed actor who would intelligently address the problems at hand, Thomopoulos could barely understand what Hoffman was saying. The actor was refusing to make eye contact and spoke falteringly, occasionally lapsing into a curious doggerel that left Thomopoulos nonplussed. And then it struck him: Dustin Hoffman had already transmogrified himself into Raymond! In true Method tradition, he'd decided to demonstrate his commitment by "playing" the savant at breakfast. Thomopoulos was dumbfounded, but delighted. It was indeed a bravura performance.

And now hope dawned anew. Dustin Hoffman had run into Barry Levinson at a circus, and even though Levinson, too, had once passed on the script, Hoffman went to work on him. Subsequent discussions were held, and suddenly the piece seemed to crystallize in the director's mind. All the issues that had obsessed the previous directors and writers were cast aside by Levinson. He didn't care whether the love story was fully resolved. He didn't care about the ambiguity of the relationship between the brothers at the end of the film. He didn't even care about the twenty-eight-year age gap between the brothers. In his mind, the story worked, and the cast was terrific. He just needed a couple of weeks with Ron Bass to iron out the glitches that stemmed from the repeated rewrites.

Bass was more than delighted to be summoned once again, but with a writers' strike about to be called, he was worried whether he would have the time. Perhaps the rewrite would have to wait till after a strike.

UA was hysterical once again. What had once been looked upon as a Christmas 1987 release could now be slotted in for Christmas 1988, but not if everyone sat around waiting for a strike to end. Levinson and Bass were told to get to work on the script, even if it became a day-and-night proposition.

That's exactly what it became. Working around the clock, Bass delivered his final rewrites scratched out in his personal handwriting—there was no time for typists before the strike deadline. At last, all systems were "go."

Paradoxically, while peace had finally settled in on the production, war was breaking out at the upper reaches of UA. Since *Rain Man* had been an on-again, off-again proposition for so long, members of the executive committee had never really pondered the economics of the project. But now that it had unexpectedly become a reality, Stephen Silbert and the others were "running the numbers," and indulging in some serious second-guessing. This was, after all, a $30 million project, the executive committee reminded everyone—probably the most expensive film ever undertaken by the company outside of the Bonds and *Rocky*s and, of course, the dread *Heaven's Gate*. Further, UA had paid dearly for its stars. Hoffman and Cruise would make over $10 million up front in salaries, and would also receive a staggeringly high percentage of the film's gross receipts. Hoffman's complex deal called for his escalators to change at seven different levels, going from 10 percent of the gross to as high as 21 percent as the film pulled in more and more income. Indeed, the two stars and their director between them would stand to make an aggregate of $30 million when the film brought in $100 million in rentals. At the $100 million level, in fact, the "talent" would have made considerably more than the company that had risked its money to finance the project.

As the senior UA officials examined their computer runs, they realized how deftly CAA had turned its packaging contributions into hard cash. The agency would stand to make as much as $5 million on its *Rain Man* commissions.

Peering at the numbers, Silbert and the others demanded to know why Rich and Thomopoulos had made such lucrative deals. The two stars, after all, had wanted so desperately to do the picture that they'd hung in there through all forms of adversity. Yet, examining their deals, one would think they'd been lured in against their will.

Rubbing salt into these wounds also was the realization that UA would be penalized in some of its ancillary deals. The overseas video rights to *Rain Man*, for example, had been granted to Warner Bros.—rights that would ultimately be worth some $25 million. Wherever they turned, the executive committee seemed to discover that UA was leaking money.

Rich and Thomopoulos bristled over this second-guessing. UA's bargaining position with CAA, they argued, had been undercut by the fact that UA desperately needed the project. If UA had failed to meet the agency's demands, the project could easily have been switched to another studio. Moreover, Rich pointed out that he wasn't responsible for the Warner Bros. video deal, or for other deals involving ancillary markets. These arrangements had been struck by prior regimes; Rich was merely unfortunate enough to inherit them.

Despite these persuasive arguments, the debate over *Rain Man* grew more rancorous. At one staff meeting, Rich accused Silbert of "going around him" to poison Kerkorian's mind about the project. Thomopoulos, too, accused the attorney of using "intimidation tactics."

Even as accusations flew back and forth, *Rain Man* edged ever closer to principal photography. No one on the executive committee was willing to accept responsibility for calling it off. And Kerkorian, despite pleas from aides, decided to remain as aloof as always.

Rain Man never really received its coveted "green light." There was only a flickering yellow.

CHAPTER FIFTEEN

■

JOURNEY'S END
1988

B<small>Y</small> early summer, the rumors were all over town. MGM or UA, or perhaps both, were on the block yet again. Less than two years after dismembering his company in the Ted Turner negotiations, Kerkorian was ready to deal once more.

Rich, Ladd, and Thomopoulos looked on with mixed emotions. It was stressful, of course, to pick up the newspaper each morning, knowing they might be learning the identity of their new boss. On the other hand, any new owner would at least offer more stability than Kerkorian had.

The Sony Corporation, it was reported, was on the brink of closing a deal. Then word leaked out that the Japanese had declined to meet Kerkorian's price.

Another potential suitor was N. V. Philips, the huge Dutch electronics manufacturer and owner of Polygram Records, but Philips, too, melted away.

Ladd was in Rome with Goldwyn and Kanter when he received a startling late-night phone call disclosing that Kerkorian had finally closed a deal. But the purchasers were not Sony or Philips— far from it. No, the supposed new owners of MGM were, in fact,

Peter Guber and Jon Peters, the executive producers of *Rain Man*. And they hadn't exactly bought the *company;* they had just bought a *piece* of it.

If Ladd was getting confused signals, so was everyone else in the company. News was hard to come by, and the little that seeped out didn't make sense.

Hurrying back to Los Angeles, Ladd tried unsuccessfully to clarify the situation. Finally, after several false starts, he succeeded in setting up a Sunday afternoon meeting with Guber and Peters. Arriving ninety minutes late, the two producers carried themselves with the hauteur of two men who had just pulled off an extraordinary deal. Indeed, they exuded confidence and elation. But when Ladd pressed for information about the structure of the new company, they became oddly noncommunicative. Nothing had been worked out, they replied evasively. When more information became available, Ladd would, of course, be the first to know.

The next morning, Ladd did in fact learn more details, but not from Guber and Peters. A friend tipped him that MGM had just sent out a press release announcing that Guber would be chairman of MGM and Peters, president. Ladd's title and role were not mentioned. Indeed, so far as the MGM announcement was concerned, Ladd had become a nonperson.

Furious, Ladd decided impulsively to drive to Kerkorian's office and force a confrontation. If he called for an appointment, he knew he'd get a runaround. As Ladd marched through the lobby of the UA Building, the doors to an elevator were just about to close. To Ladd's surprise, standing inside, sandwiched among several strangers, was Kirk Kerkorian.

Pushing onto the elevator, Ladd did not greet Kerkorian, nor did his boss's leathery face reflect any change of expression. "We've got a few things that need straightening out," Ladd rumbled in an ominous monotone, eyes burrowing into Kerkorian. Having made a career of avoiding this sort of confrontation, Kerkorian glanced uneasily around the full elevator. The passengers seemed to be leaning forward, expectantly.

"My office..." Kerkorian offered at last. "We'll talk in my office." Ladd was already feeling some satisfaction. He had nailed his elusive target at last.

The moment the elevator doors parted, the conversation started once again. Neither Kerkorian nor Ladd raised their voices, yet their terse, blunt remarks resonated like body blows.

"How do you expect me to continue working here when—"

"Don't do anything hasty. Things will be worked out in a few weeks."

"A few weeks! I don't even know whom I'm working for."

"The announcement had to be rushed out. The SEC has its rules...."

"I was told nothing had been decided, then the press release..."

"Things were misinterpreted...."

"Someone else will be doing my job! It's as simple as that!"

Ladd kept pressing for clarification. What was the exact deal with Guber and Peters? Had he really turned over control of MGM in return for just $100 million, or was there something else involved?

But it was like punching pillows. Either Kerkorian himself didn't understand the deal, or this was just his way of stonewalling Ladd.

After Ladd left Kerkorian's office, he tried to corner other UA officials, hoping they'd have more to offer. No one, however, could really explain what had taken place.

All he could determine was that the Guber-Peters negotiations had been sandwiched into only a few hurried meetings amid a curious fly-by-the-seat-of-your-pants atmosphere. The instigators of the negotiations apparently were Silbert and a former law partner, Terry Christiansen, who from time to time had represented Kerkorian, as well as the two producers.

The attorneys had lauded the producers' entrepreneureal zeal, and Kerkorian had been duly impressed by such recent films as *The Witches of Eastwick* and *The Color Purple*. And he also knew that Guber had been involved in the still-unreleased *Rain Man*, which had stirred so much debate within his company.

By and large, the principals had fared well during their sessions, despite vast differences of style and nuance. While the gregarious producers often digressed into personal anecdotes, the austere Kerkorian was all business, never allowing a single personal reference or allusion to drift into his conversation. Now and then, Kerkorian would marvel at the ability of the hyperkinetic Guber to bundle more words into a limited span of time than any other human being he'd ever observed. As a young man, Guber had collected college degrees as others would collect baseball cards, and his frenzied erudition revealed itself as the negotiations grew more complex.

In contrast to Guber's frenetic but high-spirited presentation, his partner displayed a swaggering, almost surly style. Having worked for years at his mother's side in their beauty salon, catering to clients with the requisite obsequiousness, Jon Peters now seemed determined to compensate. On a couple of occasions, when the trigger-tempered Peters seemed to belittle the performances of some of Kerkorian's prior production chiefs, "the boss" quietly but firmly set things straight. "Those men gave it their best shot," Kerkorian cautioned sternly. Peters's onslaughts quickly subsided.

The financial base of the two producers was a small, publicly held company named Barris Industries, the "industries" consisting of such quiz shows as *The Gong Show, The All-New Dating Game,* and *The New Newlywed Game.* Chuck Barris, who had dreamed up these shows, had long since departed the company, but Guber and Peters had joined forces with a businessman named Burt Sugarman to pump new financing into the venture (Sugarman's own investments ranged from the cinema to cement plants). Hence, the Guber-Peters-Sugarman scheme was to pledge some $100 million in Barris funds as working capital for MGM in return for a major piece of the studio. How "major" was the subject of intense maneuvering.

Guber wanted to negotiate his way into a situation where his group would own 40 percent of MGM, Kerkorian would own 40 percent, and the remainder would be held by the public. Kerkorian, however, was willing to grant only a 25 percent stake, along with the titles of chairman and president. In other words, they could run the company, but they couldn't control it. And if Kerkorian deemed their work exemplary, Kerkorian would then grant "performance bonuses" that would boost the producers to their desired 40 percent level.

From Kerkorian's point of view, the spinning off of MGM could also create a renaissance at UA. The combination of the Guber-Peters $100 million and the $200 million Kerkorian had pledged would greatly reduce indebtedness. Also, the cost of sustaining the distribution and marketing operations could now be divided with MGM, and other steps would be taken to reduce UA's overhead. The company would have a chance of success once again.

Guber and Peters felt they, too, had made a terrific deal, but as details of the arrangement began to seep out, they were unnerved by the skeptical questions being hurled from all directions. How were they going to finance a new slate of films? friends and critics alike asked. How were they going to turn out enough product to feed the distribution company?

The "product pinch" was especially vexing to the producers, since both knew how difficult it was to "crank up" a slate of instant winners. During the past two years, the two had quietly tested their ability to step up their output, and the results had been disastrous. Instead of focusing on their high-priced Warner Bros. projects, they had spread themselves thin around town, turning out a cluster of inexpensive films such as *The Legend of Billie Jean, Head Office,* and *D.C. Cab.* The failure of these small films had shaken their sense of infallibility.

Guber, a onetime production chief at Columbia, also knew the product shortage would worsen if the company experienced a major exodus of executives, as was now rumored. Even though he didn't have an especially high opinion of the executives or producers under contract, he nonetheless realized that they would keep product in the pipeline.

Hence, even as they savored their new positions and the lavish offices into which they would be moving, Guber and Peters were both seized by sudden doubts. They had wandered into an arena much more complex and dangerous than anything they had experienced before.

Having stoked themselves into a state of high excitement, they now accepted the grim reality that their deal simply didn't make sense. Though putting up their $100 million, they would still be employees of Kirk Kerkorian. They would be struggling with the same problems that had faced all the other ambitious men who had undertaken the job before them. And, in all likelihood, they, too, would probably be defeated by them.

They decided to make the call together. On the other end of the line, Kerkorian was, as always, courteous if cryptic. It was a short conversation. And it was to be the last they would have.

The sudden dissolution of the Guber-Peters deal sent shock waves through the company. Silbert and his colleagues had considered it a "done deal." Acting on what he interpreted as Guber-and-Peters dictates, Silbert had already started the machinery in motion to notify producers and directors under MGM contracts that their deals would be terminated. Another writers' strike had now been called, and this provided the smokescreen under which Silbert invoked the "force majeure" clause in their contracts—this meant that the deals could be invalidated in the case of extraordinary circumstances or acts of God.

The turmoil increased. Lee Rich, for one, was enraged that the negotiations had taken place behind his back. It was not only bad corporate manners, it was also a violation, Rich felt, of Kerkorian's pledges. When Rich had made his deal with "the boss," Kerkorian had promised to stop trading assets, and, rather, to support Rich in his effort to build a solid company. Now, just as significant progress was being made, Kerkorian was back on a deal-making binge once again.

In Rich's mind, the whole affair had become a nightmare. He'd put in the most strenuous two years of his life, and all for naught.

On July 18, 1988, just one week after the Guber-Peters announcement, Lee Rich submitted his resignation to Kerkorian. Kerkorian received the news in stony silence. He'd seen it coming.

There were, to be sure, some important details to be worked out. Rich had not signed a contract when he'd joined the company. Kerkorian had told him he'd "been burned" by contracts and that his handshake was more meaningful—a reprise of the speech he'd delivered to Jim Aubrey twenty years earlier. Now, Rich wanted Kerkorian to live up to a key part of the "handshake" agreement.

When Rich had joined the company, he'd borrowed some $11.8 million, just as Jerry Weintraub had done, to buy a million shares of unregistered MGM/UA stock. Thomopoulos had acquired one hundred thousand shares—also, he claimed, with Kerkorian's assurance that if anything went wrong, "the boss" would buy them back.

With events unraveling quickly now, Rich and Thomopoulos informed Kerkorian they wanted to sell their stock. Weintraub had sold $12 million in stock and repaid his bank loan upon leaving the company. But Kerkorian was not going to be so accommodating this time around. "I'll take care of it," he told Rich, somewhat vaguely. "Steve Silbert will handle it," he told Thomopoulos.

As days rolled by, however, it became clear that no one was handling it. Having moved out of the UA Building, Rich was now finding it difficult getting either Kerkorian or Silbert on the phone.

In frustration, Rich filed suit in U.S. District Court, demanding that Kerkorian reimburse him the $11.8 million. Kerkorian's attorneys tried in vain to get the suit dismissed. Finally, in July 1989, with batteries of attorneys demanding to take his deposition, Kerkorian gave in. Both Rich and Thomopoulos, it was agreed, would be permitted to sell their stock and get their money back.

Company insiders deemed it a curious paradox that Weintraub, during his tenure, had not got a single film off the ground, while Rich had propelled MGM/UA ahead of Columbia, Universal, and Orion in terms of box-office receipts. Yet Rich had to go to court to get the same amount of money that had been accorded Weintraub without so much as a whisper of protest.

* * *

With the departure of Rich, Kerkorian's "damage control" squad again sprang into action. Early in September, Stephen Silbert told a *Wall Street Journal* reporter that "the company is stronger than it has ever been." As though to underscore his point, he filed a new limited partnership called Star Partners II, aimed at raising $100 million to finance new movies.

Summoning his remaining executives to a "morale" meeting, Silbert proposed throwing a cocktail party for MGM/UA employees to bolster team spirit. Ladd, who himself was halfway out the door, responded sarcastically, "Our people don't want drinks, they want to know what's going to happen to them."

Silbert uttered some words of reassurance about maintaining the forward thrust of the company. But only hours after the meeting had ended, producers under contract to MGM started receiving their "termination notices" from Silbert.

Indignation was running high. Never before, producers argued, had a writers' strike been cause for cancellation of producer deals. Ladd was critical of Silbert for sending out the coldly worded legal letters rather than invoking more mannerly methods—a phone call or even an office visit, for example.

When Ladd called one old friend, Richard Zanuck, to apologize for the fiasco, he found Zanuck both indignant and bemused. The last time Zanuck had been fired was when he was head of production at Twentieth Century-Fox—and his father, Darryl, had done the firing. If Stephen Silbert wanted to lay him off on the grounds of force majeure, Zanuck advised Ladd, he should read the contract more closely, because Zanuck's deal didn't contain a force-majeure clause. Weeks later, MGM/UA offered to reinstate Zanuck, but he didn't want any part of it.

Two producers were spared what had quickly become known as the "Friday Night Massacre." One was Cubby Broccoli, who was presiding over a new Bond picture. The other was Irwin Winkler, the co-producer of the *Rocky* films. Indeed, Winkler was in preproduction on the lone new UA movie entitled *Dessa Rose*, which concerned the friendship of two women just prior to the Civil War. The film was to mark Winkler's first directing effort, and he felt passionate about its prospects.

Though Winkler hadn't received Silbert's termination notice, he was about to receive even more dire news. Silbert had decided to cancel his film!

Winkler was stupefied. A hundred members of the cast and crew were standing by in Charleston, South Carolina, to begin principal photography. Indeed, only three hours before getting word of Silbert's cancellation, he'd hired Donald Sutherland to play a leading role in his film for a fee of $600,000—a deal that had just been approved by Tony Thomopoulos. There was no way of canceling the deal, nor others involved in the film. MGM/UA faced a certain loss of at least $4.6 million.

It didn't make sense, Winkler argued. Indeed, Winkler even offered to put up some $2 million toward the cost of the film as an advance against foreign revenues.

Silbert was sympathetic but unbending. The studio, he said, would do everything it could to help Winkler switch his project to another company, but it would not finance the picture. Silbert, Winkler could see, was behaving like a man who'd been tossed into a pressure cooker.

The downward spiral was accelerating now. In addition to the producers and directors who'd been lopped off, some two hundred other studio employees were now summarily discharged. Alan Ladd, Jr., too, had finally had enough. In announcing his departure, he also advised Kerkorian that he would devote his efforts to raising money to buy MGM away from him. To underscore his determination, he enlisted the professional counsel of a forty-five-year-old investment banker from Merrill Lynch, Jeffrey Barbakow, to help him line up possible backers.

In the space of a few short weeks, Kerkorian's empire had shrunk dramatically. At UA, Roger Birnbaum had left, and Thomopoulos was effectively sitting out his contract. At MGM, Ladd was gone, and holdovers like Richard Berger and John Goldwyn were trying to figure out where to turn. Two films were shooting—the Bond film and a Jane Fonda picture—and the ever-controversial *Rain Man* was in postproduction, but other than that, the pipeline was empty. The only remaining properties in the once-vast library consisted of a few post-Turner projects, the best of which were *Moonstruck* and *A Fish Called Wanda*.

Indeed, much to Kerkorian's intense dismay, a small cloud surrounded even his most cherished possession—the MGM/UA logo. Though Kerkorian hadn't realized it at the time, the Walt Disney Company had negotiated a deal with Frank Davis, MGM/UA's senior business-affairs executive, to use the MGM name on new Disney theme parks both in Florida and in Europe. A possible Disney-MGM Studio tour, rivaling the highly successful Universal tour, was also contemplated for Burbank, California. (That plan was ultimately dropped.)

Disney's notion was a sound one: Even though MGM's future as a filmmaker was open to question, the logo still projected an aura around the world of glamour and glitz. The combination of the Disney and MGM names carried much more marketing clout than Disney alone.

From the MGM/UA standpoint, it seemed like a harmless deal. The company itself had no plans for its own theme parks. This seemed like an easy way to pick up some much-needed fees.

Until Kirk Kerkorian heard about it, that is. Showing up unexpectedly at a meeting of the MGM executive committee, the normally cool-headed Kerkorian was livid. Claiming he'd never been advised of the Disney deal, Kerkorian shouted, "How could this happen? How could you give away our logo like this!" There was stunned silence in the room. No one could ever remember a tirade like this before. Indeed, no one could even remember "the boss" raising his voice, no less thumping the conference table and scattering piles of paper.

Thoroughly intimidated by this performance, the members of the executive committee professed their ignorance of the transaction, but their boss was dubious. Kerkorian knew that Frank Davis was a cautious old pro, and that he would never close a deal such as this without weaving a "paper trail" around each member of the committee. Typically, though Davis had been a senior executive with the company for two decades, Kerkorian had never had a face-to-face meeting with him. But he knew instinctively that this whole problem couldn't be dumped at Davis's feet.

Frenzied calls quickly went out to Frank Wells, chairman of Disney. Kerkorian had hit the roof, Wells was told. The deal would have to be canceled.

A tall, tough-minded attorney who climbed mountains in his off-hours, Wells was unmoved. Plans were moving briskly to open the Disney MGM Studio tour in Florida the following year, he replied, and similar ventures would open in Europe at a later date. If Kerkorian opposed the idea, he should have declared himself earlier—after all, it was his company, Wells said.

The MGM/UA aides tried to argue their case. "The boss," they explained, did not believe in hands-on management, but on rare occasions such as this, he wished to exercise veto power.

To the executives at Disney, a citadel of hard-nosed, hands-on managerial technique, this sounded like pure science fiction. There was no way, short of litigation, they explained, that Disney was going to tear up its deal simply to accommodate Kirk Kerkorian's curious idiosyncrasies.

In Kerkorian's mind, the Disney trauma dramatized the intense need to shore up management at his companies. He sensed the growing disarray on all fronts. Clearly, a new top man was needed—but what sort of man? Not a movie man, that much was obvious. Kerkorian was in a mood to sell assets once again, and was weary of maintaining the facade of making movies. He needed a strong financial man now. A trader.

Of all the financial types Kerkorian had met recently, the man who'd most impressed him had been an enthusiastic, preppylike Merrill Lynch executive named Jeffrey Barbakow. Ironically, it had been Alan Ladd, Jr., who'd brought Barbakow in to Kerkorian to discuss a possible leveraged buyout of MGM. While Kerkorian didn't go for the deal, he decided to go for Barbakow.

The deal he cut with the Merrill Lynch banker was an extraordinary one. Barbakow and two of his Merrill Lynch colleagues, Trevor Fetter and Kenin Spivak, would assume the top positions at MGM, and would undertake to run the company even though they had no experience in the industry.

Barbakow's salary would be $1 million a year, Spivak's $400,000, and Fetter's $200,000. Barbakow also would receive options on some 1.5 million shares of MGM/UA stock. Even more important, Barbakow would be entitled to receive a bonus totaling $30 million if he succeeded in making a deal to sell MGM or UA during his tenure at the company. The bonuses for the thirty-two-year-old Spivak would total $1.2 million, and for the twenty-nine-year-old Fetter, some $800,000.

These were extraordinary incentives by any standard. Top executives in industry are customarily rewarded for the skill with which they run their companies, not for selling them. But the mandate to Barbakow and his associates was made abundantly clear: Kerkorian wanted a deal.

Given these nuances, the new appointments predictably gave rise to a wide range of quips and taunts. "It's a great new studio—Metro Merrill Lynch," Irwin Winkler snapped. "Maybe they'll shoot proxy statements."

For his part, Barbakow ignored these barbs and tried to assume a managerial demeanor. "We're here to fix the company," he declared loftily, emphasizing his belief in the future of MGM/UA. During his final months at Merrill Lynch, he'd been a vocal critic of the entertainment industry. "Wall Street has lost faith in Hollywood," he'd argued at one meeting after another. Yet now, Barbakow himself had become an insider—and one who faced the prospect of a huge payoff if he could persuade the right buyer that the entertainment industry had a bright future after all.

To this end, Barbakow announced details of a $200 million rights offering to shareholders. Kerkorian himself would purchase the offering in its entirety if the public showed no interest, he promised. The money would enable the studio to finance new production and pay down its $268 million in aggregate bank debt. "Kirk has decided to remain an active participant in the film business," Barbakow declared.

Despite these pronouncements, Wall Street analysts, in the closing weeks of 1988, were circling the prone body of MGM/UA like expectant vultures, alert to every sign of trouble. Projections of a $40 million loss for the final quarter were greeted with knowing glances. The company's debt was too high, earnings were too low—who in the world was going to buy a company in this condition?

The analysts even discounted the one resource that would seem to hold promise for the company—the upcoming release of *Rain Man*. Normally, the premiere of a Dustin Hoffman/Tom Cruise picture would generate high expectation, but not this time. *The New York Times* quoted the prediction of Jeffrey Logsdon of Crowell, Weedon & Company that *Rain Man* would be a critical success but not a financial one. "It won't do the sixty million to seventy million dollars that it needs to really help the company," the analyst declared.

The conventional wisdom on *Rain Man* was that it met none of the normal criteria of a "hot picture." *Rain Man* was not sexy. It wasn't especially comedic. Its perspective on humanity was rather dark. The Dustin Hoffman character was not redeemed or transformed into a "normal" person. Indeed, the only thing the picture had going for it was that it was superbly directed and performed. And it rang true.

The analysts' dire predictions were wrong from the outset. *Rain Man* was not just a hit. It was indeed the blockbuster Kirk Kerkorian had always been waiting for. In its first eighteen days, the film registered a remarkable $42.4 million at the box office. By the end of March, five months after its release, receipts had soared to $155.7 million, thus passing *Rocky IV* as the highest-grossing picture in the history of the company (only *Gone With the Wind*, by now owned by Turner, had outgrossed *Rain Man*, through its repeated rereleases).

While these records generated high excitement among UA survivors, Kirk Kerkorian, oddly enough, seemed largely unmoved. One morning a top aide entered his office, waving a copy of that morning's *Wall Street Journal*, which featured a story extolling the progress of UA. The article particularly emphasized the role of *Rain*

Man in potentially restoring the company's prestige and financial credibility.

Kerkorian scanned the article, then handed it back to his aide. "You know what they say about newspapers," the boss remarked somberly. "You can wrap fish in them."

Rain Man's emergence as the "sleeper of the year" lent new impetus to Jeffrey Barbakow in his effort to reenergize his potential buyers. In January 1989, he issued a new ninety-three-page confidential memorandum propounding the virtues of UA to the financial community. The prospectus was packed with data about UA's illustrious history. "UA's operating units are showing tremendous growth," the document declared. As an example, UA's foreign pay-TV sales in fiscal 1988 alone represented an increase of 962 percent over the prior year, it stated. Projections of net operating cash flow (computed before debt service) showed the company's performance doubling by 1991 and increasing fivefold by the mid-1990's.

On close reading, of course, one could find the fiscal "scar tissue" representing years of wheeling and dealing. In detailing the company's nightmarishly complex video output deals, for example, the prospectus noted that, until 1992, UA would have to supply ten films a year to Warner Home Video or else pay a penalty of $200,000 per film—in other words, a penalty of $1 million if it supplied only five films. Relative to the James Bond films, the prospectus noted that its distribution fees in various media ran as low as 15 percent, and also detailed the litigation in England with respect to the continued use of the James Bond and "007" names.

But if MGM/UA seemed like damaged goods at this stage in its history, Jeffrey Barbakow did not take notice. Week after week, like a dauntless used-car salesman patiently showing his battered inventory, Barbakow shepherded a nonstop stream of numbers-crunchers through his offices. The "shoppers" included some impressive names—Disney, MCA, Cannon, Polygram N.V., Sony, C. Itoh & Co., et cetera. And remarkably, by early 1989, some tentative proposals began to take shape.

Paramount suggested it might be interested in buying MGM/UA through an overseas affiliate co-owned with MCA. Warner Communications made an offer of seventeen dollars a share. This prompted Rupert Murdoch, the Australian-born media lord and proprietor of Twentieth Century-Fox to counter with another offer a tad richer.

As the Murdoch-Kerkorian talks grew more intense, MGM/UA insiders watched fretfully. Murdoch's interest, they knew, was in assets. Specifically, he needed more programming for Sky Television, a British satellite-fed TV service. The rumor at MGM/UA was that Murdoch intended to fire the entire executive corps.

The prospect of an acquisition by Fox carried with it a certain historic irony. On at least two occasions over the years, Kerkorian had taken a hard look at acquiring Fox. In 1981, even as he was about to close a deal to buy UA, Kerkorian had one final secret meeting with billionaire oilman Marvin Davis in an effort to pry Fox away from his control. Davis turned him down.

A generation earlier, in 1931, Fox had almost been taken over by MGM's then parent company, Loew's. At the last moment Fox backed off because of the continued collapse of the stock market.

Though he knew little of these past intrigues, Murdoch was nonetheless savoring his projected acquisition of MGM/UA—until a sudden jab from Kerkorian snapped him back to reality. Even as Fox was working out final details of its deal, Kerkorian unexpectedly came up with a dark-horse bidder. It was a maverick Australian company called Qintex, which proclaimed its willingness to offer $1.1 billion for MGM/UA, or twenty dollars a share. As with the Ted Turner deal, however, the subtext of the deal involved a maze of complications. While Qintex would acquire MGM/UA's film-production company, its marketing and distribution divisions, MGM/UA home video and the UA library, Kerkorian agreed to buy back certain assets for some $250 million. These included TV production, the Leo the Lion logo, the new headquarters building under construction in Beverly Hills and MGM's thirty-four-title library. Kerkorian also agreed to invest $75 million in the "new UA." Further, once MGM started making films again, UA would distribute MGM's product for a period of some thirty-five years— a return to the unsuccessful arrangement of the mid-1970s.

No one could quite figure out why Kerkorian decided to snub the glowering Rupert Murdoch. Qintex's offer wasn't that much better—some insiders guessed the gap was as little as twenty cents a share. Under the Qintex deal, to be sure, Kerkorian would retain his favorite plaything—the MGM logo. The Fox deal would have spelled the end of Kerkorian in the movie business.

On the other hand, no one doubted Murdoch's ability to come up with the money, whereas Qintex remained a question mark. Indeed, throughout the spring and summer of 1989, Christopher Skase, the forty-year-old Australian who headed Qintex, and David Evans, his chief aide, were hurtling around the world trying to cement their financing. Their quest was complicated by the decision of Standard & Poor, the bond-rating service, to place Qintex's subordinated debt and that of MGM/UA on its Credit Watch surveillance list. MGM/UA's junk bonds already had been rated double B-minus.

In revealing its ratings, Standard & Poor noted that Qintex's debt inevitably would continue to soar in the coming year as it attempted to resuscitate UA's depleted lineup of films. The acquisition, it noted, was a huge step for this relatively obscure company. Having started in real estate and resorts, Qintex's first major plunge into the entertainment field was the acquisition in 1987 of one of Australia's three TV networks, Channel 7, encompassing stations in Brisbane, Melbourne, and Sydney (Qintex already had owned two Queensland stations). A year later the company acquired the Hal Roach Studios in Hollywood, merging it with the Robert Halmi Co., an independent TV producer. In 1989 Qintex Entertainment, the newly named U.S. arm of Skase's company, earned critical acclaim with its CBS miniseries, *Lonesome Dove*.

To help finance his future ventures, Skase in 1989 sold a 49 percent stake in two Hawaiian resorts to a Japanese company for some $350 million. While this supplied the first chunk of acquisition money, there was a continued buzz in Hollywood that Skase was having difficulty coming up with the rest. To quiet these concerns, Skase let it be known that he had a $400 million commitment from several banks and also was talking to ten investors about a private placement for an additional $500 million.

Despite these assurances, some analysts suggested Skase might ultimately be compelled to deal off certain UA assets to finance his acquisition. In mid-August, proxy material distributed to shareholders indicated that Kerkorian himself might try and sell the MGM/UA TV unit that he had reacquired as part of the Qintex deal—a disclosure that fueled rumors that new maneuverings might be forthcoming.

The rumors were valid. In mid-September, the unpredictable Kerkorian suddenly invited Rupert Murdoch back to the party from which he'd only recently been disinvited. The Qintex deal hasn't closed yet, Kerkorian pointed out, adding, in effect, "Make me an offer." A hopeful but suspicious Murdoch prepared to fly to Los Angeles from London, offer in hand.

The news hit the street amid inevitable headshaking. How could Kerkorian reopen the bidding just as Qintex was on the brink of nailing down the deal? In response, a spokesman for Kerkorian claimed that the Qintex agreement "allowed us to continue our discussions with Fox." In fact, the discussions, he added, had never really broken off.

The ever-game Murdoch now submitted his new offer—some $1.4 billion compared with the $1.1 million earlier offered by Qintex. Murdoch's representatives let it be known that they considered it "a done deal." An internal memo was circulated within MGM/UA confirming the deal, adding that Murdoch "intended to operate the MGM/UA businesses aggressively." And Wall Street analysts commented sagely that the deal was "expensive" but "strategically sound." One top trader told the *Los Angeles Times:* "Murdoch has an insatiable appetite. He's like a shark. He can't sleep."

But Murdoch's sleepless nights were just beginning. Though Wall Street and Hollywood both seemed to accept the Murdoch deal as a reality, Christopher Skase had other ideas. Forty-eight hours after the Murdoch bid was revealed, Skase upped the ante. Qintex would now offer some $1.5 billion for MGM/UA, he declared. And it would also assume $400 million in long-term debt, bringing the price, in effect, to $1.9 billion, compared to the $1.1 billion in the original deal. But this time Qintex would own the company free and clear. There would be no buy-backs and subsidies. The only exception would be that Kerkorian would buy the Beverly Hills headquarters building for some $43 million, or at its appraised value, whichever was higher. To seal the deal, Qintex delivered a $50 million irrevocable letter of credit to Kerkorian.

The fifty-eight-year old Murdoch made no effort to conceal his indignation. "We thought we had it," he told reporters in London. Instead of a deal, however, Murdoch had walked into an ambush.

When all the numbers were totted up, it was estimated that Kerkorian would reap more than $1 billion in cash for his common stock. He'd also be repaid the $180 million that he'd invested in preferred stock at the beginning of the year. Jeffrey Barbakow, meanwhile, would earn $37.5 million for brokering the transaction.

And after twenty years, Kirk Kerkorian finally seemed to be out of the movie business. Amid all the financial maneuverings, this momentous fact had almost gotten lost.

But Kerkorian allowed only a forty-eight-hour span to elapse before unveiling yet another set of plans. Though he might indeed be pulling out of movies, he disclosed, it was now his intent to enter the movie-theme-park business. His new facility would be located in Las Vegas, and would be adjacent to a new five-thousand-room hotel that he would also build. The whole project would end up costing over $600 million, it was estimated.

There was, to be sure, one small complication. What would the new theme park be called? Kerkorian wanted to use the MGM name; after all, he still owned a company called MGM Grand that ran a small airline between New York and Los Angeles, among other enterprises. But the Disney company had paid for the right to use the MGM name on its own theme park in central Florida and had also planned parks in Europe. Kerkorian had challenged the deal in California state courts and had lost. Now, he warned, he would try his luck in the Nevada court.

There seemed something vaguely pathetic about this plea. Here was the former proprietor of the once-proud MGM studios humbly petitioning for the right to use the MGM name one final time. At least Kerkorian had his billion-dollar profit to assuage his pride.

Or did he? A couple of weeks after Christopher Skase closed his deal with Kerkorian for the second time, distress flags started appearing. The Australian's far-flung network of financial backers, stretched thin by the first round of negotiations, was suddenly disintegrating. Bankers and financiers fretted that Skase had gotten carried away. In his fervor to conquer MGM, they said, Skase had ignored the instability of his own enterprise at home. A deal calling for Qintex, Ltd., to sell two Australian TV channels for $110 million (Australian dollars), for example, had just fallen through, adding to Skase's cash crunch. Interest rates were climbing and Qintex's bankers were growing nervous.

Like all good wheeler-dealers, Skase tried to put a happy face on all this, but there was one reality he could not ignore. The deadline for his $50 million down payment to Kerkorian was coming due and he didn't have the money.

When the $50 million failed to arrive in mid-October, the house of cards came tumbling down so swiftly, even Kerkorian was shocked. The MGM-Qintex deal was officially called off. Lawsuits were threatened. Skase announced that Qintex's U.S. subsidiary would seek bankruptcy protection under Chapter 11.

Rushing back to Australia, Skase made a surprise TV appearance to issue a grandiloquent public apology. "I am the captain of the team," he declared, "and I have to accept the good with the bad." Qintex, he explained, "had always been a strategy-driven company, not a deal-driven one. Most times it works. Occasionally it doesn't." And with that curious analysis, Skase meandered off the stage of the world's financial power players.

Where did this leave MGM and UA? As 1989 wound down, both companies looked more and more like threadbare anachronisms from Hollywood's dim past. MGM/UA Communications conceded at year-end that it would lose some $75 million in its latest fiscal year. The company was still pulling in some money from its TV operation, from *Rain Man,* and, significantly, from some vestiges of its distant past: The fiftieth anniversary home-video release of *The Wizard of Oz,* for example, was a big winner. But with no new films on the horizon, and with the distribution company's market share down to a pathetic 3.7 percent, prospects seemed bleak.

The only real hope resided, as usual, in the possibility that Kerkorian and Jeffrey Barbakow might line up yet another corporate suitor. The twice-spurned Rupert Murdoch was the strongest possibility, but he was now playing hardball. The sight of Kerkorian twisting in the wind was doubtless an enjoyable one for the flinty Australian. The ever-playful Ted Turner had been hinting that he, too, might be interested in another round of conversations with Kerkorian, but suddenly he'd seemingly lost interest as well.

More and more, the MGM saga seemed stuck in its tracks, while the rest of the entertainment industry was caught up in a whirlwind of excitement and change. Warner Bros. and Paramount were wrestling feverishly over the right to merge with Time Inc. Sony was annexing Columbia for some $3.4 billion, also assuming $1.4 billion in long-term debt. The Japanese giant also found itself sandbagged into paying as much as $600 million for the right to hire the producing team of Peter Guber and Jon Peters as heads of production at Columbia. Sony had tried to sign the two, not realizing they were tied into an exclusive producing deal at Warner Communications (about to become Time Warner). When Warner sued, Sony had to come up with a settlement package. The settlement included such items as Warner assuming a 50 percent interest in the Columbia House division of CBS Records, the largest direct marketer of records, plus Warner obtaining cable-TV distribution rights for all theatrical and TV movies produced by Columbia. The final item: Columbia would swap its 35 percent interest in the Burbank Studios (Warner owned the rest) in exchange for the former MGM lot now owned by Warner. Hence, Warner would come away with a lot worth some $50 million more than the Culver City land—and Columbia would move its activities to the onetime home of MGM.

The deal stirred bewilderment in the film community. Guber and Peters barely a year earlier had been willing to pay Kerkorian some $100 million for the right to head MGM. Now Sony would have to allot some $600 million to hire the same two executives, an action that gave new meaning to the word *inflation.*

With such sweeping changes overtaking the global entertainment industry, Kirk Kerkorian felt a growing urgency to close a deal, but suddenly there was no one to talk to. He had recycled his assets so many times that even he had grown bored. So, it seemed, had everyone else.

As 1990 dawned, Kerkorian took a deep breath and launched into a familiar scenario. If no one wanted to buy his company, he would fill the pipeline once again, financing as many as eight new films. One would be directed by Barbra Streisand, who'd given him *Yentl*. Another would be directed by Michael Cimino, who'd given him *Heaven's Gate* (MGM/UA would only distribute this film).

In response to this announcement, MGM/UA stock took a quick tumble and Standard & Poor's placed MGM/UA bonds on its "credit watch surveillance list." The MGM/UA story, it seemed, was on instant replay.

For Kerkorian, it seemed like the ultimate Vegas nightmare. It was as though he were stuck in a poker game that never seemed to end.

Grimly, he took out his checkbook. It was time to start writing the big checks once again.

CHAPTER SIXTEEN

■

A FINAL ACCOUNTING

O<small>N</small> April 26, 1924, a newly formed company called Metro-Goldwyn-Mayer dedicated its studio in Culver City amid the hoopla of brass bands, a military salute, speeches from politicians, and even a telegram (predictably terse) from President Calvin Coolidge. A scattering of movie stars had been corralled for the occasion, including John Gilbert, Lon Chaney, and Ramon Novarro. Even Will Rogers dropped by, albeit an hour late, apologizing that "I'd left my chewing gum in my other suit."

Despite the pomp and ceremony, many in attendance were blasé about the day's events—a fact that did not inhibit the ever-purposeful Louis B. Mayer. Movie mergers were almost an hourly occurrence in that era, and both Mayer's and Metro-Goldwyn's were fledgling ventures. Mayer's assets at the time did not approach the $100,000 level, and Metro-Goldwyn couldn't even claim the services of Samuel Goldwyn, who had already moved on to other escapades. And while the MGM studio even then was fronted by the imposing white wall and colonnades that still stand today, not much in the way of stages or facilities lay hidden behind the proud facade.

To Mayer, however, the fanfare was justified. This was to be the site of his Dream Factory—his own idiosyncratic pantheon of pop culture. Detractors could say what they wished, but in Mayer's eyes, history was being made.

Sixty-three years later, when Metro-Goldwyn-Mayer, or what little remained of it, skulked off the lot without benefit of bands, speeches, or even a press release, one could imagine the ghosts of the past shaking their heads in dismay. Observing the rites of surrender, the old gonifs must have been asking themselves, "Whatever happened to showmanship—or, for that matter, to simple chutzpah?"

And Kirk Kerkorian, oddly enough, might have been asking the identical questions. Though his maneuvers and manipulations had made defeat inevitable, this was not the way he'd wanted it to turn out. Even in the summer of 1989, amid all his feverish trading, Kerkorian was still asking a confidant, "Why couldn't I ever get it to work? Why couldn't I find the right people, the right combination?"

In the eyes of the film community, Kerkorian had become a one-man wrecking crew, but, paradoxically, no owner of a movie studio had ever actually *liked* movies more than Kirk Kerkorian. None had ever, as Kerkorian had, stood on line two or three times a week at theaters in Hollywood or Westwood and munched popcorn cheek-to-jowl with the masses.

Though Kerkorian wanted his studio to turn out hit movies, he never even came close. The reasons were part financial, part cultural. A creature of Las Vegas, he'd mastered Hollywood's numbers but not its nuances. He could figure the odds, but never understood the players. In the end, he began to resemble an aging pit boss, looking on helplessly as "the house" kept losing.

Realizing that the zeitgeist eluded him, Kerkorian steadfastly removed himself from the studio's day-to-day decision-making process. "I never pretended I could pick the movies," he would explain, but he nonetheless picked the men who made these choices—and picked them ineptly. Time and again, in true Vegas fashion, he opted for flash over substance; then, second-guessing himself, he would abruptly switch managements yet again.

The movie industry is cyclical by nature. Kerkorian's incessant changes of regime exacerbated these gyrations. But while companies like MCA or Gulf + Western had the cash reserves to ride out the cycles, Kerkorian never succeeded in marshaling these resources. Time and again, he ended up writing the checks—and cursing his fate.

Inevitably, perhaps, Kerkorian concluded that the only way to win the game was to reinvent the rules. If he couldn't build an empire, at least he could carve one up profitably. In so doing, Kerkorian transformed corporate demolition into a high art.

Proving himself the ultimate survivor, Kerkorian nonetheless left a backwash of broken careers and dashed hopes. None of his chief executives—Aubrey, Rosenfelt, Rothman, Yablans, Silbert—went on to new careers or companies. Louis B. Mayer's Dream Factory had become a land of lost opportunity. It was the studio that *almost* made *Jaws, The Sting, Terms of Endearment, Last Tango in Paris, Dirty Dancing,* and *Crocodile Dundee.*

It has been said that an era ends when its dreams are exhausted. MGM's era had clearly ended.

■ INDEX